The Making of Saints

The Making of Saints
Contesting Sacred Ground

Edited by
JAMES F. HOPGOOD

THE UNIVERSITY OF ALABAMA PRESS
Tuscaloosa

Tuscaloosa, Alabama 35487-0380

Manufactured in the United States of America

Typeface: Goudy and Goudy Sans

∞
The paper on which this book is printed meets the minimum requirements of American National Standard for Information Science—Permanence of Paper for Printed Library Materials, ANSI Z39.48–1984.

Library of Congress Cataloging-in-Publication Data

The making of saints : contesting sacred ground / edited by James F. Hopgood.
p. cm.
Includes bibliographical references and index.
ISBN 0-8173-1455-5 (hardcover : alk. paper) — ISBN 0-8173-5179-5 (pbk. : alk. paper)
1. Saints. I. Hopgood, James F.
BL488.M35 2005
306.4—dc22

2004019060

Photo credits for cover of paperback edition (clockwise, starting from upper left-hand corner): detail from photo of author Phyllis Passariello with Che images based on Korda's "Guerrillero Heroico." (Photograph by James F. Hopgood); James Dean's "rebel." (David Loehr Collection); Evita with halo. (Courtesy of Archivo del Instituto Nacional Eva Perón—Museo Evita); Elvis, Jailhouse Rock (1957). (Library of Congress, Prints and Photographs Division, LC-USZ6-2067); "Teresa Urrea, Santa de Cabora, and Early Chicano: The Politics of Representation, Identity, and Social Memory." (Courtesy of the Arizona Historical Society/Tuscon; Photo Number 1671 Santa Urrea)

Contents

Figures

Preface and Acknowledgments

This book is concerned with the miscellanea of personages who, under certain circumstances, are selected for devotion and worship—whether formally named "saints" or something else. The beginnings of this book lie in a session I organized for the 1999 Annual Meeting of the American Anthropological Association entitled "The Making of Saints: Secular, Folk, Sacred." Those presenting papers and contributing chapters were June Macklin, William Breen Murray, Carolyn Stevens, and me. Following the session the participants agreed to pursue development of the project and to publish a book. All agreed, however, that additional contributions were needed to expand the cross-cultural dimensions of the topic. Our collective search for additional contributors brought Yoram Bilu, Roberto Bosca, Erika Doss, Gillian Newell, Phyllis Passariello, and Irene Stengs to the project. Dorothy Willner, who served as session discussant, excused herself. Still, I want to acknowledge her contribution as discussant and subsequently in providing many helpful insights on the original papers and the session as a whole. Finally, I asked a longtime friend and colleague, Walter Randolph Adams, to write a concluding chapter—a demanding task he undertook with aplomb. I am most appreciative of his willingness to do so and for bringing several differing perspectives to the issues raised by the contributors.

In editing this volume I have become indebted to many but especially to the contributors for their perseverance—"saints of patience" all—with the project and their understanding through the editing process. I especially want to thank June Macklin for translating the chapter by Roberto Bosca. Besides making her own contribution she undertook this task out of her kind and collegial spirit. Among others I could mention, I want to thank Murray Wax for his introduction many years ago to the sociological foundations for the study of religion. Part of the book's editing was carried out during a sabbatical from Northern Kentucky University. My thanks go to the NKU Faculty Senate's Faculty Benefits

Committee and its chair, Clinton Hewan, for recognition of the project's value in granting the sabbatical. Thanks are due to reviewer Miles Richardson and an anonymous reviewer for their helpful suggestions. To the folks at the University of Alabama Press for their guidance in preparing the manuscript for publication and to Judith Knight, acquisitions editor, for her solid professionalism, I also extend my thanks. Finally, I want to thank Esther Hopgood, *mi compañera,* for her support, tolerance, and love during preparation of the book.

JFH

Introduction

Saints and Saints in the Making

James F. Hopgood

With the predictions of 19th-century evolutionists regarding the demise of religion in the 20th now discarded, will a postmodernist 21st century see anything other than a reformulation in time and space of key concepts of the sacred? From a vast array of those concepts, the saint holds a special place in many cultural traditions. During the current millennium, the saint and human conditions that give rise to saints can be expected to endure and find expression in new forms. The contributions here cover a wide range of saints, folk saints, "near-saints," and icons or secular saints. Saints from a traditional religious framework, such as the *tzaddikim* among Moroccan Jews, are represented along with folk saints from Mexico together with secular saints and icons ranging from Japanese rock stars to Elvis Presley. But why are some Japanese performers, Thai royalty, American actors, Mexican folk healers, and certain types of political leaders, among others, candidates for "sainthood" treatment? Do the circumstances of modernity and postmodernity presage additional forms of sainthood and types of saints to meet other concerns and definitions of the self? What commonalities exist and do these personages share characteristics with institutionalized and generic saints?

The essays in *The Making of Saints* approach how saints are constructed from several complementary perspectives. Issues of sanctification, love, emotion, power, and social relations are addressed in these explorations of the genesis of saints. Contributors examine hagiographies, biographies, mass media, narratives, symbols, the control and manipulation of space and time, and acts of devotion in reaching several challenging suggestions. Many questions are addressed about the genesis of saints and sainthood. Were their in-life acts viewed differentially by their contemporaries? How is the interpretation of a saint's past negotiated by her followers? How important are formal legitimization processes?

What devotees seek from a saint derives from factors relating to gender, class, social status, ethnicity, and personal details brought to the scene and to the interaction with the saint. From the devotees' viewpoint, often the personal issues are foremost. These contributions suggest this is where most commonalities are found: at the personal level with issues of health, well-being, love, beauty, wealth, self-fulfillment, and success. Accordingly, one proposition examined by contributors relates to those saints of the secular and folk varieties generated from the existential concerns and realities of their devotees (whether "fans" or "disciples"). In such a context, it becomes problematic to distinguish the truly sacred, the "true saint," from folk saints, near-saints, or saintlike personages. The qualities of a folk saint, such as the Mexican El Niño Fidencio, do not differ from those of a formally sanctioned, canonized saint except in certain culturally specific ways and in issues of official morality that are subject to change over time. Certainly those differences are important considerations from the perspective of an institutionalized church with routinized procedures. Yet the realities of human needs of specific communities may go unmet by such official religious institutions, only to be met by other means. This perspective also suggests that it is not necessary for devotees themselves to apply the term *saint*, or a linguistic equivalent, only that their activities, expressions, and devotions clearly mark the personage as sharing qualities with traditionally conceived saints. Nevertheless, tension remains between a traditional view of the saint and sainthood and one that suggests modification is needed to accommodate a global view of sacralization.

SCOPE OF THIS VOLUME

This introduction is followed by June Macklin's chapter called "Saints and Near-Saints in Transition," a fitting prelude to *The Making of Saints* as a whole and to many of the issues addressed by other contributors. Her chapter undertakes a comparison of two types of "sanctified heroes," or personages, using narratives and paradigms: saints and celebrities. Macklin's investigation includes, among other issues, consideration of cross-fertilization of saints and "sanctified celebrities" tied to processes of modernization and globalization. Building on recent work of Chris Rojek (2001), Macklin notes that organized religions have taken on many media techniques and other devices associated with the music and film industries and considers the current pope's canonization of an increasing number and variety of saints. Macklin's analysis leaves little doubt about indicators of the convergence of a variety of saint types and sanctified secular saints.

Charisma is a significant determinant in the life histories of persons referred to as saints. Yoram Bilu in his chapter takes issues of charisma as central in his exploration of Jewish Maghrebi legacies of saint veneration. Bilu's aims are to place current Jewish Moroccan saint worship in Israel in its historical context, examine the basis for saint worship, and explore the basis of the saint's power as a special spiritual force that continues after the death of these Jewish charismatic rabbis (*tzaddikim*). Bilu also explores how charisma is "manufactured, maintained, and contested" in present-day circumstances. This is a central issue in the temporal and substantive maintenance of all types and forms of saints and sainthood. His exposition indicates the critical role of tradition and its accommodation/manipulation, how new forms of sainthood arise, and how the use of modern media and technology are employed.

Irene Stengs's focus is on the role of images and their mass production in the process of saint-making in contemporary Thailand. Stengs's attention is directed to King Chulalongkorn (who was King of Siam from 1868–1910), a Thai saint of great veneration since the 1980s. The king is not "canonized" by any official Buddhist action—he is much like a folk saint. Stengs's concern is his portraits, their appearances in a myriad of forms and locales, and the social and cultural contexts of their use and value. The portraits are linked to the contexts of narratives about his heroic deeds and personal qualities that constitute a body of myth and a hagiography. One of the more powerful of these "narrative portraits" concerns an equestrian statue of the king and portraits of the statue. Stengs's analysis ties the king's personality cult to traditional Thai Buddhism and the "Ten Kingly Virtues." However, going beyond those connections, Stengs demonstrates the relationship of the king, as righteous ruler, via the narratives and portraits, to the concerns of the Thai people.

Roberto Bosca's engaging chapter on Eva Perón, or "Evita," explores her "political canonization" and "embodiment of lay sainthood." Evita presents the case of a charismatic sinner-to-saint who aroused love and hate and was venerated by the Argentinian masses in life and death. Following her death, political moves by Juan Perón, her husband and self-proclaimed "father" of "his" people, included efforts to institutionalize her as a saint and her cult. Her efforts in life for the masses of Argentina were often characterized in the light of the Virgin Mary. Her sanctification and political canonization, as Bosca shows, could not keep the Peronists in perpetual power, but her myth and the continued devotion to her by many Argentinians continued for many years along with periodic efforts to revive her role as saint.

Evita could be constructed as a saintly, loving, and caring figure in the image of the Virgin Mary, but how is it that the hard-living, womanizing, revolutionary, and combatant Che Guevara can be elevated to secular sainthood through popular canonization? Phyllis Passariello undertakes a pilgrimage—as scholar and pilgrim—in search of answers to that perplexing question. Like many other contributors, Passariello shows how narrative and image interact in the creation of the icon and saint—in this case a hero/antihero. Passariello brings Lord Raglan's (1934) suggested hero pattern of 22 traits plus Victor Turner's (1969) concepts of *liminality* and *communitas* into her discussion of mythical narratives surrounding Che Guevara. With this potent mix, she analyses "el Che" as pan–

Latin American hero, culture hero, icon, and secular saint. Che's image is seemingly everywhere in Cuba and Passariello's examination of Che as icon and secular saint includes an in-depth exploration of Che's *image* as a semiotic and as an "ethnographic fact." His image is a powerful marker and "an active, dynamic instrument in the creation, maintenance, and perpetuation" of Che's cult.

A case of failed sainthood is the subject of Gillian Newell's chapter on Teresa Urrea (1873–1906), known as "La Santa de Cabora." Newell details efforts by Chicano writers of the 1960s and 1970s to resurrect Teresa, as a Chicana saint, long after she was forgotten by most Mexicans and Chicanos. Efforts to "re-present" Teresa failed despite the many characteristics she shared with saints everywhere. Newell's analysis uncovers the processes and contradictions involved in attempts to resurrect Teresa from her historical traces and narratives found in Chicano "social memory" and indicates why these efforts failed.

William Breen Murray's chapter, "Spirits of a Holy Land: Place and Time in a Modern Mexican Religious Movement," examines the role of place with regard to the Mexican folk saint El Niño Fidencio. Espinazo, a small desert pueblo in northern Mexico, is the major pilgrimage site for Fidencio's followers and its sacred landscape provides his followers with the setting needed to contact his spirit. The setting also furnishes the necessary structural supports for the maintenance of Fidencio as saint, despite changing expectations of pilgrims from Mexico and the United States. Along with changes in the physical landscape of Espinazo, Murray explores alterations in the *fidencista* movement itself as it shows signs of maturation.

With my chapter, "Saints and Stars: Sainthood for the 21st Century," the contributions shift to issues involving another manifestation and type of popular sainthood: one that focuses on celebrities. This chapter was anticipated by June Macklin's contribution and anticipates the next two chapters, which deal with HIDE (pronounced "hee-day"), a Japanese rock star, and Elvis Presley. My chapter provides a transition by comparing the Mexican folk saint El Niño Fidencio to the American actor and icon James Dean. Similarities in their lives, personal attributes, characteristics attributed to them by others, their respective forms of adoration, and their respective sociocultural contexts suggest a structural equivalence, with both being emotive "targets" of questing and devotion by their followers. The issue of visual appeal via photographic images, and certain key images in particular, is addressed as an example of one special element contributing to Fidencio's and Dean's successes.

"I Quit My Job for a Funeral: The Mourning and Empowering of a Japanese Rock Star" is an apt title for Carolyn Stevens's case study. This study helps bridge a gap in coverage between the beginnings of adoration and certain subsequent problematic developments. Her investigation of the mourning of HIDE, a Japanese rock star who committed suicide at age 34, adds to the discussion of key elements involved in the making of a saint or icon from contemporary celebrities. His act created a number of dilemmas for his fans and Stevens raises the question of how suicide might be considered a saintly act. From that act, his fans began to construct a view of him as engaged in a deep struggle of self-discovery and exploration, a view that helped maintain a close personal identification with HIDE among his fans. Finally this struggle became, in Stevens's words, a "manipulated narrative for both youthful and middle-aged angst in this postmodern society."

In "Popular Culture Canonization: Elvis Presley as Saint and Savior," Erika Doss provides much rich detail on the adoration of Presley, from the candlelight vigils at Graceland to individual cases of faith and pilgrimage. Expressions of devotion also include private altars and shrines and establishing churches in his name. Doss addresses the question of "Why Elvis?" and examines ways in which the adoration of Presley amounts to a religion or a religious cult. There is Elvis's charismatic, "magnetic image," which continues to draw a full range of followers, yet there is much more.

Walter Randolph Adams, in the final chapter, seeks connections not explored or seen by contributors and then weaves two differing perspectives into the task. The first is a micro-macro interaction approach applied to issues of cult and sect, as related to issues of individual involvement and organizational complexity. The second comes from medical anthropology and concerns the treatment of "disease." Both perspectives bring concomitant insights to the issues of individual commitment and adoration and the role and trajectory of organizations created in the adoration of saints and icons. Adams also addresses a number of issues and problems overlooked or in need of additional attention.

ORIENTATIONS AND CONCEPTS

Though it may be routine to think of saints, legitimate or otherwise, in the contextualization of specific religions it is clear in these contributions that the human desire and "impulse" to find and fashion what is desired in the other often settles on someone outside normal bounds. Consequently, to use the standards applied to sainthood from one or more established religions may be counterproductive. The authors here work within, without, and in between traditional religious frameworks. In some cases, the framework of religion is a hindrance for a proper understanding or for framing the varied manifestations of adoration, while in others it provides an appropriate and necessary background. Religion involves more than belief, adoration, and cult and includes an institutional framework, a hierarchy, and the associated exercise of authority and power. Yet, what of those human impulses and actions, so clearly seen by William James (1902:31), that are at the center of religion and, in a basic, foundational, or developmental sense, lay the basis for religion? Answering those impulses on the contemporary scene are a wide range of New Age expressions, new sects in the major world religions, revitalization movements, a host of new religions, the rediscovery or recreations of old religions (e.g., Wicca), and so on. Each is an existential expression of diverse human desires, needs, and circumstances.

My purpose now is to provide a few thoughts on the range of issues, theoretical and substantive, raised and demonstrated by the collection. The first goal of the collection is to fill an obvious gap in studies of saints, folk saints, near-saints, and their followings or movements. This includes an effort to consider cases outside strictly Western traditions and, in fact, outside what may be viewed as religion. The approach represented here considers the convergence of forms, often viewed as separate kinds or categories of things—saints and certain other adored ones, such as icons, celebrities, and other near-saints—and seeks commonalities in the impetus, context, development, expression, and structure among them. And, as will be shown, this involves much more than issues of "sacred and profane." Such goals overlap other efforts, as seen in a special issue of the Dutch journal *Etnofoor* (Ede 1999).

These chapters explore many topical categories of anthropological and sociological analyses, such as communitas, the liminal, popular and folk, sacred and profane, and charisma. And consideration of the subject matter—saints, folk saints, icons, celebrities and their followers—coincides with and takes us into a variety of fields of study including popular culture, sociology of culture, religious studies, culture and media studies, and the anthropology and sociology of religion.

The essays in this collection are also informed by several theoretical orientations derived from the work of Max Weber, Émile Durkheim, and Victor Turner, as well as infusions of scholarship from folklore, semiotics, structuralism, and symbolic and interpretative anthropology. Many of the contributors cite the works of Clifford Geertz, Roland Barthes, Anthony Giddens, Pierre Bourdieu, Robert N. Bellah, Harvey Cox, and many other influential theorists.

From Victor Turner (1969), concerns of liminality and communitas, the creation of community through ritual and other social actions, prove to be useful concepts in Macklin, Hopgood, and Passariello and indirectly in most of the contributions. It is instructive, for example, to view the iconic figures of Che, Evita, Presley, and Dean and folk saints like Fidencio and Chulalongkorn, the Thai King, among others, as "liminoid" in many cultural and societal contexts (Turner and Turner 1978:1–35, 38). Issues stemming from Max Weber's classic work on charisma are found in Bilu but are implicit in most other contributions. The political-religious interface with charisma is also seen in the chapters on Evita, Che, and Chulalongkorn, with their images and stories being elevated to saintlike status, even if successfully only for a brief time as in the case of Evita. Durkheim's (1915) view of religion and society is seen as an undercurrent in many of the contributions but is most apparent in those by Macklin and Hopgood. The semiotic approach grounded in the work of Charles Sanders Peirce and Roland Barthes is seen in Passariello's approach to Che, though complemented by her attention to the literature on heroes and pilgrimage. Stengs's, Passariello's, and Hopgood's contributions in their analyses of images (photographically based) are informed by pictorial semiotics. The manipulation of Evita's image by Perón and other political interests provides a contrasting view of the semiotic. Issues of text and narrative, certainly a focus of Stengs's study of Chulalongkorn, are also notable in Macklin, Newell, and Passariello.

There are also several specific concepts and terms—saints, folk saints, and icons, charisma, and pilgrimage—in need of further clarification to assist in the readings of this collection of essays.

SAINT, FOLK SAINT, ICON: THE SACRED AND SECULAR?

Is it necessary to have firm conceptual divides between a saint and a folk saint or between an icon and a folk saint, and so on? One position, and the one I maintain, is that it is not necessary except for cases of analysis in which the distinction is necessary, as found in June Macklin's discussion in her chapter of various saint types through time, or for understanding issues of sainthood in a specific tradition, as in Yoram Bilu's chapter on Moroccan Jewish saints. To maintain a steadfast adherence to a conceptual divide indicating two typological poles will distort what is observed and knowable. In exploring human behavior in the area of the sacred and in religion, it is best to use concepts with few constraints. Such dichotomies, like Durkheim's sacred and profane, are useful guides to investigation and limited analysis, but little else.

The usage of the term *icon,* it must be noted, is especially problematic. In part this is due to the popularity of the term in recent years. It seems to be everywhere in popular media, applied to a wide range of phenomena, and, as with popular usages generally, this often only confounds what is meant. And the term also has a wide range of meanings within the scholarly community. The breadth in both domains, in fact, is too far-ranging for coverage in these pages. Usages here cluster around *icon* as image and representative or indicative of a configuration of meanings associated with a particular personage. It is also applied as an equivalent to "secular saint." The popular canonization of Elvis Presley created a secular saint, but that saint is likewise an icon and is treated as such by his devoted followers. Images of Presley serve as icons and Presley is iconic of, among other qualities and attributes, androgynous sexuality (cf. Doss 1999:127). James Dean is iconic as a prototype of "the rebel," of what it is to be "cool," among other attributes. The folk saint El Niño Fidencio is iconic of a special type of mestizo Mexican folk saint. Each is quintessential and serves as a marker by which others are compared and judged. The difference, then, between an icon, secular saint, or church-canonized saint is not resolved, but that is the point of

The Making of Saints and its contributions. Icons and saints of all stripes are the field on which a seemingly perennial struggle for and over the sacred and the iconic is fought by followers, among themselves, and by their critics and defamers.

It is very clear that established saints, officially recognized, many folk saints, and icons of all sorts remain in flux with respect to their meanings to their devotees. As several essays in the recently published *Velvet Barrios* (Gaspar de Alba 2003) clearly show, veneration of a range of figures important in Chicano culture continues with unabated vigor. These saints, heroes, and icons (Virgin de Guadalupe, la Llorona, la Malinche, El Pachuco) are being "rewritten" to deal with an ever-changing Chicano reality. From a more traditional setting, John Monaghan (1995:307ff), in an ethnohistorical study of the Mixtec of Oaxaca, Mexico, links local sociocultural change with the appearance of new saints. In fact, changes in conceptions of local saints specifically reflect the "changing material circumstances of their lives" (Monaghan 1995:361) and allow the "reinvention" of self and community. These same processes apply to the saints, sacred, folk, and secular, considered in these pages.

It is clear that much current and recent research on celebrities treads similar ground. Confusion may result from the observation that some celebrities may become icons and saints. Nevertheless, a thorough review of such work, much in popular culture studies, of celebrities (movie stars, rock stars, "personalities") cannot be undertaken here. Macklin's chapter, however, does cover much of this ground. It is of interest to note a study of Hollywood by anthropologist Hortense Powdermaker (1950) over half a century ago. She drew attention to many of the ingredients of fandom by noting the functional role movie stars play in the lives of their fans, along with the role of film in providing the contemporary equivalent of the myths and legends of preindustrialized peoples (1950:248–251). Rojek's work *Celebrity* (2001) bears noting again for its comprehensive coverage of the celebrious and celebrification. Studies of fans and fan culture are of interest, such as the edited work by Lisa A. Lewis (1992); the recent effort by Matt Hills (2002) provides an excellent overview of such work and points in a number of interesting directions, including study of "scholar-fans," "cult media," and issues of subjectivity and objectivity, among others. Many working in the arena of media and celebrity studies, like Hills and Rojek, in fact, often draw on a religion metaphor in their analyses.

CHARISMA AND ROUTINIZATION

The role of charisma is a direct concern of Yoram Bilu in his chapter on the making of saints in Israel, yet it is implicit in all the contributions. Because charisma is unstable, Bilu focuses on its institutionalization, what Weber referred to as "routinization of charisma" and "charisma of office" (1968:246–249), and charisma as hereditary. This concept from Max Weber is now standard fare in the anthropology and sociology of religion from studies of new religious movements to historical cases to political and religious studies, and so on. Of course, not all charismatic leaders are followed by institutionalization or routinization: consider the case of Santa Teresa, La Santa de Cabora, in Gillian Newell's contribution. The charisma associated with political figures, celebrities, icons, and others may never be routinized or institutionalized in the Weberian sense. And it may be too early in many cases to judge the persistence of any current icon or saint. How many forgotten folk saints are there?

However, as Lindholm states, "Charisma is, above all, *a relationship*, a mutual mingling of the inner selves of leader and follower" (1990:7). And, in the cases here, it does not matter whether the leader is living or dead. Elvis Presley remains the "author" of his messages as received by his followers from recorded music, film, photographs, sayings, and relics. Between James Dean as icon and the inner-directed Deaner a dynamic of personalized interaction exists. This important characteristic of charisma in the relationship between leader and follower, however communicated, needs attention. In Espinazo, a *materia* in a trance receives the spirit of El Niño Fidencio and cures as he did, providing another example of the relationship dialectic. Where institutionalization is occurring, or has occurred, further dialectics exist between institutions and the charismatic leader as remembered, interpreted, textualized, iconized, and imaged.

In Newell's study of Santa Teresa, Chicano writers and intellectuals could not re-create a Teresa who met the needs of their intended following. Dormant or moribund charisma cannot be easily resurrected. But who will survive the initial period of discovery and frenzy and continue as a subject of adoration? Princess Diana, for example, is a case that bears watching. Despite the outpourings of love, grief, and adoration and the pilgrimages undertaken because of her, will her elevation to popular sainthood survive (cf. Merck 1998)? All elevated celebrities simply do not survive the initial adoration bestowed upon them. Perhaps the need met is fleeting, or the intense moment of loss cannot be made concrete or universal, or that special, "magical" appeal cannot be sustained.

If incipient quasimovements based on charisma do not institutionalize, then what forms do they take? They certainly go beyond mere events, "happenings," or concerts. In the manner of Victor Turner, I suggest that such incipient movements are best viewed as "liminal," seemingly in transition, never fixed, betwixt and between, and ambivalent. The *fidencistas,* followers and devotees of El Niño Fidencio, until recently, could be viewed in this way. But, with efforts underway to institutionalize a church in his name, routinization is a possible outcome.

The adoration and iconization of figures like Dean, Presley, and HIDE suggest something along the lines of Thomas Luckmann's *Invisible Religion* (1967:48–

49, 69), with an image of the individual striving for transcendence. When established institutions—religious or otherwise—fail to meet the needs of sectors of society, people may turn to the charismatic, iconic figures. This fits reasonably well in Luckmann's discussion of "private spheres" (1967:97ff). And such "individualization" of the quest for meaning and transcendence is in keeping with the current "postmodern" age. Certainly the New Age religions, best referred to as New Age "questing," are good candidates for this sort of characterization. It is also clear that these considerations do not apply only to Western societies.

A differing psychological basis of this phenomenon is found in Lasch's (1979) "culture of narcissism" and Lindholm's (1990:83–85) use of Lasch's concept in reference to charisma. This view points in another direction for unraveling these trends and how they may be manifest, but this will not detain the current discussion except to note the obvious role of emotion and other psychological states in those attracted to charismatic leaders. Related to this view is "Sheilaism," a situation in which everyone may have a personal, private religion (Bellah et al. 1985:221). These observations refer primarily to the United States, and a further point to note is the seemingly continuous evolution toward the "privatization" of religious expression in the United States, clearly seen by Bellah and colleagues (1985:219ff) and anticipated by Luckmann. The works here do not fully explore those depths, yet they are anticipated.

PILGRIMAGE

Pilgrimage is not the specific topic of any of the contributors here, though Passariello comes close, yet pilgrimage is the stage on which much devotion plays out its script. The being-there of pilgrimage—where so-and-so lived, walked, was schooled, worked, appeared, healed—is of great importance. Those places become shrines. Her image becomes an icon, her life iconic, and her things become sacred, or at least extraordinary, relics. The line between museum and shrine disappears. Pilgrimage is one of the major signs or indicators of impending devotion. But what distinguishes a pilgrim from a tourist? The recognition that "a tourist is half a pilgrim, if a pilgrim is half a tourist" (Turner and Turner 1978:20) is an important one with respect to the construction of saints and to the question of what it is that takes people to locations regarded as religious, famous, or even notorious. But, somewhat contrary to the Turners' (1978:234–237) view from the late 1970s, when the counterculture seemed everywhere on the landscape, today's postmodern pilgrims at Graceland, Fairmount, and Santa Clara seek the iconic and the sacred within a liminoid experience. The Turners did note, however, the "pilgrimage impulse" (1978:241) and the various forms it may take.

In American popular culture, trips to Graceland in Memphis may count as a "must-do," along with trips to Disney World and Las Vegas, among many others. For thousands, however, a trip to Graceland is much, much more than a requisite vacation—it is a highly spiritual experience, if not an unabashedly spiritual one. Graburn (1989:24–27) and MacCannell (1976:43–46), among others, have covered some of the issues attendant upon a too-conventional view of touring as a secular act. The sacred-secular divide cannot be approached until the issue of "for whom?" is decided. This would seem to be a clear issue: without knowing the purpose and meaning of a visit to Graceland or Che's shrine in Cuba for a particular person, it cannot be said whether what transpires for that person is sacred, secular, ambivalent, or something else. The same issue applies to why pilgrims/tourists leave objects of devotion or tribute at graves, shrines, and other sites (Richardson 2001). Passariello, in the present collection, exemplifies this dilemma well.

Finally, the contributions in this volume do not cover all varieties or forms of sacralized persons. The subject is too broad for one volume; still, we hope our coverage will be effective in broadening the discussion on the issues of sanctity and the sanctification of persons and the desires and wishes they are asked to address. The saints, folk saints, sinners, and icons here are sought for answers to the same questions and for solutions to the same problems and to somehow speak to the same inner yearnings that gods and heroes have always addressed in one form or another. In the postmodern, globalized milieu, who or what is to answer our quests, our sufferings, and our need to suffer? Who or what will offer faith for the faithless, something *extraordinary* and of awe and wonder, and above all answer the quest to touch the sacred?

The Making of Saints

1

Saints and Near-Saints in Transition

The Sacred, the Secular, and the Popular

June Macklin

Forty years ago, the prescient Orrin E. Klapp surveyed American society in *Heroes, Villains, and Fools: The Changing American Character* (1962) and arrived, inductively, at various social types that serve prominently as our major role models. Reflecting the cultural ideals of American society, they were and are both models *of* and models *for* human behavior. His still-valid "hero" types now are being retrofitted as if they were transcendent, sacred figures as either "group servants"—holy persons who are self-sacrificing, cooperative, helpful toward others, and dedicated to "group service and solidarity"—or "splendid performers"—those who shine before an audience, thereby "making a 'hit.'" The purpose of this chapter is to describe, compare, and contrast these two kinds of sanctified heroes on the basis of two premises: first, that "the pursuit as well as the perception of holiness [mirrors] social values and concerns" (Weinstein and Bell 1982:6) and, second, that they can be analyzed as "root paradigms" (V. Turner 1974:15).

In the beginning of this essay, I will limit my discussion to the vitae, the narratives created for the group servants, both for officially recognized Christian saints and for folk saints, those who are locally revered but who do not have sufficient support or economic wherewithal to attract papal attention. Together with their audiences, they comprise a surprisingly diverse lot and speak to the "common believer" as well as the "tutored elites" (Woodward 1990:18). Then, by comparing their narratives briefly with those of selected splendid performers, who emerged as a type of celebrity/hero only during the 19th century "within the context of no context" (Trow 1997), I will approach a remaining puzzle: How have our imagineries so changed that we now sanctify the images of some splendid performers, finding them intelligible and imitable as we go about our identity work in the 21st century? Originally well known primarily for their "well-knownness," to borrow Daniel Boorstin's (1961) condescending description, how have these performers (stars, icons, or celebrities) been transmogrified and given *holy* biographies, so that they become one choice among the many in the global religious marketplace? How is it that *their* storytellers have been able to strut into the "social dramas where conflicting groups and personages attempt to assert their own and deplete their opponents' paradigms" (V. Turner 1974:15)?

The narrators negotiating for the power and authority to define what is and what is not authentic among the lot of our heroes are a major part of the captivating, dramatic stories the saints have left us. The data suggest two final propositions. First, traditional saints' narratives provide their own followers, those of the folk saints, and fans of the splendid performers with a sentimental education, meanings for the sacred objects related to them, and rituals with which to approach the adored and venerated. Second, ironically, as the dialogical processes of modernization and globalization—promulgated through print and electronic media—have loosed both religious imagineries and the modern self from their institutional moorings, the culture of the splendid performers has lent new forms, new styles, and new content to the veneration of officially recognized new religious saints.

THE SAINTS GO MARCHING IN

The dynamic negotiations and processes that produce suitable stories and reject the rest have created a bewilderingly diverse crew of saints, at once dazzling, sometimes ascetic, sometimes virtuous, and often obedient. But frequently they also offer us controversial, rambunctious, rebellious, gender-bending, miracle-working, and pretentious holy men and women—their halos slightly askew—who also garner their share of veneration. Over the *longue durée* the saints' lives, like prisms, refract and illuminate many issues of contemporary concern. The vigorous production of new saints as well as the vitality of recent scholarly interest in them belies Max Weber's observation that secularizing societies no longer need saintly intervention.

Saints' stories may be seen as the discourses produced by the three major categories of narrators, each vying for control. First, there is the individual aspiring to sainthood, along with the conditions he or she must exhibit to qualify as an honored, powerful heavenly resident; second, the would-be saint's devotees, whose stories and "cult" (i.e., *cultus* or veneration) are necessary for their hero's wider recognition; and third, those with the power and authority to shape and tailor the final story to fit (or modify) prefigured models, approve it, and turn the saint into a mnemonic unit. Of this storytelling triad, the aspiring saint is the least important. Of course, the diverse discourses reflect the religious, economic, and political climate of the era in which canonization is conferred, not necessarily that of the era in which the individual lived and died.

Originally, the two major criteria by which religious authorities identified sanctity stipulated that candidates must have lived lives of "heroic virtue" and they must have had the charismata, the gifts, that are signs of God's grace and are the means by which they can turn "their holiness into miraculous actions" (Head 2001:xiv). Relevant to my entire discussion is Thomas Head's explanation that "it is no accident that in Latin the single word *virtus* (which can be translated variously as *virtue* or *power*) was used to denote both pious actions and miracles which transcended the rules of nature" (2001:xiv). The criterion stipulating the need for doctrinal purity was added later, at which point the less the aspiring saint said or wrote, the more likely he or she was to leap the necessary hurdles into the ranks of sainthood.

THE FRIENDS OF GOD: ATTRIBUTES

The earliest recognized saints were the "red martyrs," their deaths for their faith having imitated that of Jesus and therefore having "publicly demonstrated" their sanctity. Reborn in heaven at the moment of their perfect sacrifice, the red martyrs enjoyed everlasting life as "friends of God" and soon were "recognized and proclaimed by the churches to which they belonged" (Vauchez 1997:13). No further scrutiny was necessary: *vox populi, vox Dei*. The death of a saint was remembered with joy, for his death marked his *dies natalis*, his "real birthday" into his heavenly existence. His "heroic virtue" was meant to serve as an example for others. At this time few women were in the position to become sainted martyrs, regardless of their piety.

When the persecution of Christians ceased and Constantine accepted Christianity in C.E. 313, the Church was then at peace. New types of sanctity were needed and new kinds of saints, known as "white martyrs," confessed or taught the faith. They suffered but did not die for their faith. For these confessors, ascetics, and other holy persons, it was required that they perform miracles either during their lifetimes or after their deaths, such power usually "being associated with their tombs or their relics" (McBrien 2001:604). The shift away from saints as *exempla* or *imitanda* is clear by the sixth century. The confessors become saints because of the miracles performed and the more amazing the miracles "the greater the sanctity" (Cunningham 1968:18) reputed to the admired persons, the *admirandi*.

Again, few women were permitted to occupy positions in the social hierarchy from which they could become confessors, although those of high social status and wealth were able to found religious orders and be recognized for their holy devotions (cf. Mooney 1999; Schulenburg 1998). Otherwise, they were forced to seek other routes to earn recognition for sanctity, a distinction important to this day as one attempts to understand the impact of gender on definitions of sainthood.

For the first four centuries of the Christian era, local communities constructed the discourses creating the saints' lives and realities; all saints were effectively saints of the folk. By the eighth century, the popularity of such saints and their cults challenged the Church and its "leaders and theologians to keep the veneration of saints, angels, and the Blessed Virgin Mary in line with the central truth of Christian faith" that the only mediator between mankind and God is Jesus Christ (McBrien 2001:6). The struggle over who controls the stories continues to mark the making of saints. The creation of contemporary folk saints and revered popular icons outside any hierarchical control continues to demonstrate the vitality of such challenges.

It was only with the Catholic Reformation, during which the Congregation of Rites in 1588 was given "responsibility for preparing canonizations and authenticating relics," that the pope gained greater control (McBrien 2001:7). Those procedures, solidified in 1634 under Pope Urban VIII, detailed precise procedures to distinguish between beatification and canonization and gave the Church's authorized saint-makers final control over the saintly narrative (cf. Cunningham 1968; McBrien 2001; Woodward 1990).

IMAGINERIES AND BEHAVIORS: PROCESSES, NARRATORS, AND THEIR CONSEQUENCES

In sum, then, during the first Christian millennium, all saints were de facto popular or folk saints, the Vatican gaining ever-tightening control only during the succeeding six centuries. The initiative in matters of sainthood still came from the people and early on their choices received almost pro forma episcopal guidance and blessing. Once this had occurred, the body of the saint-in-process was dug up and "translated" (transferred to the local church) where it was placed on the altar for future veneration. The saintly biographies were composed, copied, and read aloud to the bishop, an act tantamount to canonization. These stories, with the local bishop's imprimatur, "became more familiar to people than the Scriptures themselves [thus] *contributing to the shaping of the Catholic imagination of the Middle Ages*" (McBrien 2001:6, emphasis added). They retain a viselike grip on the religious imaginary of the present. Canonizations were rare during this era, with only 35 occurring between 1198 and 1434 (Kleinberg 1992:13), but by the mid-15th century, canonical authorities had begun to dismiss both bodily preservation (the absence of decay and disintegration) and the retention of flexibility ("incorruptibility"), along with fragrance, as proof of sanctity. Nonetheless, both beliefs ooze on into the present as "evidential." Many living saints are said to have given off the "sweet odor of sanctity," and awed reports of apparent incorruptibles still emerge.

The role of collective memories in the making of the saints' stories can be significant. For example, in the 1980s, the Church, always cautious to "root out fake relics," asked for a scientific examination of the apparently incorruptible body of the 13th-century Italian mystic St. Margaret of Cortona. Papal investigators were astonished to discover that her remarkably preserved body had long incisions streaked along her thighs, abdomen, and chest, all "clearly made after her death." Her internal organs had been excised and her skin "drenched in fragrant lotions," techniques that recalled those used by early Egyptians (Pringle 2001:257). Further research showed that at the time of her death the followers of the miracle-working St. Margaret publicly asked the Church to preserve her body, a *traditional* request at the time. They hoped that the record and memory of her life might literally be embodied in their town. However, once the collective memory of her having been embalmed was lost, secular knowledge was transformed into sacred incorruptibility. Several centuries of devotees read her "miraculously" intact body to be evidence of her sanctity. Of course, not the least of her compatriots' concerns in maintaining the myth of her incorruptibility was that the city might continue to benefit both economically and spiritually "from the miracles God might choose to perform in its presence" (Pringle 2001:257). Regardless of current official Church positions, many medieval beliefs and practices are imbricated in the attributes of and devotions directed toward both 19th- and 20th-century folk saints' tombs, as well as those of the sanctified splendid performers.

COMMODIFICATION OF SAINTS, THEIR PARTS, AND THEIR SPACES

The commodification of objects associated with medieval saints blurred the distinction between relics and souvenirs, and to this day items infused with the charisma of contemporary folk saints and sanctified heroes whet consumer appetites and feed burgeoning markets. Of course, the remains of the saints themselves participated, metonymically, in their miracle-working. Any part of the body, anything they had used or touched, was deemed to be powerful. By extension, then, objects belonging to the faithful (with which they themselves could touch the tombs), or to other powerful places associated with the saints, also took on some of the saints' power. When a reputed holy person died, the faithful rushed to his home, where "some tore the clothes of the deceased to pieces, whilst others pulled out their hair and nails." The cult of relics, "many of which were sold, traded, falsified, stolen and fought over[,] became increasingly important" (Cunningham 1968:16).

The practice of the translation (transfer) of relics from tombs to churches throughout the Christian world became more common, and the Church itself encouraged veneration of relics among the newly evangelized. The lack of a tomb or relics could "seriously inhibit the kind of popular devotion which produces miracles, and therefore hobble the making of a saint" (Cunningham 1968:16).

GENDER AND SAINTHOOD

The perceived threat from holy women to Church hierarchy was—and continues to be—quite real. In spite of religious claims to spiritual egalitarianism "beyond the grave," the celestial realm continued to be organized according to the customs and values of secular society (Schulenburg 1998:404). The female saint was considered to be a male manqué (Warner 1982:149). It is important to note that the laity clearly not only had come to believe that popular male saints were loci of intercessory power but also began to question the negative religious screeds on the nature of female saints as well. In early pagan and Christian communities alike, women's gifts of miraculous healing and prophecy were considered appropriate; they could function "as charismatic, inspired leaders with their special authority based on divine revelation" (Schulenburg 1998:102).

In her study of religious women in the later Middle Ages, Carolyn Bynum (1987:266–268) reports that the reputations of holy women were more often based on supernatural charismatic authority than were those of men. Mooney extends this view: "holy women were depicted as conduits through whom divine knowledge flowed to humanity. They are called 'vessel' far more often than men"; many folk saints refer to themselves as "vessels" who "lend" their bodies to the possessing saint or deity, be they male or female. Mooney adds, "The sanctity of men tended to be based more on their 'this-worldly' offices and achievements . . . [while] holy women's sanctity derived more from their relatively easy access to the other world through visions, locutions and divinely infused forms of knowledge" (1999:69; cf. Macklin 1988).

The routes to official sainthood for women remain limited and include pain—from physical illnesses, flagellation, and severe penances to the wounds of the stigmata—patterned after the suffering of the Passion of Jesus, as they literally embody a fervent desire to join Him in ecstatic union. Such signs are much more frequently exhibited by women than men. But their private pains needed to "be expressed in a culturally meaningful idiom," recognized by their communities, as well as by the narrators in charge of editing their vitae as they positioned themselves "in the contexts of the drama of salvation" (Kleinberg 1992:105).

By the early 16th century a different official religious climate was emerging. The period was one of growing suspicion of popular religious movements and especially mysticism, which affected the narratives being constructed from holy women's lives, most of which were controlled by their male confessors. Bynum traces these changes: "The model of the female saint, expressed both in popular veneration and in official canonizations, was in many ways the mirror image of society's notion of the witch" (1987:223), a distinction these women share with those shape-changing, shamanic figures whose "betwixt and between" liminal ambiguity has caused anxiety throughout history. Deemed to be "little women" of "mental incapacity and gullibility," they were seen as "prime candidates for diabolical intervention" (Schutte 2001:44–45).

An important concomitant change appeared at this time, providing for an increased emphasis on scholarship among the male Minors and Preachers (Vauchez 1997:354). Bynum connects these points, observing that almost all the males canonized were clerics, while the model of holy behavior offered to the Catholic laity was almost exclusively female (Bynum 1987:21).

As early as the end of the 13th century, then, the issues of today were joined with tensions emerging over "faithlessness to doctrine and the freedom of the spirit, which no one, not even a saint, was able to resolve" (Vauchez 1997:473). I have attempted to describe their characteristics and show how the hegemonic discourse—suffering its own internal dialogic processes—always has had to deal with the dramas and the discourses that contest it. The saintly "heroic group servants" among that number who are allowed to go marching in qualify for the honor according to an evolving "*virtus*": they have moved from martyr, to threatening mystics and miracle-workers, to learned bureaucrats, and, more recently, to the obedient servant who does good works. However, to this day one cannot hope to climb the saintly ladder without the power to work miracles.

In the ensuing sections, I suggest some partial answers to the rueful question posed by one American Catholic theologian: "What happens when formal canonization procedures no longer give us the saints we need?" (Woodward 1990:19).

FOLK SAINTS, SEERS, VISIONARIES, AND MEDIUMS

"Mighty *poderosos*, blessed powerful ones . . . Santisimo Niño Fidencio, Gran General Pancho Villa, Bendito Don Pedrito Jaramillo, virtuosos John F. Kennedy, and blessed Pope Juan Pablo." With this fervent plea, a character in Sandra Cisneros's *Woman Hollering Creek* (1991) appeals for help to the important supernatural beings in her own richly endowed pantheon of spirits. It is a familiar litany, comparable to those to which I have been listening for the past 40 years, on both sides of the Mexico–United States border and as far north as Ohio, Illinois, and Michigan. Two of the powerful 20th-century spirits she invokes, El Niño Fidencio and Don Pedrito Jaramillo (Garza Quirós 1980; Heliodoro y Fabiola 1997; Macklin 1967; Romano 1965), are folk saints; the others, powerful males all, represent military, political, and religious worlds, and all descend regularly to assist today's mediums. But they are drawn from the "feminine" model, mystical, gifted with abilities to transcend natural law, nurturing, and caring, which prefigures the discourses embodied by the folk saints of the past century or so. I will focus here on that quintessential Mexican folk saint, El Niño Fidencio, who probably will languish in unofficial limbo forever (Macklin 1967, 1974a, 1974b, 1988, 1997). Although the focus here is on the discourses surrounding Fidencio, I will draw data from others and, taken together, their stories suggest relevant working propositions about the phenomena.

A QUINTESSENTIAL "LIVING" FOLK SAINT

My returns to the fiestas venerating El Niño Fidencio Síntora Constantino (1898–1938), the Mexican *curandero* and thaumaturge, always evoke a disorienting sense of having emerged through a time warp into a place redolent of the 13th century. That milieu is palpable in 2004, despite the presence of hundreds of trance mediums (*materia*)—the receiving "vessels" (*cajas* or *cajones,* meaning "boxes") for his spirit—their devotees, other supplicants, and the curious, along with various wandering social scientists, *their* students, journalists, and professional filmmakers, all toting expensive video camcorders. El Niño Fidencio's tomb and the other sacred loci are a palimpsest of saintly pasts and, like other saints, his *dies natalis* is celebrated on the day of his death, regardless of the November 13, 1898, date on his birth certificate.

I began in the early 1960s to record and try to understand the discourse that swirls around the "living" saint El Niño Fidencio. At that time, fortunately, I was able to interview many who had known him personally, *en vida,* not only in Espinazo, Nuevo León, where he lived and healed during the last two decades of his life, but also in Ohio, Indiana, Texas, and Monterrey, Mexico. Their lived experiences with him lent both authority and prestige to them and their stories. The focus of their stories was not on "historical" events; rather, it was on the relationship they had with him. To be included in Fidencio's story secured for the narrators a modicum of immortality. Ergo, the "tacit 'pact' between saint and community [was] constantly renegotiated" (Kleinberg 1992:6). Putting oneself in the saint's story is true both of the narrators of today's folk saints and of those with stories of sanctified star/icons.

Significantly, like sufferers in the 13th century, Fidencio's devoted followers have entered into a dyadic contract with the saint before visiting his tomb, in which they promise to offer gifts, including the gift of the pilgrimage itself, in exchange for the help they have solicited. And today, as then (Vauchez 1997: 466), many resort to such a celestial intercessor only when all else fails, when they have been "abandoned by the doctors" to an unhappy fate (Kleinberg 1992:6).

The most popular hymns and prayers locate him firmly within the Catholic Holy Family: Fidencio, the Son of Joseph and Mary. He, himself, identified closely with Jesus, a conflation expressed in the most sacred and popular icon associated with his cult. Known as "El Niño Guadalupano" (Figure 1.1), it is a composite photograph that comprises the face and figure of Fidencio, his (or Jesus's?) right hand raised in a priestly benediction; all is ensconced in the blue, starred cape and distinctive rays of Our Lady of Guadalupe—the "indigenized" version of the Dark Virgin Mary of the Apocalypse, Our Lady of Revelations. The Sacred Heart of Jesus is superimposed on this hierarchy of power. Through the icon, the supplicant appeals to God/Virgin, Jesus, Fidencio, and, finally, the medium/*materia:* multivocality writ large.

But two additional points must be emphasized: first, the Sacred Heart is a feminine symbol, representing the redemptive love of Jesus, and expresses the "dignity and importance of the family" (Moell 1967:812) and, second, this symbol stresses the love of a father for his children and wife as well as "pre-figuring the messiah's sacrificial love in the new Covenant" (Moell 1967:815). El Niño Guadalupano also embraces another central and recurrent theme to be found in saint-making: the sexual ambiguity of sanctified heroes of all stripes. Fidencio was and is widely described as having been effeminate and Espinazo has long been known as a gathering spot for gays. He reportedly was known as one who enjoyed work appropriate to women: he was a good cook, and he liked to clean and arrange the hacienda, which he left looking "brand new." One of the children for whom Fidencio cared told me he always addressed him as "Mama," to which Fidencio always responded, "Yes, my son?" (Macklin 1967:546; author's translation).

El Niño Fidencio and other folk saints imbricate the patterns of two of the most beloved Latin American female saints, Santa Rosa of Lima and Santa Mariana of Quito. They and San Martín de Porres, the "black" mulatto saint of Peru, are the only figures from the Latin American panoply of saints to join the Church-approved community of saints without being full members of an organized religious order. Like folk saints, all three gained their power through their identification with and service to the poor, the sick, and the outcast; all three assumed responsibility for the sins of the world, dedicating their lives to others.[1]

Although the age at which folk saints have died is irrelevant, always they are perceived as having died in the service of others. All were marginal to the social and religious power structures by reason of gender, class, race, or legitimacy of birth (San Martín). All of these "unquiet souls" (Kieckhefer 1984) successfully resisted being bureaucratized by the Church. Their very marginality permitted independence of action and they always operated in *spaces outside* those controlled by the Church. In that way they successfully contested the hegemonic discourse and exercised the power of the weak. To this day, official and unofficial saints following this model are the most revered, venerated, and attended and

Figure 1.1. Fidencio "Guadalupano." (James F. Hopgood Collection)

most frequently invoked. These figures all embody the "warm" charisma of supernatural powers that some individuals claim through a "special, non–formal relation with the divine," rather than the "cold" charisma of office (Kleinberg 1992:64). Always "betwixt and between," they fall into the liminal and threatening interstices between stable hegemonic structures and the hurly-burly of daily life. Folk saints are forever being retrofitted to accommodate modern concepts and spiritual needs and thus remain relevant to the lived experiences of ordinary people.

The threatened institutions—established religious, familial, economic, and governmental—must be always vigilant, shaping, controlling, and domesticating these powerful mavericks, for such power is both political and economic in its consequences.

MODERNITIES, GLOBALIZATIONS, SECULARIZATIONS, THE MEDIA, AND MODERN SELVES

To return now to our focus, how have our worlds and our imaginaries so changed that we now sanctify some splendid performers and find them intelligible, imitable icons? Where do they fit into "mechanisms of self-identity which are shaped by—and yet also shape—the institutions of modernity" (Giddens 1991:2)? Here I will limn only those changes that appear to be related directly to the admission of new stars to the saintly constellations analyzed above.

Scholarly consensus accepts that premodern, "paleo-Durkheimian" societies were more cohesive than post-Renaissance and post-Reformation "modern" societies. People lived and created their social identities within communities in which public and personal lives were more likely than not to be religiously expressed and sanctified. It is also clear that the highly touted "disenchantment" of the world has never been complete. In fact, it is estimated that the number of church adherents in the United States has *risen* from 17 percent in 1776 to about 60 percent today (Finke and Stark 1992:15–16). And contemporary mediums and visionaries continue to create quasitraditional communities, fictive and ephemeral though they may be, in a fragmented, postmodern world. Nonetheless, others seeking transcendence have been left cold by the established creeds of their youth and increasingly refer to themselves as "spiritual" people within whom "God" resides; but when they speak of "religion," they see it as evil, greedy, materialistic, powerful, and manipulative. Nonetheless, during the 1990s, 90 percent of all Americans still identified themselves as religious, "vastly" more than do contemporary Europeans (Moore 1994:4).

A critical difference between "traditional" and "modern" ways of thinking is that the latter's "form of discourse *interrogates the present*" (Gaonkar 2001:14, emphasis added), with important consequences for the making of saints. The Enlightenment having midwived the birth of science, and knowledge now being construed as power, churchmen began to interrogate the nature of the miraculous and simple explanations are no longer sufficient (Hayward 1999). For example, when the Congregation for the Causes of Saints must determine whether or not there has been a healing miracle on the basis of inexplicability, a medical member of the group always immediately consults Medline, a worldwide internet survey, to examine all articles on the disease, its prognosis, and "citations of remissions" (Cornwell 2001:232–233).

R. Laurence Moore's *Selling God: American Religion in the Marketplace of Culture* (1994) traces another important connection between religion and show business: the impact of Protestant revivalism on the style of influential preachers from the 18th century forward. They had to imitate the "talents and training of professional actors" (which they abhorred) if they were to attract the people's attention, and they "became entangled in controversies over commercial entertainments which they both imitated and influenced . . . and shoved American religion into the marketplace of culture" (Moore 1994:43). The sanctifying of selected splendid performers provides just one more choice in the dizzying religious smorgasbord we are offered (Fiske 1992).

Pragmatic humans have always found religion useful in diverse ways. As recently as 1999, a leading publisher reported a "surge in books about the lives of saints or books about people's religious experiences"; he added that "the great thing about religion publishing is that it now includes *business* books, *parenting* books, *dieting* books and *relationship* books" (Carvajal 1999, emphases added). Religion is expected to produce a "kind of spiritual euphoria . . . a comfortable feeling of divine-human 'chumminess,'" in which God is envisioned as a "Friendly Neighbor" (Herberg 1955:282–283). Although there is a notable absence of the *mysterium tremendum* in this view of God, it is a view that invites Elvis Presley and company into the *sanctum sanctorum*. We have come to expect the same kind of 20th-century therapeutic panaceas from all our saints, including sanctified splendid performers.

Andrew Delbanco avers the most striking feature of contemporary culture may be an "unslaked craving for transcendence" (1999:114), but these cravings are highly individual, not collective. Individualism itself and the right to express it is not new, nor is it peculiar to Western society (B. S. Turner 1994:193).[2] What *is* new is the search for transcendence through *expressive* individualism, and this "new kind of self-orientation *seems to have become a mass phenomenon*" (C. Taylor 2002:80, emphasis added). William James emphasized that the real locus of religion is "in individual experience, and not in corporate life" (C. Taylor 2002:7) and that "individuality is founded in feeling" (James 1902:501). James's insights illuminate why the experiences offered by mystical, nurturing, religious heroes who serve others have always been adored; they also suggest why it is that the splendid performers who help us to make sense of our complex quotidian experiences have become the focus of contemporary veneration.

The anthropology of mass media "recognizes the sociocultural and global significance of these phenomena in our everyday lives" (Ginsburg et al. 2002:1) and must be given brief attention here. Contemporary electronic technologies have changed our perceptions of our selves and our worlds, offering new resources and new disciplines for the "construction of imagined selves and imagined worlds," according to Marshall. "They are resources for experiments with self-making in all sorts of societies, for all sorts of persons. They allow scripts for possible lives to be imbricated with the glamour of film stars and fantastic film plots and yet also be tied to the plausibility of news shows, documentaries, and other black-and-white forms of telemediation and printed text" (Marshall 1997: 4–5). Important here is Marshall's conclusion that the imagination becomes "a collective, social fact (following Durkheim's notion that collective representations are social facts), and transcends individual volition" (1997:4–5). As such, it plays a newly significant role.

Although the iconic celebrity/star performer emerged in the middle of the 19th century (cf. Braudy 1997; Garelick 1998), the universal spread of Freudian ideas and the popularization of the Kinsey report on human sexuality, along with the challenges of feminism, the queer, the young, and those clamoring for Black, Red, or Brown power in the post–World War II era, paved the way for their extensive impact. Add the relaxation of film censorship and the stage is set for new heroes, antiheroes, and new views of the self (cf. Doss 1999:128; Dyer 1998:22; Pountain and Robins 2000:70, 138).

Whether our venerated ones are religious figures, race-car drivers, pop singers and performers, soccer players, or movie stars, the practices and behaviors with which we approach them are striking in their catholicity and Catholicity. Although some of these practices (e.g., votive offerings and the widespread burning of candles and incense) predate Catholic Christianity itself, many others derive from the latter tradition and are predictable whether or not the devoted have been brought up Catholic, or even Christian. Although Protestants have been known historically for their hostility to Catholic rituals, there has been a countercurrent since the 19th century in the United States. Among other things, many Americans have been attracted to the "beauty and spiritual realism of Catholic ritual and to its power to create *community and overcome the isolation associated with American individualism*" (Porterfield 2001:62, emphasis added).

The splendid performers have been able to assume their place in the constellation of the venerated in part because the vaguely churched, suspicious many in America see organized religion at best as a benign but mostly empty concept.

As H. J. Muller sums it up, it is "a religiousness without religion . . . a way of sociability or 'belonging' . . . a 'belief in believing'" (1966:235).

THE SELF-MADE SELF

Perhaps now we are ready to address what kind of self must be constructed in order to cope with this complex, fragmented world, in which the guidelines of identity have been cut. What kinds of needs do we now have and whom will we sanctify to meet them? Zygmunt Bauman's analyses (2000, 2001) of our "liquid modernity" show that human nature is no longer seen as the product of divine creation (2001:140). This self has *agency* and must *make* meaning, that is, it is a self that "authors" the world. But, as Dorothy Holland cautions, this 'I' is not a "freewheeling agent, authoring worlds just from creative springs within. . . . Rather, the 'I' is more like Lévi-Strauss's 1966 *bricoleur,* who builds with preexisting materials" (Holland et al. 2002:5) and from those multiple pasts outlined above.

We all inhabit Anthony Giddens's uncertain, shifting, unpredictable, late modern, "post-traditional" world "where uncountable traditions, beliefs and customs mingle with each other" (1991:215). The creation of fragmented, impersonal human relations driven by economic concerns, this self is fit to survive industrialized, modern, secularized, and profane societies. Having little commitment to others or to the public good, the self is ego-centered, lonely, isolated, and alienated. The solipsistic plaint is "Yes, but what about *ME? What about* MY *needs?*" (Russo 1999:85). Accordingly, religious belonging is becoming more and more unhooked from our political, ethnic, regional, and corporate societies (cf. Garelick 1998). This, Ann Swidler concludes, generates "new forms of spirituality" and "a reconfiguring of religious imagery within established, mainstream religious traditions" (2002:41). In such post-Durkheimian worlds—inimical to grand narratives—it is this self-made self that characterizes the new saintly star heroes (Heelas 1996).

Finally, and in summary, it is important to tie theory to praxis: do the above points affect how we act in the real world? Evidently they do. Andrew Delbanco recalls that 60 years ago, 50 thousand children between the ages of 6 and 16 were polled on the question, "Who do you think is the most loved man in the world?" They put God second to Franklin D. Roosevelt. And in 1999 a poll revealed that Bill Clinton and the pope were the two most admired men in the world. Delbanco's conclusion? "Having slipped the yoke of historical validation . . . 'representative men' [have] become reworked into a democratic myth of humble beginnings followed by . . . hard work, discovery and stardom" (1999:98). *Image* capital takes over from *symbolic* capital, to borrow Stuart

Ewen's (1988:38–39) terms, informing representations not only in religion but also in political, economic, and familial institutions. Such societies are likely to produce solipsistic social icons: our splendid performers, our celebrities, stars, and some quasars.

SPLENDID PERFORMERS, CELEBRITIES, STARS, AND QUASARS

So it is that the processes of modernization and democratization and the decline of organized religion along with postindustrial consumer capitalism have created a plethora of bereft, self-absorbed individuals, hungering for meaningful symbols and self-transcendence. But it is a yearning in search of content. Simply to hypothesize a "yearning" for self-transcendence scamps the question: why have we come to expect our splendid performers—stars, icons, idols, or, to use the more generic term, celebrities—to provide that content? Sociologist Chris Rojek demonstrates that it is important to understand the role of celebrities in society because they are "an integral element in the conduct of everyday life, and like the myths of the gods among the ancients, they provide us with role models" (2001:16).

Fame and the qualities it takes to achieve it have fascinated humans since the beginning of recorded history (cf. Braudy 1997; Marshall 1997). Of course, splendidly performing iconic heroes also depend on effective narrators to tell their stories. And the narrators must construct sufficiently meaningful discourses to attract audiences; the latter, then, also want to have a say in shaping their heroes' stories. A significant difference emerges between our two kinds of stories, however. "Group servants" must create a delicate balance between showing proper humility and the equally compelling need to make their extraordinary experiences public, occasionally playing the *faux naïf* (Ferrazi 1996; Schutte 2001). Such modesty is not an issue for either splendid performers/celebrities or their storytelling agents.

Nowadays, the sanctified among the ranks of celebrated icons include individuals as disparate as Elvis Presley, James Dean, Marilyn Monroe, Diana, Princess of Wales, Evita Perón, the Mexican American pop singer Selena (Arraras 1997), and race-car driver Dale Earnhardt (to cite only a few). Although the qualities of stars/icons/idols in many ways stand in binary opposition to those of official religious and folk saints, their devotees bestow on them holy attributes. For example, simply by touching the grave of former First Lady Jacqueline Kennedy, "hundreds of sick and dying Americans [were cured] of everything from arthritis to terminal cancer" (Jefferies 1994), and Elvis Presley reputedly had "healing hands" (Doss 1999:170).

It is clear that although icon/idol/celebrity culture may appear to be secular, its roots lie in the sacred. Rojek suggests that many of the symbols of "success and failure in celebrity draw on myths and rites of religious ascent and descent" (2001:74), as the following case materials show.

If El Niño Fidencio can be considered to be the quintessential folk saint, surely Elvis Presley qualifies as the quintessential celebrated, sanctified quasar. I present his case briefly, comparing its data with those of others to tease out generic star-saint qualities; here I rely heavily on Erika Doss's 1999 analysis in *Elvis Culture*. Doss shows how the faith of fans demonstrates the "important links among popular culture, cultural production and religiosity in America's contemporary public sphere" (1999:113). She reports that comments like "it's a religious thing" tend to dominate the discourse surrounding Elvis's abiding cultural presence in contemporary America and around the world. Quasireligious factors and conditions that seem to confirm Elvis's contemporary deification include sacred "texts" (his recordings), disciples, prophets, and relics and pilgrimages to his birthplace in Tupelo, Mississippi, and his Graceland grave-site shrine (cf. Hopgood 1998b, 2000 on James Dean). As early as 1957 there were attempts to start an Elvis Presley church and now many exist. As recently as 1995 a group in St. Louis, Missouri, sought his canonization (Doss 1999:77). Followers see in him many Christlike qualities, including belief in his resurrection, a conviction shored up by frequent "sightings." Ritual activities in Memphis each August reinforce such ideas. Some followers copy the look of Graceland in their own homes (as Fidencio's followers do with Espinazo) and celebrate him through the stuff of consumer culture, as they set about constructing and reconstructing their own identities.

The multivocality of the star/icon image, deriving from its ambiguity, provides a tabula rasa onto which the "great army of the rudderless" (Barzun 1959:163) can project multiple identifications, massive wish fulfillment, diverse dreams, fantasies, and hopes. Simultaneously, one can enjoy a frisson of the forbidden. By embodying many counter-cultural values that circled the globe from the mid-1950s forward, stars invite audiences to rethink conventional understandings of reality. As Sarah Benton's analysis of the death of Princess "Di" notes, "the defining contradiction of any contemporary mass movement . . . [is that] to be universal it must be *diverse*" (1998:94, emphasis added). The stars' physical icons make visual their semiotic diversity. For example, today Elvis Presley is "imaged" as a dark, swarthy rock-and-roll mariachi for Mexicans and a "lean and energetic guitar-playing samurai" for Japanese audiences. So it is that various racial and ethnic groups can claim, "He's just like one of us" (Doss 1999:178).

Primary among those narrators who construct the discourses of the splendid performers are their professional press agents, who are their most important "confessors." Taking a cue from C. Wright Mills's classic 1956 work on "the power elite," Ewen goes so far as to assert that "no contemporary analysis of social and economic power can avoid the devices of press agentry and image management . . . the message [being] that the 'underlying population' can achieve the status of 'those on top'" (1988:94). And because the fans of folk saints as well as of star saints are so dependent on the "materiality" (Doss 1999:249) of their idols, they are also dependent on those who produce the "marketable stuff" they want. Doss's observation that even devotees' "personal and hybridic images of Elvis do not operate completely apart from the 'official' commercial image" (1999:249) controlled by Elvis Presley Enterprises, Inc., is true of all of the other hero categories considered here.

While it is imperative that *religious* group-servant hero-saints must have died "well" (or *be perceived* as dying well in service to their faith and others), the *age* at which they died was irrelevant. Sanctified stars, it seems, *must* die young, as did Elvis. Thus to die "surrounded by an ambiguity that supports continuing tragic . . . speculation" is considered to be a "good career move" (Schickel 2000:128). The death of Diana provides an exemplar par excellence: speculation concerning her demise abounds with conspiracy theories. She will not age; she will continue to glow, "forever young, forever vital, in the hearts of those she touched" (Newey 1998:148). Her very identity seemed to consist of her image, of being photographed and being looked at, as if she were a virtual person.

Followers of sainted stars expect dramas and tragedies in exchange for the celebrity they confer (Lapham 2001:152). We revel in the schadenfreude offered by their troubled lives: we see that the glamourous, rich, and greatly admired are sufferers—even as we are—in a post-Freudian, therapized, victim-speak world. True, some of the *religious* saints may be "victim-souls," but they sacrifice themselves for the salvation of others (Freze 1989, 1991), a concept quite different from that embodied by the "victim-stars."

The victimhood of the popular star/icons can be inferred from the *content* of their deaths. The death of a sanctified group-servant is transformed by the grand narrative of sainthood into a grand celebration of a sacrifice made for the redemption of others. The death of a sanctified star stands in stark contrast: all of the narratives of the stars' deaths construe the objects of their adoration as victims—of dysfunctional families, of society, of demanding followers, of the press, of the paparazzi who hounded them—in short, as victims largely of their own celebrity. They share with folk saints an almost obligatory narrative piece in which they are presented as having suffered poor, lonely, outsider childhoods, neglected (often) by alcoholic or absent parents, which cripples them in later life, psychically or physically. But their routes to redemption are quite different. Would-be saints are saved by means of supernatural intervention, and their deaths redeem others. The stars often must turn to substance abuse, suffer a major fall from grace, and be applauded when they triumph. We, too, can suffer with and through their anguish.

The simulation of appropriate religious behavior extends to memorabilia. The relics of *all* sainted stars, including "genuine fake relics" (e.g., false bits and pieces of Elvis's hair and fingernails), are cherished and sell briskly at the festivals accompanying rituals marking key dates in their lives. As is true of things associated with official and folk saints, the relics also have value added if they were found in, purchased in, or simply touched the *sacred space* in which the saintly one lived and worked.

The devotees of both religious and star saints view them as mediators, intercessors between themselves and other devotees and God. Typical is the comment of an Elvis fan: "There is a distance between human beings and God. That is why we are close to Elvis" (Doss 1999:70). But the ambiguity of sanctified stars' images offers alternative, sometimes rebellious, models of behavior to their audiences. Their lives test the limits of hegemonic discourse. Perhaps it is fitting that a song, "Live Fast, Love Hard, and Die Young," composed and popularized by the late, influential Faron Young, epitomized for many a more radical challenge to the established order than available political movements could offer (Pountain and Robins 2000:67; Rojek 2001). James Dean is often quoted as having said, "Live fast, die young, and leave a good-looking corpse" (Grant 1991:62). And gender-bending has *always* been a part of Christianity and *always* has caused cultural anxieties for both Catholics and Protestants, whose binary theology has clear boundaries between masculine and feminine representations.

Enter the sanctified stars of the mid-20th century, who blur these uncomfortable boundaries further. Few of today's Elvis impersonators imitate the hypermasculine image he sometimes projected; it has never been a favorite among his fans, Doss (1999:155) tells us. In his self-conscious yearning for fame, he identified with Liberace (Doss 1999:155), creating a more "transgendered" sexual image than those of other male entertainers of his era. In so doing, he offered an androgynous figure that "helped to de-stabilize conventional understandings of masculinity" (Doss 1999:126). He studied the work of James Dean and Montgomery Clift, "both of whom were gay" (Dyer 1998:53).

In short, these star heroes helped to shift the model for ideal manhood from that of the super-macho "frontier individualist and gung-ho patriot John Wayne" (Pountain and Robins 2000:70) to a more vulnerable, emotional, sensitive, feminized model. Although Elvis's gender-slippery image—both tender and tough—subverts "the essentialist view of male and female sexuality," it also allows men to claim him as "a rebel stud and women as an intimate friend," a cultural representation "attractive to both gays and lesbians" (Doss 1999:151).

A final trait important to this analysis is that most official saints, *all* folk saints, and *all* of the star saints on whom I have data spoke little. When they did, their pronouncements were predictably vague and difficult to verify as having originated with them. Fans imbue their heroes with great wisdom, but inasmuch as almost nothing of their own words are reported, their "texts"—whether deemed to be "philosophical" or "theological"—are as vague and open-ended as those their multivocal images offer. The "sayings" followers repeat overwhelmingly come from the stars' songs or the scripted dialogues from their films. Rojek notes that any attempt to "articulate or codify [stars'] creeds . . . usually falls flat" (2001:69). When stars try "to express a creed of living, [their thoughts] are confused and often embarrassing" (Rojek 2001:70). Stars' messages can replace easily the equally vague messages of the most popular official saints. Consider one of Mother Teresa's "quotable quotes": her interpretation of poverty informs us that "it is very beautiful for the poor to accept their lot. . . . The world is being much helped by the suffering of the poor people" (Hitchens 1995:11). One surely cannot get into trouble following such "theological" advice, which—with both saint and star icons—provides a tabula rasa onto which one can project one's hopes and wishes and, in return, feel "real good."

By way of summary, one must conclude that while the stars/icons/saints do not introduce a new discourse, they extend and make acceptable some existing basic, but hardly subversive, themes. We learn that being "like you and me" (Hopgood 2000:355–356; cf. Gamson 1994), *humanness*, is one of the distinguishing characteristics of the sainted star performers, while that which traditionally has been demanded of religious candidates for sainthood is precisely their "otherness." The laity always has been expected to emulate the latter, even though such saints are at once imitable and inimitable. Celebrities/icons/idols reinforce the conception that they are imitable, there being no barriers in contemporary democratic culture that a determined individual cannot overcome (Marshall 1997:246).

THE SAINTS REDUX: LEAPING, LURCHING, AND LANGUISHING

On Sunday, June 16, 2002, Pope John Paul II used his "divinely guided ability" (Woodward 1990:17) to "recognize" that Padre Pio is now among the elect. The miracle-working Italian peasant–become–Capuchin friar, *né* Francesco Forgione, henceforth is to be known as St. Pio de Pietrelcina. Having died as recently as 1968, St. Pio had marched smartly along to join the more than 400 others already canonized by John Paul II since he became pope in 1978. In what some have criticized as "halo inflation," this pope has recognized more saints than all his predecessors of the past ten centuries combined (Woodward 1990:118; cf. McBrien 2001:49). As of March 22, 2004, the number reached 476. Some disenchanted critics have referred to the Vatican as the "saint-machine," one journalist going so far as to call John Paul II's saint-making "a holy rampage, a beatific binge" (cited in Schulenburg 1998:394). The bracingly matter-of-fact

Father Richard P. McBrien, whose lapidary aperçus enlighten every discussion on the subject, agrees in suggesting the pope should consider a "moratorium" (Henneberger 2002).

Thanks to the impact of electronic media, there has been a filtering up of attitudes and beliefs, tying popular figures and democratic attitudes to saint-making; John Paul II must be lauded for listening to some insistent modern voices. Multiculturalism is *in*. An indefatigable globe-trotter, he is the most-traveled pope in history. Clearly he is interested in diversifying the demographic profile of candidates he elevates; he has increased the scope of his choices geographically (specifically in the Americas, Africa, and Asia) (cf. Arce Gargollo 1992) and in socioeconomic background, gender, and occupation. He has sought out those who represent marginalized or minority peoples who have had no saints to celebrate, such as the Rom (Gypsies) and the indigenous peoples of the Americas.[3] It is also noteworthy that John Paul II can take credit for having canonized 63 percent of the women on the roster of saints.

A quantitative, demographic view of recent beatifications and canonizations might lead one to infer that the present pope has at least one foot planted firmly in the camp of modernity. That having been said, however, a brief content analysis of the homilies accompanying these "new" models suggests an alternative conclusion. If sanctified laity are rare, happily *married* lay saints are even rarer, as there continues to be a positive identification of sanctity with virginity (Woodward 1990:337). Not a footling matter, it was not until 2001 that a pope beatified the *first* married couple and declared "venerable" a second—but for highly traditional reasons. Also, at first glance, it might appear that the slightly increased number of laywomen among those beatified in the 1990s could serve as rallying symbols for the Church and be role models for women. Alas, all so elevated have been praised primarily for their obedience and humility, regardless of other accomplishments. The not-so-innocuous remain unlikely to receive official recognition, regardless of their saintlike selflessness.

Nowadays the *populus* and the specialists alike speak in bluntly critical, raucous voices. Item: the July 31, 2002, canonization of the Aztec (Nahua) Indian Juan Diego Cuauhtlatoatzin, Mexico's 29th saint and the first Native American to be so honored, may be taken as paradigmatic of the struggle among those contesting, strident voices. To emphasize his Indianness, his mother's Nahua surname was often used in news reports of his saintly recognition. Juan Diego is a saint for "nobodies," it is said. Some deem him worthy of sainthood for having been the divinely elected conduit for the 1531 message of the ever-miraculous, nurturing Dark Virgin of Guadalupe; others see St. Juan Diego as "a vindication of our Indian people . . . so long subject to injustice, so vulnerable" (Weiner 2001). Yet other contemporary narrators—both in and out of the hierarchy—denounce Juan Diego as an "invention" of the Spanish friars and accuse the

Holy Father of having bequeathed to the Church "a holy ghost" (Dreher 2002; cf. Wills 2002:249–252).

But the October 6, 2002, "recognition" of John Paul II's 468th saint, Josemaría Escrivá de Balaguer (1902–1975), stimulated more internal criticism than any other. The latter has been described as having exhibited a "lack of humility, a foul temper, and vanity" (McBrien 2001:53). The rebarbative founder of the secretive, elite, conservative Opus Dei in 1928, he is a particularly arresting but polarizing figure. Even his "stunningly hasty beatification" (McBrien 1997:442) evoked strong criticism: it has been bruited about the Vatican that "it was known that the pope had the power to dispense with the requirement for miracles in a canonization process, [but] it was not known that he could also dispense with the requirement for virtue" (McBrien 2001:54).

Clearly, the Final Arbiter of Stories continues to reign, albeit shakily. The power of the papal homilies continues to promote a very traditional agenda, the apparent diversity of those elevated notwithstanding. Obedience and support for papal authority continue to rank highest among desirable saintly virtues.

SUMMARY AND CONCLUSIONS

From Christianity's first millennium and a half, when a holy person's hierophants determined who should join the celestial chorus, to the present, when we see the official saint-makers frantically "recognizing" new models, vigorous other voices have contested the choices. Many of the rudderless are content to form a "dyadic contract" with their own powerful, caring saints, as George Foster (1967:233–235) observed, to communicate with him or her directly. For some, beautiful, ever-young, solipsistic saintly stars/icons suffice. The search for models around which we can "author" a self in an uncertain, fragmented, fraught world goes on (Wuthnow 1994) even as the grand narrative of sainthood is unraveling.

I have described and interpreted "the strength and vitality of certain 'root paradigms,' and the social dramas where conflicting groups and personages attempt to assert their own and deplete their opponents' paradigms" (V. Turner 1974:13). I have also revealed some of the processes through which the religious paradigms represented by saints and near-saints are "continually reinvested with vitality and . . . maintained by the periodic emergence of counter paradigms which under certain conditions become reabsorbed in the initial and central paradigm" (V. Turner 1974:15).

Finally, the impact of religious saint-making processes and rituals on the treatment of stars/icons/celebrities has been described. Chris Rojek, discussing star/celebrity culture, brings my argument full circle when he notes that organized religion has succumbed to celebrity culture's emphasis on "bigger and brighter," citing John Paul II's "ritual kissing of the soil on alighting from his aircraft." He opines that "the staged authenticity of mass rallies and live TV links clearly borrow many of the ceremonies and devices refined by Hollywood and the rock industry for the presentation of celebrity to the public" (Rojek 2001:97). Even the redoubtable Mother Teresa scurried after photo-ops—her eyes always modestly downcast—with the rich and powerful, the famous, and the infamous. After having been photographed with the shady John-Roger Hinkins, for example, she permitted a scrim of Calcutta's slums to be slipped in, which added symbolic, but inauthentic, value to the picture. John-Roger claims to have a "'spiritual consciousness' that is superior to that of Jesus Christ" (Hitchens 1995:7). So Rojek gets it exactly right when he adds that although "celebrity culture is no substitute for religion, it is the milieu in which religious recognition and belonging are now enacted . . . celebrity culture provides the scripts, prompts and supporting equipment of 'impression management' for the presentation of self in public life" (2001:97). Hiroshi Aoyagi concludes his analysis of pop idols and Asian identity with the gnomic observation that "the times seek the idols and the idols lead the times" (2000:318).

NOTES

1. These folk Catholic-based cults appear to share many of the functions Josef Meri describes for Muslim saints: they flourish where there is an absence of effective centralization and "exercise control over the living through dreams and visions," their tombs becoming public space where the folk can interact with saints, "spiritually, physically, and ritually" (1999:273).

2. Bryan S. Turner's analysis of "the self and the reflexive modernity" argues that the "historical and artistic research" from China belies the claim of an exclusive Western individualism. He sees the "focus of *Western* individualism as a persistent feature of orientalism (1994:193–194, emphasis added). Ronald J. Morgan's (2002) analysis of the public role of Roman Catholic institutions from the late 19th century on, in "the rhetoric of identity" in Spanish and Portuguese America, is valid for other countries as well.

3. He can take credit for having beatified the first Native American, Kateri Tekakwitha (1656–1680), in 1980. Of Algonquin-Mohawk ancestry, she became a Christian in 1677.

2

The Making of Saints and the Vicissitudes of Charisma in Netivot, Israel

Yoram Bilu

In recent years Israel has witnessed an astonishing revival of hagiolatric traditions. Old-time saints' sanctuaries are glowing with renewed popularity, new ones are being added to the native "sacred geography," and the list of contemporary charismatic rabbis acknowledged as *tzaddikim* (sing. *tzaddik*, a pious man, endowed with holiness) is constantly growing (Gonen 1998). The cult of the saints in contemporary Israel clearly exceeds narrow ethnic boundaries, but the imprint of the Jewish Maghrebi legacy of saint veneration has been evident in many of its manifestations (Bilu 2001).

Given the central role of Moroccan Jews and their descendants in this hagiolatric revival, my aim in this chapter is threefold. First, by way of introduction, I situate Jewish Moroccan saint worship in the proper historical context and present its current manifestations in Israel. Second, focusing on the vicissitudes of Maghrebi-based sanctification in one setting, the town of Netivot in southern Israel, I explore the processes by which charisma is manufactured, maintained, and contested under present-day "modern" and "postmodern" circumstances. Noting that Weber, in introducing charisma to the social sciences, asserted that "charismatic authority" may be *alleged* or *presumed* rather than actual (Weber 1946:296), I take a constructivist approach to charisma, viewing it as tenuous, processual, and amenable to calculated use and manipulation. Third, shifting my gaze from processes and mechanisms of charismatization to the setting where they have been deployed, I seek to account for the fact that these activities have been thriving in places such as Netivot, situated in the urban periphery of the country.

JEWISH SAINT WORSHIP IN MOROCCO AND ISRAEL

Saint worship played a major role in the lives of the Jews in traditional Morocco and constituted a basic component of their ethnic identity. In form, style, and prevalence this cultural phenomenon clearly bears the hallmarks of indigenous saint worship, perhaps the most significant feature of Moroccan Islam (Crapanzano 1973; Eickelman 1976; Geertz 1968; Gellner 1969). At the same time, however, it was also reinforced by the deep-seated conception of the *tzaddik* in classical Jewish sources (Goldberg 1983; Stillman 1982).

Most of the Jewish Moroccan saints were charismatic rabbis, distinguished by their erudition and piety, and were believed to possess a special spiritual force, which did not fade away after death. This force, akin to the Moroccan Muslim *Baraka* (Rabinow 1975; Westermarck 1926), could be utilized for the benefit of the saints' adherents. In contrast with their Muslim counterparts, most of the Jewish Moroccan *tzaddikim* were identified as such only after their deaths. Therefore, their miraculous feats were usually associated with their tombs. At the same time, however, the strong sense of inherited blessedness inherent in the Jewish notion of *zekhut avot* (literally, the virtue of the ancestors) allowed for the emergence of some dynasties of *tzaddikim*. The best known were the Abu-Hatseiras, the Pintos, and the Ben-Baruchs (Ben-Ami 1984).

Generally speaking, the presence of the saints was a basic given in the social reality of Moroccan Jews, a central idiom for articulating a wide range of experiences. The main event in the veneration of each saint was the collective pilgrimage to his tomb on the anniversary of his death and *hillulah* (celebration) there. In the case of the more renowned saints, thousands of pilgrims from various regions would gather around the tombs for several days, during which they feasted on sacrificial cattle, drank *mahia* (arak), danced and chanted, prayed, and lit candles. All these activities, combining marked spirituality and high ecstasy with mundane concerns, were conducted in honor of the *tzaddik*.

In addition to collective pilgrimages, visits to saints' sanctuaries were made on an individual basis in times of plight. As intermediaries between God Almighty and the believers, the saints were considered capable of solving problems that included the whole range of human concerns. The presence of the saint was also strongly felt in daily routine, as people would cry out his name and dream about him whenever facing a problem. At home, candles were lit and festive meals (*se'udot*) were organized in his honor. In many cases the relationship with the saint amounted to a symbiotic association spanning the entire life course of the devotee. Rather than a frozen set of cultural vestiges, however, Jewish Maghrebi hagiolatry was a dynamic system, accommodating to shifting circumstances, in which new saints and shrines successively emerged, sank, and resurfaced.

The social fabric of Moroccan Jewry, including their hagiolatric traditions, was ruptured following the massive waves of immigration from Morocco to Israel during the 1950s and 1960s. To the predicament of homecoming, fed by cultural shock and the enormous economic difficulties (Cohen 1983; Deshen and

Shokeid 1974), one could add the traumatic disengagement from the saints whose tombs had been left behind. Indeed, in the first years after immigration, Jewish Moroccan *hillulot* (pl.) underwent a process of diminution and decentralization, being celebrated in small groups, mostly at home or in the local synagogue (Stillman 1995; Weingrod 1985). Once the newcomers became more rooted in the local scene, however, and more confident in their Israeli identity, hagiolatric practices were forcefully and ingeniously revived as emblems of ethnic pride, compatible with the resurgence of ethnic sentiments in many immigrant-absorbing countries (Bennett 1975; Gans 1979). The renaissance of Jewish Moroccan hagiolatry in the new country was made possible by the availability and flexible employment of several compensatory substitutes for the deserted shrines.

Most accessible among these alternatives were the tombs of local *tzaddikim*, mainly from the Biblical and Talmudic eras. The "Moroccanization" of these old-time pilgrimage traditions has been particularly noted in the popular, all-Israeli *hillulot* of Rabbi Shimon Bar-Yohai in Meron near Safed and of Rabbi Meir Ba'al HaNess in Tiberias (Brown and Mohr 1982; cf. Bilu and Abramovitch 1985). In addition, Maghrebi Jews living in development towns (*arey pituah*), hastily built throughout the country to accommodate newcomers, have adopted burial sites of native *tzaddikim* in their vicinity.

A second avenue of saint worship renewal, directly coping with the painful disengagement from the old Maghrebi *tzaddikim*, has been the "symbolic translocation" of saints from Morocco to Israel (Ben-Ami 1981; Bilu 1990). This alternative, restorative rather than merely compensatory, has involved men and women of Moroccan origin who erected sanctuaries for *tzaddikim* buried in Morocco after inspiring dream encounters with them. Several development towns in the urban periphery of Israel now boast shrines of Maghrebi saints transferred to their new locales via dreams.

Because of the opposition of the Moroccan authorities, the more palpable restorative method of digging the graves of saints buried in Morocco for reburial in Israel is underrepresented in Israel's sacred geography. Of the few sites in this track, the most noteworthy is the quadripartite shrine in the town of Kiriat-Gat housing four sainted figures of the noble Pinto family.

Given the dynamic nature of saint veneration in Morocco, it is not surprising that in Israel new cult centers have been established around the tombs of contemporary rabbis and their living descendants. Unlike the previous alternatives, all of which dealt with existing traditions of longtime *tzaddikim*, this one involves making new, modern saints. One of the early cases in this category was the emergence of Rabbi Hayyim Houri, a Tunisian rabbi who died in 1957 in Beersheba, as the saint of this southern town (Weingrod 1990). Impressive though it was, the adulation of Houri was soon eclipsed by the cult of the saints that evolved in nearby Netivot, first around the shrine of Rabbi Israel Abu-Hatseira (affectionately known as Baba Sali), a descendant of a virtuous family of southern Morocco, and later around other sanctuaries.

It is the making of new saints in Netivot that is the concern here. The vicissitudes of charisma in the town are portrayed as a two-act drama. First, referring to a study conducted in the late 1980s (Bilu and Ben-Ari 1992), I present the entrepreneurial efforts of Baba Sali's controversial son and heir, Baruch Abu-Hatseira (Baba Baruch), to propagate his father's charisma and to bask in his glory. Second, I discuss the arrival on the local scene of new contenders for saintly status, focusing on a recent case of "postmodern sanctification." I seek to highlight the complex interplay of creative and inventive processes that facilitate sanctification in a modern industrialized setting and the fragile and ephemeral aspects of charisma that curb it.

PROPAGATING LINEAGE CHARISMA: THE ABU-HATSEIRAS OF NETIVOT

The death of Baba Sali in January 1984 in Netivot, at the age of 94, has been the most decisive event in the renaissance of saint worship in Israel. By the late 1980s, Baba Sali's grave site had already become a pilgrimage center of national importance, on a par with the old-time sanctuaries of Rabbi Shimon in Meron and Rabbi Meir in Tiberias. Bustling with supplicants throughout the year, the grave site draws tens of thousands of celebrants from all parts of the country during the *hillulah* of the *tzaddik*. More than any other *hillulot*, the festival in Netivot is the object of intense "promotion campaigns," replete with media coverage, official invitations, special bus lines, organized markets, and government backing. It seems that these modern means have been quite instrumental in facilitating Baba Sali's rapid sanctification and in transforming him into a sainted figure of national caliber.

In terms of family background and lifestyle, Baba Sali lent himself easily to aggrandizement and mythologization. As the grandson of Rabbi Yaakov Abu-Hatseira (1808–1880), the first exponent of piety and holiness in the celebrated Abu-Hatseira family, Baba Sali was the present-day epitome of the family's blessing with his profound devotion and unswerving asceticism. Given his longevity—born in 1890 and still active in the early 1980s—he could easily become a substitute for the saints "deserted" in Morocco. Yet the mechanisms underlying his swift and pervasive genesis as a saint of Israel are worth exploring. For a contemporary rabbi, virtuous and venerable as he may have been, to transcend the bounds of historical reality within a mere half-decade appears extraordinary indeed. The massive and effective recruitment of the modern means of the media, the state, and large bureaucratic organizations appears to have played a decisive role in facilitating his rapid glorification.

When the limelight turns from Baba Sali to his son and successor, Rabbi Baruch Abu-Hatseira (Baba Baruch), the prime mover behind the undertaking in Netivot, the question of sanctification becomes all the more intriguing. Unlike his virtuous father, Baruch did not devote himself to scholarship and asceticism but pursued a political career. He joined the Religious National Party and was elected deputy mayor of the town of Ashkelon. During this period he was party to a much-publicized adulterous affair and, in his capacity as a deputy mayor, was accused of corrupt practices, found guilty, and sentenced to a long period in prison. On being paroled after five years, he joined his father for the last three months of Baba Sali's life.

Despite the corrosion of his public image, Baba Baruch managed to take his father's mantle and possession of his father's house in Netivot, and he arranged for Baba Sali's burial in the local cemetery. In a short time he transformed the informal network of his father's supporters in Israel and abroad into a very efficient organization. Relying on the generous financial aid of these adherents, he built a magnificent sanctuary to cater to pilgrims at the burial site. While Baruch's public image has remained controversial, it is safe to say that he has been accepted by a wide circle of Moroccan Jews as his father's legitimate successor and as a possessor of the family's special blessing. Baruch's notorious personal record as a former convict and adulterer makes the issue of his legitimacy all the more compelling. Even in the eyes of veteran devotees, Baruch's ample blessedness (*zekhut avot*), akin to lineage or clan charisma (Tambiah 1984:326), could not automatically cleanse him of his problematic background. In what follows I am concerned with the sophisticated means Baruch has employed to gain support and validation, as well as with the lingering precariousness of propagated charisma and the challenges it might face.

Since Baruch has premised his actions on his inextricable bond with his late father in seeking recognition for his claim, we should turn now to the image of Baba Sali, as molded and propagated by Baba Baruch. In the plethora of stories about him, Baba Sali is depicted as an ascetic and withdrawn figure, entirely free of mundane concerns. He is said to have seldom left his house, having his synagogue and ritual bath located within its confines. Devoting much of his time to solitary prayer and learning, often accompanied by week-long fasts, he radiated an image of humble self-sufficiency, constriction, introversion, and "invisibility." While the rabbi's image was clearly shaped by actual conduct, what is of importance is how his behavior has captured the imagination of the masses and produced a fertile matrix for mythologization.

Superimposed on the rabbi's passive image, in the eyes of the followers, is a representation at once complementary and antithetical. In this representation, which Baba Baruch took pains to promulgate and make known, each minor detail in the rabbi's life is portrayed as partaking of cosmic significance. Thus his excessively penitent behavior on the eve of the 1967 War was described as instrumental for Israel's swift victory, and his finally settling in Netivot was accounted for as an emulation of Abraham the Patriarch, who erected his tent in nearby Gerar more than three millennia ago. This transcendence of historical bounds was facilitated by the fact that Baba Sali is also said to have been a practicing Kabbalist, deeply immersed in Jewish mysticism.

In order to bask in the glory of his mythologized father and enjoy the lineage charisma, Baruch had to actively reconcile the moral stains in his biography with the familial aura of holiness. This he has managed to do by constructing an autobiographical narrative that creatively dwells on, rather than disregards, the darker aspects of his former life. Using a Biblical metaphor, Baruch likens prison to a furnace in which the dross was separated from the gold and eliminated from his soul. Likewise, he presents the dire consequences of his short-lived political career as a heavenly trial, part of a mystical plan to test, purify, and transform him into the worthy heir of his sainted father. In highlighting the role of prison as a penitentiary, he seeks to make a virtue out of his failings.

Taking advantage of the fact that he was alone with his father during his final hours, Baruch presents this critical time as the matrix for his self-transformation and symbolic rebirth. He maintains that just before the departure of his soul, his father kissed him on his lips and thus, in resonance with the Maghrebi notion of holy grace as concrete and transferable (Crapanzano 1973; Eickelman 1976: 160), endowed him with his spiritual gifts. In this vein, emphasizing the essential similarity and continuity between father and son has been one of Baruch's central rhetorical strategies. Since his position is clearly dependent on this perceived similarity, Baruch has been adamant to convey the notion that his every move is inspired and closely monitored by his father, mainly through visitational dreams. Moreover, he also hastened to wear his father's mantle and shoes and to grow a beard like his. The physical similarity, together with Baruch's adoption of the title "Baba," has had a strong impact on many common believers, further reinforcing the idea that Baba Sali's soul now inhabits his son. Baruch also embraced his father's peculiar curing mode, a special blessing uttered over water, which Rabbi Yaakov presumably bequeathed to his descendants. The widespread distribution of miraculous stories regarding Baba Baruch's healing water further substantiates his claim that he enjoys his ancestors' blessing.

This is the background for the emergence of the thriving shrine in Netivot in terms of the dramatis personae involved. However, to account for the swiftness and scope of the sanctification of father and son, we shift our analytic lens from Baba Sali and Baba Baruch themselves to the means by which their stories have been passed on. We pass, in other words, from charisma to its production.

PRODUCING CHARISMA

The conscious planning evident in the sanctification of Baba Sali and the development of his site in Netivot (Weingrod 1990:20) highlights the extent to which charismatic qualities can be actively promoted and propagated (Shils 1975:128). This emphasis on intentionality and purposefulness may lead us to expand Weber's (1968:241ff) classic treatment of charisma by using the analytical metaphors of "manufactured charisma" (Glassman 1975) and "synthetic charisma" (Ling 1987). Both terms, provided by scholars dealing with charisma in complex, industrialized societies, seek to convey the central role of the various media and technologies in creating and propagating claims to charisma. These scholars have focused almost exclusively on the charismatic "packaging" of political figures, tacitly assuming that charismatization in the religious realm is somehow still a pure, "real" charisma that is not actualized by any artificial means. My purpose here is to go beyond their exclusive focus on political figures and to suggest that a similar process of manufacture can be discerned in regard to the charisma of religious figures. To that end, I will explore the effective system for selling the saint that Baba Baruch set into motion.

Baba Baruch's organizational efforts capitalized on the proximity between his residence (formerly his father's) and the Baba Sali burial site in Netivot, which enabled him to exert a close control over the shrine and to monopolize the intentional use of his father's "assets." The space between the house and the tomb, about half a kilometer, was originally empty, so each site could be extended toward the other. On one side, the tomb was enclosed in a spacious whitewashed sanctuary and an opulently decorated synagogue was erected next to it. This impressive edifice, visible from a distance, is now part of a larger, walled enclosure that includes a parking lot, a picnic area, a restaurant, vendors' booths, and other facilities. On the other side, the father's (now Baruch's) residence was enlarged and the foundations for Kiriat Baba Sali, a big religious campus, were laid. Today the campus includes several buildings housing the headquarters of Baba Baruch's organization, a *yeshiva* (religious academy), a *talmud torah* (religious school), and a kindergarten. These were built in a distinctively Moorish style, sharply at odds with the plebeian neighborhood surrounding them.

In order to implement his plans, Baba Baruch has founded Amotat Baba Sali, a nonprofit, tax-exempt organization composed of public figures, rabbis, lawyers, and accountants. The board of directors meets irregularly in the rabbi's house to discuss projects designed to "cultivate and deepen Baba Sali's heritage," as one brochure puts it, but the board usually just rubber-stamps Baruch's plans. Baruch also controls a small staff of executives, aides, and secretaries who administer the institutions bearing Baba Sali's name. Complete with computers, fax machines, and cordless telephones, the offices of this staff are marked by an atmosphere closer to that of a quietly run, efficient business firm than that of a center of religious zealots.

Clearly, the unparalleled sanctification of Baba Sali owes at least some of its success to the peculiar "selling" of this saint. Recall how constricted, home-bound, and "invisible" Baba Sali's actual life was. To achieve the power of a national myth, a private story had to go public; the invisible had to be placed under the spotlights, within the public eye. Thus, both the hidden, ineffable details of Baba Sali's life and the elaborate projects of Baba Baruch had to be highlighted and publicized. This publicity has gone far beyond anything that can be achieved by word of mouth. A rich variety of literary products—periodicals, monographs, and book series using the latest types of graphic layout, printing, and binding—recount the miraculous deeds and life story of the late patriarch. Some texts are specifically written for children, while others, translated into French, are designed for the Jewish Moroccan diaspora abroad. In addition, as the annual festival approaches, the country is subjected to a media blitz: special notices are published in major newspapers, and the day's program is posted on billboards all over Israel. By granting interviews to newspapers and journals and securing regular radio and television coverage, Baba Baruch achieves name recognition. Every year the big dailies carry color spreads of the *hillulah*, complete with pictures of Baba Baruch, political dignitaries, and "typical" believers caught up in the ecstasy of the festival.

Like the media, the numerous objects that carry Baba Sali's image or that of his shrine also help to manufacture charisma. A partial list of these products, marketed on the site and around the country, includes *mezuzot*,[1] prayer books, clocks, candles, cups, plates, pictures, postcards, photographs, holograms, key chains, audio cassettes with songs praising the saint, and videotapes of the *hillulah*. While Baruch does not control the entire production and marketing of the sacred objects, he virtually monopolizes sales around the shrine, and he encourages the introduction of new products every year. The proliferation of the Baba Sali sacred "industry" clearly reflects a creative and entrepreneurial spirit underlying the "selling" of the saint. These mementos, souvenirs, postcards, and photographs procured at Netivot help to propagate the saint's charisma in two ways: they are a means of "bringing the saint home" and they are icons of the contemporary Jewish Maghrebi version of nostalgia (Stewart 1988). These items are part of what Douglas Cole calls "procurable culture" (Dominguez 1986:547), which serves as a means of remembering, strengthening, and creating membership in so-called "ethnic" groups.

Thus far, Baba Baruch's success in sanctifying his father and aggrandizing his burial site in Netivot has been mainly attributed to his skill in manipulating the Israeli media, commerce, industry, and politicians to manufacture charisma. In this process of the "selling of the saint" he managed to extend his own basis of legitimacy by propagating and highlighting his image as a physical and spiritual replica of his father. Nevertheless, found behind the elaborate facade of similarity and identity are striking differences in the divergent lifestyles of father and son. These incompatible careers radiate distinct images of piety and virtuousness and emanate from altogether different sociocultural contexts. Unlike the purely spiritual image of Baba Sali, Baba Baruch radiates expansion, dominance, and activity. Extroverted and energetic, his image is that of a strong-willed entrepreneur always seeking to expand his territory. Ambitious, opinionated, and overbearing, Baruch is deeply engaged with matters extending outside the religious realm, including municipal and national politics. Unlike his passive, humble father, Baruch is mobile, visible, and involved. Even though he dresses like his father, he does not look like an ascetic. Full-bodied and unabashedly fond of gas-guzzler American cars, alcohol, good food, and imported cigarettes, he appears self-indulgent and even hedonistic—despite his spiritual reawakening.

Baruch's expansive style reflects a problem from which his father, the personification of piety and virtuousness, was altogether exempted. Unlike Baba Sali, Baruch has had to impress people by employing "'conspicuous creations,' devices for mobilizing, attracting, focusing and ordering attention" (MacAloon 1982:262). Thus, the *hillulah* and the invited guests, the American-made car and the entourage, the politicking and the public speeches about his father may all be seen as props, scenery, and dramatic action in Baruch's play to appear powerful. In Glassman's terms, they are all part of "stage-managing the charismatic process" (1975:618).

Yet, Baba Baruch's entrepreneurial and expansive style is not merely a defensive maneuver intended to compensate for an initially inferior position in the pursuit of legitimation. Baba Sali's image as a sainted figure germinated in the Jewish society of southern Morocco and was sustained in Israel, frozen in time, as an exemplar of a lost and idealized past. In contrast, Baba Baruch, whose road to sacredness was paved in contemporary Israel, is a "saint for our time." As a child of the Israeli political system, he seems to patently espouse and expertly employ the values, norms, and symbols that govern public life in Israel. Baruch's involvement with politics is particularly evident in Baba Sali's *hillulah*. Against the spontaneous and apolitical spirit that dominates most of the other *hillulot*, including those conducted by the saint impresarios (Weingrod 1990), the festival for Baba Sali includes a very tightly scheduled public event, replete with public addresses given by the most important figures in Israel. Baba Baruch uses the occasion to show politicians (from the two leading parties) his support and potential power, as well as to signify to his followers his centrality in the country's political life.

Unlike his father, then, Baba Baruch may be seen as representing something quintessentially Israeli. Beyond his general willingness to participate in state-regulated politics, he espouses specific models for actions derived from the Zionist ethos. Likewise, he focuses attention on the Jewish Moroccan diaspora as a potential source of financial support. Like other leaders, Baruch sees that community as a "mobilized diaspora" (Armstrong 1976) and an economic frontier, capitalizing on the Sephardi diaspora's growing sense of responsibility for their Sephardi brethren in Israel.

In addition, like many other public figures in Israel, Baruch constantly seeks to make his mark on the country's landscape, changing the actual physical topography of Netivot (and other places) by erecting and developing various institutions bearing his father's name. Although inspired by a traditional idiom, he follows the Zionist ethos that emphasizes "making" Israel by building and transforming the country's landscape.

In conclusion, Baba Baruch's project in Netivot demonstrates how charisma can be "manufactured," using modern means, in order to achieve premeditated goals and in line with expectations in public life in contemporary Israel. These means include the media, which broadcast claims of charisma; industry, which creates material objects for the cementation of charisma; and the political machinery, which may render contested charisma legitimate by linking it to the society's symbolic centers and foci of power. Note again, however, that this large-scale "stage managing" through which charisma is manufactured, propagated, and negotiated also posits it as strained and fragile. In transforming Netivot into a sacred precinct and in using modern technological and administrative means to amplify processes of charismatization, Baba Baruch unwittingly paved the way for rival saint impresarios (Bilu 1990; Brown 1981) eager to stake a claim in the sacred territory he furnished for himself. And among those is Rabbi Ifargan, the most popular contender for holiness in Netivot.

RABBI YAAKOV IFARGAN: THE MAKING OF A POSTMODERN SAINT

Rabbi Yaakov Ifargan, dubbed "the Roentgen" for his piercing eyes and celebrated diagnostic skills,[2] made his debut as a miracle-worker in the mid-1990s, when he was only 30 years old. A native of Netivot of Moroccan extraction, he had led a mundane, unnoticeable life before emerging as a great Kabbalist and healer. Indeed, some local inhabitants have found it hard to reconcile his old, unassuming persona with the mystical transformation he putatively underwent and the saintly status it accorded him. Aside from being in the vulnerable position of a prophet in his hometown, and suspiciously young for mystical pursuits, Ifargan also lacks the impressive lineage charisma of the Abu-Hatseiras and has never been ordained as a rabbi.[3] Still, he managed to attract many thousands of followers outside Netivot and to undermine Baba Baruch's hegemony in town. Ironically, the Roentgen owes much of his success to the example set by Baba Baruch in effectively propagating his father's charisma and in deftly crafting his own. The juxtaposition of the two cases affords a better view of the fluctuations of the sacred in modern settings, where the commodification of charisma renders it liable to contestation and fragmentation (Eade and Sallnow 1991).

Ifargan started his mystical career as a diagnostician who could putatively disclose any ailment and discern its etiology and prognosis by merely scanning the client's body with his piercing eyes. Pursuing a "medical" trajectory based on personal charisma seemed apt for an aspiring self-taught Kabbalist devoid of impressive background at a time when alternative medicine and esoteric healing were gaining unprecedented popularity in Israel (Beit-Hallahmi 1992). In pursuing his role as a healer Baba Baruch made it clear that he was painstakingly following the unique curative method that Rabbi Yaakov Abu-Hatseira, the source of the family's blessedness, bequeathed to his descendants. In contrast, Ifargan's method of choice appears to rely on extraordinary personal resources, more resonant with the classic Weberian notion of charisma, yet cloaked in the prestigious aura of modern medical technology.

Actually, the traditional notions of ancestral virtue and mystical piety were important weaponry in Ifargan's arsenal too, but he has been less bound by the Jewish Maghrebi ways of conduct, which is made clear by his appearance and followers. While Baba Baruch is wrapped from head to toe in a traditional Moroccan gown, highlighting his identification with his father, Ifargan dresses in typical Ashkenazi ultraorthodox black garments. In terms of followers, the popularity of Baba Baruch is ethnically based, relying on *Mizrahi* (Middle Eastern) devotees, mostly of Moroccan extraction; Ifargan's following clearly transcends ethnic and religious boundaries and includes many young nonobservant middle-class Israelis who defy the accepted characterization of the traditional member in the cult of the saint.

Ifargan's unprecedented success in reaching out to the Israeli secular mainstream stems from the nightlong mystical gatherings he has been conducting on a weekly basis, first at a popular shrine in northern Israel and later in Netivot (Zarfati 2000). The appeal of these gatherings derives from their syncretistic nature, combining revivalist, mystical, and therapeutic themes, in a highly charged atmosphere. They allow young Israelis, alienated from established orthodoxy but thirsty for unmediated spiritual experiences, to enjoy a nightlong respite from their professional routine and partake of *tikkunim* (sing. *tikkun*), mystical ceremonies designed to "rectify" misfortunes and adversities on both individual and national levels. During these meetings Ifargan recites an endless litany of petitions while feeding a gigantic pillar of fire with thousands of candles. Flanked by the participants' intermittent shouts of amen and sporadic chanting and hand clapping, he gradually builds up their emotions toward the climactic end of the meeting, when he commands one of the crippled adherents in wheelchairs flocking around him to stand up and take a few unaided steps. While skeptics have raised doubts regarding the authenticity of these miraculous feats, the participants, energized by the emotional bonding and resultant atmosphere of *communitas* (V. Turner 1969), cherish the nightlong celebration as a genuine spiritual experience.

Focusing our analytic gaze on the production of charisma, it should be noted that these popular gatherings, although articulated through a traditional idiom, are deftly concocted and professionally marketed performances, palatable to the New Age sensibilities of young, spiritually deprived Israelis. In line with Ifargan's brazen businesslike orientation (see below), air-conditioned buses ship the participants to the meetings and professional guides prepare them on the way to the exciting mystical adventure that awaits them. This professional packaging makes the *tikkunim* all the more attractive to Israeli yuppies eager to indulge in a time-limited, easily accessible spiritual exploit.

As noted previously, much of Ifargan's success rests on perfecting the organizational and technological methods that Baba Baruch, his bitter adversary, had introduced to promote and legitimize his own charisma. Given the growing popularity of mysticism and the occult in Israel—a trend facilitated in part by the ascent of the Abu-Hatseiras—media figures were intrigued by the diagnostic and therapeutic claims of the young mystic and the esoteric rituals he initiated. Availing himself of their interest, Ifargan forged special relations with some of them, assisted by a polished public relations agent, and was rewarded with a crop of positive reports in the newspapers. Written from a "pseudoethnographic" perspective and investing Ifargan's miraculous feats with factuality tinged with exoticism, these solicited reports were instrumental in bringing the Roentgen's name to many homes in Israel and in drawing to him many Israeli celebrities, first from the entertainment industry and later from other domains.

Businessmen, in particular, have been noted among those seeking Ifargan's advice and blessing. For certain top figures in Israel's economy and industry, from senior bank executives to general managers of high-tech companies and construction firms, Ifargan has become a personal guru. Aside from businessmen and pop stars, high-ranking military officers, key media figures, senior civil servants (including public attorneys and judges), and politicians can be observed at Ifargan's public events. The list of political figures who have sporadically frequented his house includes Israeli presidents, prime ministers, cabinet ministers, the speaker of the Knesset (the Israeli parliament), and party leaders from the whole political spectrum. They all partake of a cultural climate in which paying tribute to Kabbalists and miracle-makers has become an asset rather than a liability. As noted in the Abu-Hatseiras case, both parties enjoy the name recognition entailed by media coverage.

The social processes underlying the exaltation of the esoteric and the mystical among contemporary Israelis are not difficult to identify. They are associated with the gradual disintegration of the collectivist Zionist ideology that once inspired and cemented Israeli society; the growing sense of malaise and insecurity following years of "military deglorification" since the 1973 War; and the strengthening of sectarian religious and ethnic sentiments in a social ambiance of competing cultural visions (Horowitz and Lissak 1989; Kimmerling 2001). It should be noted that the triumph of the occult has been an accumulative process in which Baba Baruch, by gaining legitimacy for his own project, also contributed to moving mystical and folk-religious beliefs from the society's periphery to its symbolic centers. Again, Ifargan and other New Age, second-generation charismatics could walk and extend the road paved and legitimized by Baba Baruch.

Aided by a professional team of agents, accountants, lawyers, spokesmen, and secretaries, Ifargan runs his fast-expanding ventures as a skillful entrepreneur. His nonprofit tax-free associations take care of an impressive array of projects and activities designed "to buttress Jewish heritage" all over the country. While few of their lofty objectives have been realized thus far, the nonprofit associations are resourcefully used to launder the monies Ifargan receives for individual healing services and collective *tikkunim*. Capitalizing on the fact that in Israel Kabbalists and folk healers are operating in a legal gray area, Ifargan's lawyers and accountants cloak income and apparently enormous contributions for charity. Moreover, claiming a perennial deficit in their budget, they apply for and receive government and municipal support for advancing Jewish education and religion.

Perhaps the most impressive of Ifargan's ventures has been his ability to furnish himself with a lineage charisma by retrospectively glorifying his forebears. His father, Rabbi Shalom, who passed away in 1988, was respected in Netivot for his piety and humility, yet not for erudition or mystical power. Ifargan, however, has been relentlessly promoting his image as a hidden *tzaddik*, a great mystical luminary with ample *zekhut avot*. The comparison with the Abu-Hatseiras is striking in this regard. While Baba Baruch established his legitimacy by bonding himself with his venerated ancestors, Ifargan had to gentrify his forefather in order to gain a respectable, "deep" past. The "invented tradition" of the Ifargans gained salience through the mass production and aggressive marketing of publications, posters, and other artifacts depicting the hallowed images of Rabbi Shalom and his ancestors (cf. Hobsbawm and Ranger 1983). It is evident that some of these images were unabashedly modeled on the popular iconography that dominates the Abu-Hatseira holy industry.

To anchor the emerging family tradition in a noticeable *lieux de memoire* (Nora 1989), Ifargan transformed his father's modest tomb in the Netivot municipal cemetery into a magnificent mausoleum. The supermodern truncated pyramid, built in marble and encompassing a spacious, air-conditioned burial hall, faces Baba Sali's Maghrebi-style sanctuary, with its whitewashed dome, as a constant reminder of the pluralization of charisma in Netivot. For Baba Baruch, the fact that Ifargan meticulously followed his steps in building the monument made the encroachment on his territory all the more irksome. Ifargan took pains, first, to bury his father in a remote plot, in an interim zone between the cemetery and the surrounding farmland, thus securing the space—like Baba Baruch before him—for future mass gatherings. With the help of supporters in key public positions he managed to take control over more than eight acres adjacent to the cemetery, and on this the mausoleum has been erected, together with ample facilities for visitors. A special road leading from the main highway to the shrine allows the pilgrims to reach their destination without going through Netivot.

The new shrine has become the epicenter of Ifargan's diversified activities. Aside from the annual *hillulah* of Rabbi Shalom, it now hosts the weekly *tikkunim* and is frequented by a perennial stream of supplicants. In accord with the plural, nonexclusive spirit of saint worship, many of the visitors to Rabbi Shalom's shrine hasten to enjoy the blessing inherent in Baba Sali's sanctuary, and vice versa. But for Baba Baruch the success of the shrine that Ifargan built for his father was a blow he could not take. He sued Ifargan for conducting the *hillulah* for Rabbi Yaakov Abu-Hatseira, Baba Baruch's great-grandfather and the origin of the family's blessing, at Rabbi Shalom's mausoleum—an audacious undertaking viewed as "trespassing" (cf. M. Marcus 1985). Having lost in court, where Baba Baruch's traditional idiom of family-sealed charisma could not hold against the sanctimoniously egalitarian counterargument of Ifargan's lawyer that "Rabbi Yaakov is held in high esteem by all Jews," Baba Sali's confidants sought to smear Ifargan in the media, accusing him of witchcraft and sexual abuse. But these allegations could not be confirmed and, in fact, acted as a boomerang, depicting Ifargan as a martyr and lending him more public support.

It is hardly conceivable that the cult of Baba Sali, which has become fairly institutionalized by now,[4] could be ousted as a result of Ifargan's growing popularity. Nor can we rest assured, given the precariousness of manufactured charisma, that Ifargan's popularity will last. For the current historical moment, however, the municipal cemetery in Netivot boasts two major shrines of national caliber, plus several minor sanctuaries. Hierophany of this magnitude is quite exceptional in present-day Israel, but it is compatible with the fact that most of the new saints' sanctuaries in Israel's map of holy geography are located in the urban periphery of the country. What accounts for this peculiar geographical distribution?

NETIVOT AS THE BENARES OF ISRAEL: THE SANCTIFICATION OF DEVELOPMENT TOWNS

In seeking to situate the renaissance of Maghrebi hagiolatry in the wider context of contemporary Israeli society, the fact that most of the urban arenas for this revival were development towns like Netivot appears highly significant.[5] The peak of the population dispersion policy initiated by the Israeli government in the early 1950s coincided with the first massive waves of *aliya* (Jewish immigration; literally, "going up") from the Maghreb. Consequently, many Moroccan Jews found themselves relegated to these hastily built, "planted" communities in the periphery of Israel, where they were assigned pioneering roles that veteran Israelis were unwilling to assume (Inbar and Adler 1977). As the largest ethnic group placed in development towns, their sharing of the Zionist dream was marred by the many ills of such disadvantaged communities. These included limited occupational opportunities due to an underdeveloped infrastructure and reliance on one type of industry based on manual, low-paying jobs, an almost total dependence on government services, a poor educational system, and a high rate of population turnover in which the more resourceful, upwardly mobile inhabitants left the towns while the poor and the less able tended to stay (Aronoff 1973; Semyonov 1981).

Many of the socioeconomic and political ills that characterized these towns in the 1950s and 1960s still haunt them today. At the same time, however, the inhabitants who did stay in the towns, despite the social and economic difficulties, have slowly developed genuine attachments to the localities. The growth of these natural sentiments of belongingness and rootedness in one's own community finds expression in and is further enhanced by the appearance of saints in these towns. This presence grants metahistorical depth to places that were without a recognized and validated past, thus making them a more integral part of Israel. The *tzaddik* endows the town with an aura of sanctity, and the residents' sense of attachment is placed within a larger meaning-giving system, based on the idioms encoded in their Maghrebi traditions.

This process of sanctification has been quite widespread. In some development towns, local denizens have adopted longtime saints' sanctuaries located in their vicinity and transformed them into local centers of cultic activities. In other cases Jewish Moroccan saints originally buried in Morocco were transferred into new abodes in development towns following a dream inspiration (cf. Bilu 1996, 2000).

In the case of Netivot, the most impressive instance in this process, the peripheral, backward town became the sacred abode, in life and death, of Baba Sali, a mystical luminary and scion of a venerated family of *tzaddikim*. This acquired transcendence, skillfully propagated by Baba Baruch, has generated "reverberations of holiness" in the town, most impressively reflected in the ascent to saintly status of Rabbi Yaakov Ifargan. The mushrooming of the sacred in Netivot has led a renowned Israeli writer to designate the town "the Benares (Varanasi) of Israel." This deriding designation reflects the mixture of condescension, mild disdain, and paternalistic concern with which development towns were viewed by mainstream Israelis (Goldberg 1984); yet for many local denizens the saints represent an urban transformation that is congenial and welcome. Evaluating the changes in the town following the death and rapid sanctification of Baba Sali, one local inhabitant said with a modicum of pride, "A town that was 'outside' of Israel's map, is now not only 'on' the map, thanks to Baba Sali it is also 'above' it."

This process whereby sacred cities are being added to the country's landscape is strongly associated with the changing context of ethnic consciousness in Israel. The folk veneration of saints (along with the preservation or revival of other practices associated with *Mizrahi* Jews, such as ethnic festivals and ethnic music) provided many Maghrebi Jews with a set of cultural means to deal with their situation. By discovering and establishing sacred sites associated with the saints, they express their integration into Israeli society. In this sense, the *hillulot* in various sites partake of the nature of "ethnic renewal ceremonies" (Weingrod 1990). They reflect the growing confidence of an émigré group in being part of the contemporary Israeli scene while at the same time indicating a strong sense of ethnic distinctiveness.

A leading Israeli social scientist has designated the renaissance of Maghrebi-based saint worship in the new country a "symbolic diasporization" of Israel (Cohen 1983). Note, however, that in planting the cult of the saints in the contemporary scene, the *tzaddikim* are reconstituted in a reality quite remote from that of traditional Morocco. The diachronic alignment of the saintly careers of the Abu-Hatseiras and Rabbi Yaakov Ifargan conveys the dynamic process in which traditional notions of saint worship are being accommodated to the changing cultural idioms and religious sensibilities in contemporary Israel.

Admittedly, the hallowed image of Baba Sali is quintessentially "traditional," having been anchored in the Maghrebi past; still, it was effectively marketed by his son using modern means. Baba Baruch, born in Morocco but at home in Israeli public life and political culture, represents the entrepreneurial spirit of a "modernist" saint impresario who actively seeks to expand his influence and visibility and leave his mark on the landscape, in accord with the Zionist ethos of expansion and building. Israeli-born Rabbi Yaakov Ifargan is a "postmodern" *tzaddik*, less attached in appearance, style, and following to the Maghrebi past or *Mizrahi* ethnicity and more audacious in inventing traditions and glorifying his forefathers. In a post-Zionist society (Kimmerling 2001), where once-denigrated mystical quests and interest in the occult are now more welcomed, he was able to furnish himself with a social network that includes prominent figures from most public spheres. His New Age sensibilities, evident in the syncretized rituals he concocted and his creative confounding of mystical and medical terminology, resonate with the spiritual taste of many young Israelis coming from varied ethnic and socioeconomic backgrounds.

DISCUSSION AND CONCLUSIONS

The scope and dynamism of saint-making processes in Netivot may become more apparent through a closer comparative look at Baba Baruch (given that he is the prime mover behind his father's sanctification) and Ifargan. The two appear as active agents, well adapted to the respective social milieus in which they operate and skillful at promoting their hallowed images through modern, "rational" means that involve the media and the political machinery. It might be argued that both men cultivated an entrepreneurial, scheming style, with special alertness to appearance and impression management, because sanctity was not guaranteed for them at the outset of their careers. Baba Baruch was a scion of the venerated Abu-Hatseira family, but he had to grapple with and neutralize serious past moral failings in order to be deemed worthy of his forefathers' blessing. Ifargan sought to make himself a name without a celebrated family tradition or a recognized background of erudition and piety.

The difference between Baba Baruch's and Ifargan's initial predicaments has shaped their divergent tactics in pursuit of holiness. While Baba Baruch struggled to reduce the painful gap between his problematic past and the hallowed image of his family, Ifargan had to craft his image from scratch. In his attempts to present himself as a physical and spiritual replica of his father, Baruch settled in his father's residence, in walking distance of Baba Sali's resting place, borrowed his father's title of "Baba," and hastened to wear his father's mantle and shoes and grow a beard like his. He has also embraced his father's particular curing formula inherited from the family's source of piety and blessedness, Rabbi Yaakov Abu-Hatseira. Notwithstanding these mimetic practices, Baba Baruch's semblance of holiness is still worlds apart from his father's traditional image, given his political involvement and quintessentially Israeli style of action. But the weighty legacy of the Abu-Hatseira family, which is the source of his claims for legitimacy, is also a constraint, forcing him to cast his healing and spiritual activities in the past-oriented, ethnically based Maghrebi mold and drawing to him primarily *Mizrahi* followers of traditional background. Even the Moorish architecture of Baba Sali's whitewashed, domed sanctuary and of the opulently stylized Kiriat Baba Sali, said to be inspired by the Moroccan sultans' royal palaces, reflects the same conservative tilt to the Maghrebi past. Noblesse oblige—particularly when one's share in the lineage charisma is in doubt!

If Ifargan's ascent to hallowed status appears more daring and innovative than Baba Baruch's, it is partly because he was able to make a virtue out of his initial lack of resources. Unconstrained by a lofty family tradition and imposing ancestors, he could use his creative imagination, interpersonal skills, and managerial capacity to carve himself a unique role as a mystic and healer. Dressed in the standard black ultraorthodox apparel, devoid of any ethnic marking, he developed an impressive kit of modern and mystical healing devices, relatively liberated from the traditional healing modes of blessings and written amulets. Significantly, Baba Baruch viewed his glorious family tradition as a prerequisite for his pursuit of saintly status and tied to it his every move. Ifargan, in contrast, started to aggrandize and lavishly commemorate his forefathers only after he had gained some name as a wonder-worker, seeking to further deepen an already established charisma. Lastly, the architectural style of Rabbi Shalom's sanctuary, with its bold contours and truncated pyramid shape, is innovatively modern, altogether liberated from the Maghrebi aesthetic legacy.

A synchronic comparison between Baba Baruch and Ifargan is not entirely in place since the fact that Baba Baruch preceded Ifargan in his claims for saintly status bears two significant consequences. First, the transformation of Baba Sali into the "national saint" of the 1980s was in itself instrumental in creating a more favorable attitude toward mysticism and saint-worship in Israel. Ifargan could therefore propagate his claims in a more auspicious atmosphere. Second, Baba Baruch unwittingly served as an exemplary model for aspiring young Kabbalists such as Ifargan. Indeed, many of the latter's achievements—the deft use of the political system and the media, the association with celebrities, the businesslike managing of the "holy industry," and the cultivation of the father's sanctuary—appear to be informed by, and at times blatantly copied from, Baba Baruch's initiatives. Motivated by the idea that "everything you can do, I can do better," Ifargan constantly strives to broaden the horizons of sanctification set up by Baba Baruch, solidifying his social networks, multiplying his tax-free associations, and expanding his mystical and educational projects. Whereas Baba Baruch sought "to cultivate Baba Sali's heritage," Ifargan is looking "to cultivate Jewish heritage," no less.

The conclusions derived from the synchronic deployment of Baba Baruch and Ifargan should be taken with a caveat. The comparison has captured a particular historical moment in which the attempts of a young, enterprising, self-made Kabbalist to encroach on the sacred territory of an established dynasty of *tzaddikim* and to make himself a name as a mystical luminary have been crowned with success. But the volatile history of saint-making in general and the tenuousness and precariousness of constructed charisma, in particular, instruct us that this success might be short-lived.

To sum up, the vicissitudes of charisma in Netivot demonstrate how images of holiness can be manufactured, commodified, appropriated, and transformed in a modern industrialized society. In stretching the careers of the three saintly protagonists on a spectrum from "traditional" to "modern" and then "postmodern" imagery, I argue that charisma is historically situated; it is creatively molded in line with the dominant zeitgeist and cultural expectations. Whatever shape the renaissance of the saints in Israel is going to take in the future, all of its current manifestations signal a vision of peoplehood and society entirely at odds with the secular collectivist-Zionist ethos that shaped Israeli society in its formative years.

NOTES

This chapter is informed by a two-decade-long study on Jewish Moroccan saint worship in Israel, started in 1981. Data on the Abu-Hatseiras were collected in Netivot between 1986 and 1989. Data on Ifargan were collected in 2000–2001. I would like to thank my colleague and friend Eyal Ben-Ari for permitting me to use excerpts from our joint article on the Abu-Hatseiras (Bilu and Ben-Ari 1992) and Leora Zarfati, whose Master's thesis (2000) alerted me to Ifargan's nightlong rituals of rectification.

1. *Mezzuza* (sing.), a small case attached to the doorpost containing a rolled piece of parchment bearing a text from Deuteronomy.

2. In Hebrew, X rays are called *karnei Roentgen* (Roentgen's rays), after the name of the discoverer of X rays.

3. While Ifargan is always addressed or referred to as "Rabbi Yaakov," the title is merely an honorific. The term *Rav* indicates formal rabbinical ordination.

4. In 1996 the Ministry of Religious Affairs officially declared Baba Sali's sanctuary a holy site and the Jewish National Fund transformed the precinct into a national park in the form of a *hamsa* (a palm-shaped amulet).

5. In Israel, only urban settlements with a population over 20,000 are accorded the status of a town (*yir*). None of the development towns had obtained this status in the 1950s and 1960s, but throughout the years most of them, including Netivot, have crossed the threshold of 20,000 inhabitants and have been declared towns. However, in terms of size and significance, they are still far behind established cities like Tel-Aviv, Jerusalem, or Haifa.

3
Presence of the King

The Vitality of the Image of King Chulalongkorn for Modern Urban Thailand

Irene Stengs

The mass production of objects is inextricably linked to present-day saints. These objects include such items as photographs, posters, badges, and statuettes with the image of the venerated person. Regardless of the secular or religious background of the cult, portraits clearly have a potential that meets a very fundamental need of devotees. However, the common appearance of a person's portrait does not necessarily indicate sanctity or popularity, as the massive display of the leaders' images in dictatorships (e.g., Stalin, Kim Il-sung, Saddam Hussein) may demonstrate—but the power holder's display of portraits probably stems from the same particular potential of a person's image. Portraits are, to follow Marin (1988), powers of presence. In Marin's study concerning the representation of the absolute monarchy through portraits of Louis XIV, as well as in modern forms of absolutism, the image presented is the power of the state. When studying cults that emerge independently of any state or other central institution there is an issue as to what is provided by the presence of portraits and images. Here I will address this question by tracing local concepts about the powers of the portraits of one particular Thai saint, King Chulalongkorn the Great, king of Siam from 1868 until 1910.[1] He is the object of a nationwide personality cult that began in the late 1980s.

A MYRIAD OF PORTRAITS

To the eye, the cult of King Chulalongkorn is most manifest through the innumerable quantity of King Chulalongkorn portraits. The king's portraits are found all over the country but particularly in urban areas. Wherever one goes—offices, restaurants, shops, private homes, temples, spirit shrines, railway stations, or other public buildings—there is always an image of the king and generally as a portrait or statuette.

Portraits may be obtained at one of the many "portrait shops" selling framed copies of photographs and paintings of historical kings, members of the present royal family, and famous monks. In the city of Chiang Mai I counted 20 such shops, and even in the smallest provincial town there is at least one shop. King Chulalongkorn's portrait is more abundant than those of any other king or monk in these shops. Furthermore, a wide range of objects such as clocks, necklaces, coffeepots, key rings, stickers, embroidery patterns, and even jigsaw puzzles bearing the image of the king are also for sale. King Chulalongkorn objects are found at markets and in bookstores, department stores, fancy fairs, temple shops, and amulet markets. They are also available through the many door-to-door statuette vendors, from children selling homemade King Chulalongkorn stickers in restaurants, and in the mail-order catalogs. In addition, organizations such as banks and the army regularly issue King Chulalongkorn images in a variety of forms, including King Chulalongkorn commemorative coins or statuettes that may be either for sale or distributed free at a special event.

The profusion of King Chulalongkorn portraits raises a question regarding needs they satisfy. Why do so many Thai possess King Chulalongkorn portraits? What is the role of these King Chulalongkorn portraits in his cult? What meanings do these King Chulalongkorn images carry for those who possess them? As the material presented will demonstrate, the role and meaning of portraits can be understood only in the context of the narratives that exist about the king.[2]

THE GREAT BELOVED KING

Similar to the mass reproduction of portraits, King Chulalongkorn narratives are endlessly reproduced in a wide range of media. The narratives are taught in schools as part of the history curriculum, they appear time and again in popular magazines and books, and they are retold in radio and television broadcasts. Of equal importance is their reconfirmation in the daily experiences of many of the more dedicated worshipers. The experiences of these worshipers, particularly spiritual encounters with the king, may themselves live on as narratives. In the course of such encounters the king acts and speaks in accordance with the patterns established in narratives, as the cases below demonstrate.

The body of King Chulalongkorn stories consists of several major narratives, each representing a different theme from the king's biography and addressing particular emotions. Since each of these narratives depicts the king in one of his particular capacities, they can be regarded as "narrated portraits." This chapter will demonstrate the vital, intrinsic connection between pictorial portraits and narrated portraits in the emergence of this personality cult.

Because of their repetitive character, the continuous recounting of the same details, events, and heroic moments, and their constant mutual reference, the narrated King Chulalongkorn portraits must also be understood as components of an indivisible whole. Together they constitute the myth and hagiography of the "Great Beloved King" (*phra piya maharat*), an epithet actually given to King Chulalongkorn during his lifetime. However, the biographical details and deeds highlighted in the narratives recount not merely the personal qualities of King Chulalongkorn but also those that are in general indicative of a "righteous ruler" (*thammarat*). Such kings are said to be guided by the teachings (*tham*) of the Buddha and to rule in accordance with the "Ten Kingly Virtues" (*thotsaphiratchatham*): charity, morality, self-sacrifice, rectitude, gentleness, self-restriction, non-anger, nonviolence, forbearance, and non-obstruction.

The Buddha provides the exemplary background of the *thammarat* concept. Before reaching enlightenment he is believed to have been reborn as a king many times. Such beliefs are well within the tradition of Buddhist hagiography (Tambiah 1985:326–327, 1988:111–118). The King Chulalongkorn narratives elaborate on ancient Theravada Buddhist conceptions of kingship, yet at the same time they are incorporated in a powerful modern nationalist ideology. As ideology the King Chulalongkorn myth derives its potency, to follow Kapferer (1988:79–84), from being based on vital elements of an "ontology" shared by those in power and the general populace. In Thai Buddhist ontology power relationships are ordered in a hierarchical system, with the king at the apex. Thai nationalist ideology is founded on the intrinsic linkages between nation, kingship, and religion: the virtuous Buddhist king is the benevolent power that unites and sustains the nation (see Murashima 1988). The narratives I present here recount various components of this nationalist ideology and from these I have composed four narrated portraits. Each expresses what most Thai would consider the significance of King Chulalongkorn and they are consistent with the principal answers people give when asked why they worship King Chulalongkorn. These answers follow more or less the issues taught in standard history books at school. Yet, in contrast with the effect compulsory subject matter generally has, the subject of the king and his achievements literally gives many people goose bumps.

The first narrated portrait is "King Chulalongkorn used to visit the countryside." In Thai there is an expression that specifically refers to the king's visits: *sadet praphat ton*, which can be translated as "a person of royal descent making an ordinary (leisure) tour or visit." This portrait narrates how King Chulalongkorn was the first Siamese king to go into the countryside incognito to learn *in person* about his subjects' needs and problems. He made these trips incognito to be certain to see conditions for himself, instead of depending only on the information given by possibly untrustworthy officials. Wherever the king went, he treated his subjects with respect. Stories recount how the king stayed with ordinary villagers, had meals with them, and even invited them to his palace (cf. Chula 1960:229–230; Stengs 2000). "King Chulalongkorn used to visit the countryside" addresses the universal topic of the fatherly king and compassionate ruler who cares for each of his subjects. Similar stories are told about historical figures like Charlemagne and the illustrious caliph of the Arabian Nights. The recently crowned kings of Morocco (Mohammed VI) and Jordan (Abdullah II) acquired instantaneous popularity from their policy to inspect their kingdoms incognito.

The second narrated portrait is "King Chulalongkorn abolished slavery" (*song loek that*). During his reign the king brought an end to the *sakdina* system, a Siamese form of slavery comprising feudalism and debt slavery.[3] The abolition of slavery is celebrated as one of his major achievements. "King Chulalongkorn used to visit the countryside" usually takes the form of "old stories told, still good to hear." In contrast, the narrated portrait "King Chulalongkorn abolished slavery" is often related in a manner indicating the direct relevance of this long-ago history to the daily lives of the worshipers. The following quotations illustrate this point very well. Arun, a designer of jewelry living in Chiang Mai, told me:

> By abolishing slavery the king actually gave the people of Thailand a new life and that is the king's most important accomplishment. That the king even did this is the very reason I now live in liberty (*isara*). King Chulalongkorn was the first king who did not give thought to his own interests, but instead thought of ordinary people. One can never be sure whether any king after King Chulalongkorn would have done the same thing.

When this achievement is presented in paintings and statues, it is generally depicted as one single momentary act, with the king, seated on his throne, surrounded by grateful, just-freed slaves. Yet it is generally known that the endeavor was difficult and hazardous. King Chulalongkorn had to deal with the conservative opposition of the Siamese nobility, the power of which depended on the *sakdina* system. In contrast to what happened in the United States and Russia, the narrative emphasizes that slavery in Siam was abolished *without* civil war. This was due to King Chulalongkorn's ingenious policy not to abolish slavery immediately, but gradually. Having abolished slavery, Thailand became a member of the league of civilized nations (*araya prathet*).

"King Chulalongkorn abolished slavery" depicts the king as a very intelligent ruler with his genius being a key element of his personality. The portrait narrates the greatness of the king's compassion (loving-kindness, *metta*) for his subjects, which led to the abolishment of slavery despite the difficulties. Many present-day worshipers feel that without the acts of this king they still might be slaves. For many, the feeling of personal gratitude for being "free" in this life is a major motivation to worship the king.

A popular painting, reproduced on a school poster about the achievements of King Chulalongkorn, clearly visualizes the important elements (Figure 3.1). In this painting the slaves are kneeling at the feet of the king, emphasizing the closeness of king and subjects. The artist of this composition has situated the abolition in what is clearly a rural setting. The king is standing in the middle of a humble village, his face expressing *metta,* or "loving-kindness." For those who know the stories, the painting combines the narrated portraits "King Chulalongkorn used to visit the countryside" and "King Chulalongkorn abolished slavery." The everlasting protective powers of the king's spirit in this full-color composition are visualized with the addition of a large, sepia-hued portrait of the king's face shown as if rising from the earth.

The third narrated portrait is "King Chulalongkorn saved Thailand from becoming a colony." This portrait recounts how the king's diplomatic capacities enabled him to establish friendly relationships with influential European leaders of his time. These personal contacts counterbalanced the threats that were presented by the British and the French to independent, but powerless, Siam. Equally important were the king's efforts to show the West that Siam was not just an insignificant kingdom ruled by barbarians. The king wanted it made clear that the country was open to progress and civilization, was governed by an enlightened monarch, and was not inferior in any important aspect to the European monarchies. In fact, two journeys undertaken by the king to Europe in 1897 and 1907 can be better understood in light of these objectives. In 1997, the centennial of the first voyage was commemorated by tremendous public interest in both voyages. In the popular perspective, the two voyages have become fused into one major event or, more accurately, into a single epic recounting the king's mission and genius. Another important aspect in the narrative is that his visits to Europe are not treated as leisure trips but rather as strenuous, worrisome expeditions. There was much at stake and it was hard for the king to leave his kingdom behind for such extended periods. He made sacrifices, giving up personal comfort and pleasures for the well-being of his subjects.

These voyages, the king's vision, and his dedication to the Siamese people form the background for the initiatives the king took toward fundamental administrative and legal reforms. These were intended to organize Siam along similar lines to those of the modern states of Western Europe. The fourth narrated portrait is therefore titled "King Chulalongkorn modernized Thai society." This portrait unfolds itself like the table of contents of any book on King Chulalongkorn. In these books the history of the Fifth Reign breaks down into a

Figure 3.1. "The Abolition of Slavery" poster (fragment) with inset of King Chulalongkorn 1 Tical Thai commemorative stamp. (Prepared by James F. Hopgood)

long list of topics on the introduction of technological innovations and the reorganization of the administrative, educational, monetary, military, and juridical institutions. This narrative of the king is repeated in the way people enumerate various concrete achievements of the king in nearly identical sequence as in the tables of contents of such books. The modernizations brought by the king fit Theravada Buddhist ideas on the beneficent powers of meritorious kings, who are supposed to bring progress and improved welfare to the kingdom.

Current veneration for the king expresses a mixture of national pride for a great diplomatic king who saved Siam's independence and of gratitude—national and personal—for the reforms and progress he brought. Next to independence and modernity, the major features of King Chulalongkorn's image arising from these narrated portraits are those of the compassionate, self-sacrificing, Buddhist king: the righteous ruler.

The King Chulalongkorn narratives are vital enough to make the king, his achievements, and his personality important in the everyday reality of many Thai. People feel connected to this king, and in speaking of him they transfer and rework the narratives, contributing to the construction of collective memory. This formation of collective memory encompasses, to follow Connerton (1989:36–56), repetitive processes of knowledge of the past in textual forms (myth) and through nontextual practices (ritual). Where ritual is characterized by a high degree of fixation, myth or mythic material can be considered as a "reservoir of meanings," with a large potential of variance, reworking, and reinterpretation. Just how this process of reworking of myth by individual worshipers takes place poses a significant question. Before attempting an answer to this question I will cover relevant Thai concepts on the power and supernatural qualities of Buddhist kings. These are part of the popular imagination of the Thai people about kingship.

THE KING'S MERIT AND GRACE

The narratives exhibit the contours of King Chulalongkorn as a "righteous ruler." The king's intentions and deeds as they appear in the narrated portraits testify that King Chulalongkorn ruled in accordance with the Ten Kingly Virtues. The importance attributed to the adherence of kings to the Ten Kingly Virtues is the first clue to the Thai conception of kingship and its fundamental religious nature. In this conception, adherence to the Ten Kingly Virtues is inseparable from possessing *barami* (grace, virtue), a "charismatic power" with auspicious qualities. Equally important is the idea of a king being a man who has accumulated so much merit (*bun*) in his previous lives that he is reborn to become a king. Merit and reincarnation are central concepts in Theravada Buddhism. It is a person's "karma" (*kam*) that determines one's rebirth. According to the "law of karma" every action generates a consequence. Actions in accordance with Buddhist morals will produce merit and contribute to good karma. The more merit accumulated, the better one's karma and, accordingly, one's rebirth. Morally contemptible deeds, on the other hand, will result in demerit (*bap*), which in turn causes bad karma and an unpleasant rebirth (cf. Akin 1969:11–12; Spiro 1982:67). As the king stands at the apex of Thai society, he is perceived as the person with the greatest reservoir of accumulated merit (Akin 1969:47; Keyes 1977:288).

For the Thai people the "merit and grace" (*bun barami*) of the king are important matters, as they believe them to influence the course that society might take as well as their individual well-being. It is generally accepted that when the kingdom is ruled by a virtuous king, his *bun barami* makes the kingdom prosper and its inhabitants live in happiness and peace. However, although *bun* and *barami* overlap, they are not exactly the same and are experienced differently. The idea that the merit of a king works for the good of all is based on the belief that merit can be shared and transferred.[4] Monks transfer a share of their accumulated merit to the laity in public ceremonies and certain rituals. Laymen transfer and share merit particularly with deceased relatives or ancestors (Terwiel 1994:101–102). The extra merit deceased persons may receive in the interval between their death and rebirth through the merit-making ceremony organized by their relatives may contribute to a superior rebirth (Spiro 1982:124–125). A king is believed to have accumulated so much merit that through his compassion the merit can be shared and transferred to anyone connected with the king (Keyes 1977:287–289). Obviously, a king is connected with all his subjects and that explains the immediate beneficial effect a king's merit is believed to exert on his kingdom and its people. This belief also implies that disaster or misfortune can be understood as a weakening of the king's merit and its meritorious effect. Kings therefore are required to continue to make merit. In particular this takes the form of almsgiving to the Sangha and the construction of Buddhist monuments (i.e., Buddha statues, stupas, and temples), especially in times of crisis.

King Chulalongkorn is believed to be reborn in one of the heavenly abodes as a divine being, a "guardian angel" (*thep, thewada,* or *deva*). Through his compassion he still cares for the well-being of his kingdom and its inhabitants. And although this again leads to further accumulation of merit, contributing to both King Chulalongkorn's personal salvation and to the welfare of the Thai nation, the emphasis in the cult is placed on the beneficent effect of the king's *barami*. Different from merit, whose auspicious effect is unpredictable, the effect of the king's *barami* is direct and can be experienced particularly in his immediate proximity. The popular use of the word *barami* also refers to those effects of the king's observance of the Ten Kingly Virtues that may be experienced personally. One could translate *barami* in its popular conception as "grace," since it is considered to be a perceivable aspect of majesty. This same *barami* may also be experienced as emanating from King Chulalongkorn's portraits.

THE EQUESTRIAN STATUE

King Chulalongkorn's most significant and impressive portrait is the equestrian statue at the Royal Plaza in Bangkok. To understand the specific position of the statue in the King Chulalongkorn cult and the role of *barami,* the narrative devoted to its creation must be considered. This directly involves the writings of Prince Damrong Rajanubhab, one of the king's most intimate half-brothers. The prince published a diary (often reprinted since) on the *sadet praphat ton* visits of King Chulalongkorn. Prince Damrong accompanied the king, and he wrote on October 23, 1912: "Knowing the story of this statue makes one understand that the statue belongs to the people of Siam, irrespective of class, rank or place. . . . It was a joint effort in which everyone shared the same feeling. More than 1,000,000 baht was collected—five times more than the amount needed to erect the statue. . . . Many, many people, from everywhere, showed their love and loyalty towards the king" (Damrong 1976:35, author's translation).

The equestrian statue was erected in 1908 to celebrate the 40th anniversary of the king's accession to the throne. The unveiling of the statue on November 11, 1908, was the high point of the celebrations and still lives on in the collective memory through well-known photographs. The series of commemorative stamps issued that day, featuring an engraving of the statue, not only has become a valued collector's item but also depictions of the stamps on new stamps, posters, or on the cover of stamp albums are part of the usual repertoire of King Chulalongkorn objects (see inset, Figure 3.1).[5]

The account of the erection of the equestrian statue by the people of Siam, including how everyone, regardless of birth or background, liberally contributed, is widely known through the popular *sadet praphat ton* diary of Prince Damrong and is also inscribed on a plaque on the base of the statue. Books on King Chulalongkorn typically feature a photograph of the statue—either a recent picture or one of the photographs taken during its unveiling—and a short account of how the funds were collected. Prince Damrong's quote or the text of the plaque is also commonly included. The essence of the statue narrative is that it is a present from the Thai people to their king, with the size of the funds collected indicating the dimensions of their love.

Significantly, the inscription on the plaque is the first text that referred to the king as *piya maharat,* or the people's "Great Beloved." I have not found any direct account of Prince Damrong's role in the epithet's origin, but the idea is commonly accepted that it stemmed from the mind of the prince. As the prince was one of the members of the central committee charged with organizing the jubilee, it is logical to attribute the plaque inscription to him. The idea to erect an equestrian statue, however, came from the king himself (Apinan 1992:15–16). The money needed was collected through the sale of occasional stamps featuring a preliminary drawing of the statue.

The idea for collecting donations at large was possibly inspired by the construction of the Albert Memorial in London, which was financed by donations from the British populace. Certainly a monument erected after a successful campaign for funds may serve to give testimony to the legitimacy of the ruler. In the Thai case it made the creation of the statue an act of formalizing and formulating the love of "the people" for their king. Unlike the Albert Memorial, which in the 1990s narrowly escaped destruction, the equestrian statue has increased in significance throughout the years. But why and for whom exactly? For worshipers of King Chulalongkorn the equestrian statue gives testimony to the unique and intensive relationship between the king and his subjects, of which the "creation narrative" is a reconfirmation.

PORTRAITS OF THE KING

The importance of the equestrian statue as a focus for popular sentiments for King Chulalongkorn became apparent in the late 1980s. In that period an increasing number of people came to worship the king at the statue on Tuesdays. King Chulalongkorn was born on a Tuesday and many believe that every Tuesday night at 10 P.M. the spirit of the king descends from heaven to enter the statue. In 1992 the famous movie star Bin Banlerut sparked further interest in the cult by publicly declaring (in the *Thai Rath*, Thailand's most popular newspaper, and on television) that he had survived a terrible car accident thanks to the protective power of a King Chulalongkorn coin (*rian*) that he wore as an amulet. After Bin's declaration the number of people worshiping the king at the statue increased drastically while, as my research indicates, elsewhere in the country other centers of King Chulalongkorn worship appeared.[6] During the periods of research, thousands of people came to the statue to pay their respects to the king, particularly on Tuesday evenings but also on Thursday and Saturday evenings. The pilgrims presented offerings and asked the king for spiritual support in all kinds of worldly problems.

For an understanding of the omnipresence of the king's portraits another important aspect to the cult needs to be introduced. People explained their worship of King Chulalongkorn, almost without exception, as stemming from a need for a *thi phung* (a patron) or a *thi phung thang chai* (a mental patron). Sometimes the expressions *yut nieo* (a belief one can hold to) and *lak nieo* (a principle or a basis one can stick to) were used. These expressions indicate a need for someone who can always be turned to or relied upon. The colloquial forms used to address the king in prayers or when speaking about the king—*sadet pho* (royal father), *sadet pu* (royal grandfather), *phra piya* (beloved highness), or *pho piya* (beloved father)—demonstrate how worshipers perceive and experience their relation with the king in terms of an intimate father-child relationship. Such perceptions, of course, are elaborations of the image of King Chulalongkorn as an accessible, fatherly ruler or as the ideal Buddhist king noted earlier.

The interpretation of King Chulalongkorn as a faithful fatherly figure explains, in part, why people long to be physically close to him. In the narrated portraits this longing is expressed in the recurring theme of the immediate presence and approachability of the king among his subjects during his life. The abundance of portraits may be regarded as a material expression of the same longing for his presence. It is difficult to find a single worshiper of the king who does not own at least one King Chulalongkorn portrait. Among all the portraits, though, the meanings attached to the equestrian statue are more powerful than those of any other portrait. This is because the idea of the king's spirit descending from heaven into the statue makes the statue, at least on Tuesdays at 10 P.M., indistinguishable from the king. And the statue is not only embedded in the collective memory as "a gift from the people" and regarded as belonging to the people, but also the square where it is situated has become a place *of* the people.[7] These ideas about the statue are important in understanding why, in terms of *barami*, the statue is considered to be extra powerful and why people make an effort to come to the statue to worship the king. For them King Chulalongkorn's *barami* emanates directly from the statue, radiating equally to everyone, leaving an immediate and lasting positive effect.

Nearly everyone making the pilgrimage to the statue brings one or more King Chulalongkorn images. The portraits are placed amidst each person's offerings and are charged or recharged with the king's charismatic power. In this way the statue's *barami* with its protective and auspicious qualities can be taken home or, in the case of coins and amulets, carried. This process of transfer of the king's charismatic power into the objects is comparable to the sanctification of objects (*pluk sek*) that takes place in consecration ceremonies (*phithi pluk sek, phutthaphisek*) at temples (Nithi 1993:27). Also in such ceremonies people bring images (whether Buddhist amulets, monk statuettes, or portraits of Thai kings) to have them sanctified and charged with beneficial power. The fundamental difference, though, is that in the King Chulalongkorn cult people do not depend on expert intermediaries, such as monks (Nithi 1993:27). In a *phutthaphisek* ceremony, objects are sanctified through beneficial power, which is generated by monks chanting Pali formulae (*khatha*).

Significantly, at the equestrian statue monks are not needed to consecrate the objects—the physical nearness of the statue is sufficient. People are entirely in the position of doing this on their own, without the need for a collective ceremony. Leaflets, booklets, and tapes providing the required knowledge about offerings, rituals, and magic formulae are widely available. Nithi (1993) points to the role of such *tamra* (literally, textbooks or manuals) in enabling individual worshipers to establish a direct contact with the king. Because of them, he argues, people can do as well without as with spirit mediums, the usual expert intermediaries in cults. Clearly a significant dimension of the King Chulalongkorn cult is that direct access to the divine is open to all and is not controlled by an esoteric inner circle. While this observation is important, it requires a more detailed consideration of popular ideas about the relationship between the king's effigy and *barami*.

There is no doubt about the special meaning of the equestrian statue and its importance as a source of *barami*. Yet, for people who lack the time or live far away, the king's *barami* can also be experienced through any of his portraits. Opinions on this matter differ widely but without resulting in any conflict or schism. I spoke with people who bought King Chulalongkorn images at the square and returned them regularly to the square but also had them consecrated in a temple ceremony elsewhere. I also spoke with people who never had their King Chulalongkorn portraits consecrated in any way but were convinced of the strength of their auspicious power only because of the king's effigy. But wherever people obtained their King Chulalongkorn objects and whether they had them sanctified at the statue, in local temple ceremonies, in spirit medium sessions, or not at all, the general opinion was that only the individual's attachment to the object and his or her personal intentions really mattered. However, the latter implies that a portrait's beneficial powers will only work for those who behave morally and work hard, as the king desires.

The need to be as close to the king as possible stems from the feeling that in this way a more direct appeal can be made to him and his *barami* for support in personal matters. A portrait opens up, or increases, the possibility for the worshiper to establish direct contact with the king. The equestrian statue is but one portrait through which such a contact can be established, although it is an extraordinary portrait, "shared" by the worshipers at the square. It is irrelevant that the motivation for approaching the king is purely personal and, in fact, the reasons vary greatly. I have met a good range of petitioners at the statue seeking help: students calling upon the king for help in passing their examinations, shop owners striving to increase their sales, employees needing his help to get promotions, and people seeking relief from grief or some general distress. Of course, these worshipers—and this is the case with virtually everyone who worships the king—have their own, personal King Chulalongkorn portraits. This phenomenon actually predates the weekly worshiping of King Chulalongkorn at the equestrian statue:

> [The method] of paying homage to deceased kings in Siam remains to be mentioned: the setting of a photograph or lithograph of the particular king on a table, before which are made the usual offering of lighted candles, flowers, and incense. This is now a very popular custom, both in government institutions and private houses, since every Siamese home possesses at least a cheap lithograph and can thus show its loyalty in this easy and practical manner. But it is of course quite a new custom, since the making of royal portraits only came into fashion after the middle of the last century, after the belief that this was harmful to the person represented had been officially discountenanced. Indeed, the supposition that some part of

> the royal "soul" (if one may be permitted to use this loose term) might possibly inhabit the portrait, would be an added stimulus to paying homage before it. It is also a modern means of expressing what remains of the worship of the living King [King Rama VII, reign 1925–1932], for whenever it is desired to honor him, especially on the occasions of a royal procession, portraits of the king set up on tables may be seen at almost every Siamese doorway along the route. [Wales 1992:173]

Wales, when speaking of "deceased kings," must be referring to portraits of King Chulalongkorn and King Vajiravudh (King Rama VI, son of King Chulalongkorn), since the mass production of portraits only started during the reign of King Chulalongkorn. Apparently, contact with the divine without intermediaries was an aspect of the worshiping of kings by early in the 20th century.

In conversations with devotees of King Chulalongkorn the significance of personally owned portraits in their relationships with the king was an ever-present topic. In the following section three cases are presented to illustrate the importance of this linkage. Although the interpretation and molding of one's relationship with the king is, to a certain extent, highly personal, these relationships are also characterized by recurring themes. Here I distinguish two such themes, though there are others. The first theme is one in which certain experiences involving the king or his image occurred during an especially emotional incident or episode (whether positive or negative) in the person's life. The second theme involves the role of a material token with the king's image as proof or reconfirmation of the special relation the new devotee has with King Chulalongkorn.

SOMBUN'S TURNING FATE

Sombun's first remarks when hearing about my topic of research were "those who worship King Chulalongkorn feel desperate" and "worshiping King Chulalongkorn is a psychological thing." This made me think that he was not an active King Chulalongkorn worshiper. To my surprise Sombun (an architect and contractor) turned out to be a strong believer in the powers of King Chulalongkorn. This was not always the case, though.

In January 1991 a vendor of King Chulalongkorn statuettes came to Sombun's office. At first Sombun had no intention of buying one. But then the vendor said, "Just buy one. For you, I will make the price very low." So Sombun bought a plaster statuette replica of the equestrian statue. Later he asked friends where the right place to put the statuette would be, how to make an altar, and what offerings to make. Two weeks later he sold a parcel of land he had tried to sell for a very long time. This was during a time when Thailand was experiencing a real-estate boom, but he had been unable to find a buyer. Sombun said,

"Thus without working I earned 100,000 baht. I immediately bought a bottle of Hennessy to present as an offering to the king."[8] In a later conversation it turned out that Sombun and his wife had started as architects and contractors one year earlier and their business was doing very badly at the time Sombun bought the statuette. Sombun said, "It was after I started to worship King Chulalongkorn that we always had enough orders." When asked about his earlier remark that King Chulalongkorn is for the "desperate," Sombun said he does not consider himself to be desperate, although he did not feel well at the time he bought the statuette.

NUM'S NEW JOB

Num, a woman in her early thirties, works as an official at the Land and Water Management Department in Mae Rim, a small town in the province of Chiang Mai. Num owns a 24-carat golden medallion (*lokhet*) bearing the image of King Chulalongkorn, and she was eager to tell me how she became the owner.

After finishing her formal education in water management Num went to work for a private company. Her parents regretted this as they had hoped she would become a government official. In Thailand, to become a government official, one has to take an examination. The examination results are valid for two years only and it is during this period that a job in government service must be located. Otherwise, the examination must be taken and passed again. Encouraged by her parents, Num took the examination, but she could not find a government job and had to stay with the private company. Approximately two months before the exam's expiration date, she had a disagreement at her work (she did not want to tell me about the problem) after which she wanted to leave more than ever and began urgently to seek work as a government official, but still without success. Seeking help with this problem, her father consulted, without her knowledge, a spirit medium (*khon song chao*). Without ever having met Num, the spirit medium told her father many things about her that were true, especially that she was a woman with many "male characteristics." Num had never thought about visiting a spirit medium, but after hearing this she felt she could trust the medium and joined her father for another visit. The medium told her that in her previous life she had been a soldier of King Chulalongkorn. As a soldier she had killed many people and the accumulated sin (*bap*) resulted in her rebirth as a woman. But much of the soldier in the former life had remained in her and in her heart she was *naklaeng* (a tough fighter). The medium told her that if she wanted a job as a government official she must pray to King Chulalongkorn, as she had been his soldier.

After the session Num turned to the king on a daily basis. She prayed: "If I really have been your soldier, then please help me now." When only one week remained until her examination expired, she received a message that there was a position for her at the Land and Water Management Department. Because the king had fulfilled her wish, she felt she wanted to have something special of him. Portraits and statuettes of King Chulalongkorn were plentiful, but these all seemed very ordinary to her, so she did not buy one. In her new position Num made a friend who had a beautiful golden King Chulalongkorn medallion. Num never dared tell her how much she admired the medallion. Num found the medallion special for two reasons: it was made in a famous temple and the king was shown full face rather than being portrayed in profile as on most medallions.

One day Num noticed her friend was wearing a different King Chulalongkorn medallion, and she asked about this change. The friend said that it was very clear to her that it was Num who should be wearing the golden medallion and she wanted to sell it to her. Num could not believe her ears, but a question remained: how much would her friend ask for the medallion? Num dared not ask the price since she thought it would cost at least 7,000 baht, an amount she could not afford. She prayed to the king, asking that the price would not be beyond her reach and to her great surprise her friend only asked 1,000 baht. Now Num has the desired portrait and she feels no need for additional portraits. This medallion is all she wants. At home she has no portraits and no altar: she believes (*napthu*) with her heart. She does cross-stitched, sepia-hued portraits of the king and one small one takes her two to three months to complete. She does not keep these portraits herself but makes them as gifts for friends.

RENU'S DIRECT ENCOUNTER

On a Sunday morning many years ago Renu, now retired but at that time a secretary at the main office of Shell Oil in Bangkok, visited the weekend market (now closed) at Sanam Luang. It was a windy day. While she walked down the street near Wat Mahatat (a famous temple), a crumpled piece of paper, tossed about by the wind, danced just in front of her feet, behind her feet, and in front of her feet again. Every time she walked past it, it seemed to pursue her even faster. Finally, she stopped to pick it up and to see what was on the paper. It turned out to be a portrait of King Chulalongkorn, dressed in purple clothes. Although she never had any feelings or ideas one way or the other with regard to the king, Renu decided to keep the portrait. She ironed the paper portrait, bought a 50-baht frame, and took it to the restaurant owned by her family.

On the very same day, they hung the portrait. Later, a thief entered the restaurant. Her brother, a soldier, was standing next to the cashier. The robber pointed his gun at her brother and told the cashier to hand over all the money. But suddenly, without any apparent reason, the man dropped his gun and ran away. A few streets away he was caught and arrested by the police.

Renu later heard this story from her brother. While he was being held at gunpoint by the thief, he could see the portrait of King Chulalongkorn. He prayed to the king: "If I have to die, please let it happen in war while defending my country, but not this way." The king then raised his hand from the portrait and with an enormous power knocked the gun out of the thief's hand. The cook standing nearby had seen the king's hand, too.

This event made it very clear to Renu that it was no coincidence she had come across that particular piece of paper. The king had come to her through that portrait to save her brother. She had experienced, as she calls it, a direct encounter (*prasop kantrong*) with the king. Of course, the portrait is no longer housed in a 50-baht frame. Immediately after the incident it was reframed in a beautiful gilded wooden frame.

CONCLUSIONS

From analyzing the narratives of these experiences it is clear how each of the two recurring themes contributes to the persuasiveness of the stories. The initial lack of interest in King Chulalongkorn makes the associated events more notable and highlights the fact that involvement with King Chulalongkorn is not a fancy. At the same time, the initiative for the relationship is seen as coming from the king, implying that the resulting relationship is genuinely mutual. A crisis situation makes the king's intervention plausible and helps to demonstrate the beneficent effect of his involvement. The particular King Chulalongkorn portraits figuring in the stories not only serve to illustrate and confirm the particular relationships between the narrators and the king but also provide tangible evidence of each story's truth and hence provide an indispensable element in the narrative. At the same time we see how King Chulalongkorn stories and legends provide a "reservoir of meanings" (Connerton 1989:56) from which one may draw to reinterpret and to retell one's personal history in terms of a generally accepted framework. The personal stories "borrow truth" from the accepted body of stories and legends. For instance, Num and Renu's brother rightfully escape misery and danger because they place their lives in the context of defending Thailand's independence as soldiers, now or in the past. Sombun's story shows how becoming involved with King Chulalongkorn is instantly rewarded. Such individual elaborations in turn enhance and reinforce the persuasiveness of the general King Chulalongkorn myth. Exchanges of personal stories such as these are also vital elements in the spread of the cult.

These conversion stories clearly demonstrate how mass-produced portraits of the king may become objects of great personal value, not merely because they provide the presence of the Great Beloved King but, in particular, because they have become physical symbols of the king's personal involvement with his devotees. Finally, these cases demonstrate how the role of the king, from a historical savior of the country to an omnipresent daily problem-solver, is refashioned by individual worshipers.

NOTES

The material for this chapter was collected during my Ph.D. field research on the cult of King Chulalongkorn the Great (Stengs 2003). The research periods were from September 1996 to December 1997 and October to November 1998. The research was funded by the Program on Globalization and the Construction of Communal Identities of the Netherlands Foundation for the Advancement of Tropical Research (WOTRO). I thank Jeroen Beets for his useful comments and Rafael Sanchez for sharing his ideas with me.

1. Siam was formally renamed Thailand in 1939 when Phibun Songkhram was prime minister. The country became Siam again in 1944 under Prime Minister Pridi Phanomyong. In 1947 Phibun Songkhram took over the government again and the country's name reverted to Thailand.

2. The terms *portrait* and *image* will be used interchangeably when referring to depictions of the king in the form of painted portraits, statuettes, photographs, bank notes, coins, sculptures, postage stamps, and so forth.

3. See Akin (1969) and Brummelhuis (1995) for clear and detailed analyses of the *sakdina* system. This article also leaves no room to go into detail about the *sakdina* system or the king's precise motivations for abolishing the system.

4. This idea is in contradiction with the law of karma, but this contradiction generally is not resolved (Obeyesekere 1968:22–26; Spiro 1982:125).

5. The 1997 catalog price for the original stamps: 90,000 baht ($2,500) for the whole series of seven in mint condition.

6. My research was partly carried out among visitors to a temple and among clients of a spirit medium in Chiang Mai (about 600 kilometers north of Bangkok). It turned out that the spirit of King Chulalongkorn approached both the abbot of the temple and the medium in 1992 for the first time. Another part of the research was carried out among a prayer group praying for the well-being of the monarchy, the nation, and the Thai people at royal monuments in Bangkok. This group began its prayer sessions in 1993 at the equestrian statue.

7. Indicative of the importance of the statue is that most people do not use the square's official name (*Suan Amphon*) but refer to the square as *Lan Borommarup Songma*, "Equestrian Statue Square."

8. In addition to traditional offerings such as candles, incense, garlands, and Thai fruit, King Chulalongkorn is offered a variety of Western products. Next to cognac the king is believed to have appreciated apples, black coffee, red wine, cigars, and Winston cigarettes. Such offerings clearly express how people associate the king with Europe and modernity. For more details on these and many other aspects of the cult see Stengs (2003).

4
Evita

A Case of Political Canonization

Roberto Bosca
(Translated by June Macklin)

Eva Perón incarnated one of the most fraught and important mythical icons of Latin American political history during the past century. As such, she surpassed even the prestige of her husband, Juan Perón, then president of Argentina (1946–1955). Here I neither describe Evita's personality (already sufficiently treated in the political literature) nor analyze her role in the relations between *perónismo* and the Roman Catholic Church; rather, I consider her persona in relation to religious factors, stressing her embodiment of lay sainthood.

Converted into "Evita," she played a role in the society the importance of which today is beyond dispute. She went well beyond the claims of both her apologists and detractors. Always controversial, she was at once passionate, implacable, valiant, and foulmouthed; both wildly hated and wildly loved (Luna 2000:130). Paradoxically, she fostered and provoked tremendous resentment at the same time she aroused unconditional, fanatical support. Although such extremes have occurred in other cases that one might also classify as political canonizations, the process by which Evita rose to this status was dazzlingly rapid. She was a young woman of 27 when her husband rose to political power in Argentina (Gallardo 1995:222). When she was 33 years old—an age deemed significant by many, as it is said to have been Christ's age at his death—she became frail and was struck down by cancer of the uterus. She died on July 26, 1952.

Half a century after this tragic moment, Evita Perón has become again a cyclonic force internationally as well as in Argentina. Stage and film productions (in which she is portrayed by the enormously popular North American film and stage star Madonna) reprise Evita's life, including her fading success; these performances ratify renewed interest in her importance. Albeit a de-ideologized and postmodern return, the revival also captures her mythical nature. Novelistic treatment—*Santa Evita*, by Tomás Eloy Martínez (on Argentina's bestseller lists), and *Eva Perón: A Biography (Evita: Eva Peron a Madona Dos Sem-Camisa)*, by Alicia Dujovne Ortiz, both followed *The Passion, According to Eva*, by Abel Pose—has helped to confer beatific meaning on her person. One sees a recentering of interest on this singular and fascinating Argentine myth of which so much has been written and spoken: Evita has not died; *Evita lives.*[1]

The figure of Evita is well known; her name is mentioned with those of the great political women of the century, both nationally and internationally. She, along with her husband, was very charismatic, which permitted her to enter a kind of "mystical communion" with those she protected politically, the wretched and the poor (literally, the "shirtless," or *los descamisados*). Without doubt, there existed between her and her public a solidarity that was so strong one might call it physical (Folliet 1963:78).

THE INTERCESSION

As a way of sacralizing his political strategy, Juan Perón compared himself with the figure of the Eternal Father, one who blesses all others equally. And in her relation to her husband, one can see the multiplicity of functions Evita fulfilled in his regime. Multivocalic in significance, the symbolic Evita's principal function was that of mediation between her husband, the leader, and the masses: she took the typically feminine and maternal role of protecting her "children" from the harshness of the father and of obtaining benefits for them. Often, this same function has been assumed by the figure of a queen on behalf of her subjects. Further, according to theological teachings of the Catholic Church, the Virgin Mary, a maternal figure with whom Evita has been identified, is the universal intercessor for all of the favors of salvation for the entire human race. Historians Carlos Floria and César García Belsunce (1992:403) point out that Eva Perón occupied a singular role, albeit insufficiently studied, in the political and social processes of Peronist Argentina. A relatively recent investigation calls attention to her representation of the "myth of the Mother" during the epoch in which she shared power with her husband. She acted as an intercessor for many men, but especially for women, and broke the rigidities of party and official bureaucracy. According to a daring, suggestive psychosocial thesis, her role implied a deliberate, or perhaps unconscious, copy of the characteristics attributed to the Virgin Mary (*marianismo*) (Floria and García Belsunce 1992:403).

Vice President Alberto Teisaire, who was widely believed to have been a freemason, told Perón that he, the president, did not have to worry about a conflict with the Church, because in Argentina no one (supposedly) felt tied to the parochial priest, and in many homes, people had replaced the image of the Virgin with photos of Perón and Evita (Potash 1980). In his discussion of Latin American millenarianism, the French anthropologist Jacques Lafaye mentions that the veneration of Evita's lay image competes with that of the Virgin Mary in Argentina and "is perhaps one of the most outstanding examples" of the adoration of men and women "of flesh and bone" (1984:10).

The mythic symbol of a virgin already existed in the pre-Christian world. Pagan myths may differ radically from Christian dogmas, but in neither case are religious values isolated from social and political life. The image of the Virgin Mary, in her invocation as Our Lady of Guadalupe, has been endowed with patriotic significance and is considered a national symbol of Mexico (Lafaye 1984: 384). Although the cult of the pre-Colombian Aztec goddess Tonantzin provides an outstanding prefigurative antecedent of Guadalupe, her mythic content differs and therefore is not continuous with the national devotion to Guadalupe.[2] Other manifestations of Mary, such as Poland's Virgin of Czestochowa, also take on the character of national political symbols.

The images of the Virgin Mary vary according to the large number and enormous variety of devotions dedicated to her, each being known for the place where the cult originated. In each case, the name of the manifestation of the Virgin is always preceded by the expression "Nuestra Señora" (Our Lady). Significantly, Evita was officially listed as "La Señora" (The Lady) (Comisión de Afirmación de la Revolución Libertadora 1987:42), and she was quite conscious of her role as intercessor. Explaining how she would like to be remembered in Argentine history, she wrote in her book *La razón de mi vida,* "There was, at the side of Perón, a woman who dedicated herself to carry to the President the hopes of the people, which Perón then would convert into reality" (Perón 1951). In another passage she wrote, "I chose to be 'Evita' . . . in order that by my mediation, the people—and above all the workers—would always find the way of their Leader" (Perón 1951).

Evita saw her mediation as having the same reciprocal flow as that exercised by the Virgin Mary, who, in her evangelical apparitions, says to the people, "Do what He tells you to do" (John 2:5). Another example Evita provides concerns the Virgin's intercession for both sinners and the needy before her Son: "They have no wine" (John 2:3). But, Evita adds that "nonetheless, many times, I must tell the people, face to face, that which your Leader would say, and as a consequence of this, I, myself, also must speak to the Leader of those points the people want carried to his ears" (Perón 1951). At the end of her life, consumed by disease, she defined herself as a "rainbow of love" between the people and Perón (Page 1983:304), which parallels the same pontifical functions the Roman emperors had and emanates once more from her unique personality.[3]

During a heated parliamentary debate on May 19, 1955, in the national House of Representatives, the radical representative Yadarola read a prayer that allegedly was published in the daily paper, *Democracia,* on February 14. The truth of its publication, and of the prayer itself, was denied. Nevertheless, it is certain religious devotion to Eva Perón was and *is* real, among Peronists. Although the number of devotees has shrunk, *estampitas* (small cards, engraved or imprinted with images of religious figures and texts) bearing the sacralized image of Evita still circulate among them and bear the following message: "May God save you, Maria Eva, full of grace. All of the people are with you. Blessed be you among children, among men and women, and blessed be the fruit of your genius. . . . Saint Maria Eva, Mother of Justice, pray for us workers, now and even more in the hour of our deliverance. So be it" (Cámara de Diputados de la Nación 1955).

The prayer may have been concocted as a weapon to disparage Evita; nonetheless, one cannot ignore its kernel of truth: Evita represented something supernatural to her followers. At the very least, they saw her as a being invested with uncommon qualities, which, effectively, she was. One of the Peronist parliamentarians went so far as to swear by Eva Perón (García de Loydi 1956:31).

In the new "Peronist religion," even kindergarten children were catechized by the state's educational machinery when they were taught certain simple prayers. The first-grade students encountered "Ave, Eva" on the first page of their texts, under her picture and surrounded by angels. Second-grade texts (again following an illustration of Evita) began with the words of a small child directed to the defunct First Lady: "Our little Mother, who is in heaven. . . . How good it is that you laugh among the angels. . . . Evita: I promise you that I will be good" (J. M. Taylor 1979:108). At the death of Eva, a children's magazine led its young readers in a similar, fervent prayer: "Evita, our love who art in Heaven, may your goodness always accompany us. May you continue to protect our dreams and our games from the nearest star. . . . May you continue to intercede before God the Father Almighty so that our elders may never lack fruitful work. May you continue to teach and guide our Fatherland" (J. M. Taylor 1979:108). Thus the parallelism with the image of the Virgin Mary becomes evident in both the iconography and the content of schoolbooks. The teachers were *not* devoted to the teachings of the Church but "wrote reading texts in which they taught the children to compare *that* woman of well-known background," as Rock called Eva Perón, "with the Virgin Mary" (1993:185). The religious allusions went further. During Juan Perón's conflict with the Church, members of a group of Peronist women created a "Congregation of Our Lady Eva Durate de Perón" and dressed themselves in tunics similar to habits of the religious orders. According to some accounts of the era, a bust of Evita began to produce miraculous cures (J. M. Taylor 1979:82–83).

THAUMATURGY AND EVITA

The politico-religious monism of the ancient world shows that power always has clothed itself with religious significance. Even after the rise of Christian dualism, the bishops exercised temporal functions when civil authority disappeared. Further, those with public power often exercised ecclesiastical privileges, claiming a theological foundation for their right to do so (Kantorwicz 1957).

Many studies, such as the now classic work of Marc Bloch (1924), have plumbed the supposed curative or healing power tied to the institution of thaumaturgical monarchies. The mythology surrounding Evita includes references to her sharing such abilities. One of the most interesting narratives about Eva for its obvious religious connotations is that of her kiss on the mouth of a leper (or syphilitic, according to another version). Poet José María Castiñeria de Dios, apparently an eyewitness at one such event, wrote, "She could touch the most terrible things with a Christian attitude that amazed me, kissing and letting herself be kissed. There was a girl whose lip was half eaten away with syphilis, and when I saw that Evita was about to kiss her, I tried to stop her. She said to me, 'Do you know what it will mean that I kiss her?'" (Plotkin 2003:159).

In all of these narratives, Eva appears to be surrounded by a semireligious aura. She can touch and kiss people who suffer ostensibly contagious diseases, while refusing to take the most elementary hygienic precautions. This attitude was consistent with her image of being a saint: Eva never contracted any of their diseases. Her charisma was based in part on these quasi-supernatural qualities it was believed she enjoyed.

Eva's work in the foundation she created, in which she maintained direct and physical contact with the people, was tied to her style of unrestricted devotion and also ties her to the martyrish image with which she is ensconced in the popular imagination: "As was foreseen, this great Samaritan [Evita] of the mystical body of Christ, fell wounded in her heroic exercise of charity. Now prostrated by illness, we see her haloed with the bright light of martyrdom" (Caimari 1995:230). The body of such narratives constitutes a true mythology, in the sense that Marc Bloch uses the term. The climate of sacrifice, redemption, pain, and mysticism is reflected constantly in a large number of anecdotes, among which that of the kiss of the leper is perhaps the best known and constitutes a scene that unquestionably resonates to the Gospels.

At the initiative of Representative Héctor Cámpora, Congress agreed that an intercessor's function was appropriate to Evita's title, "The Spiritual Head of the Nation." As I noted above, she participated in the same messianism her husband epitomized. Still, the title she was given was not merely an honorific: Evita truly was a spiritual guide for many, many people. Years after her death, a nurse who had worked at her side used a religious concept to refer to this spiritual leadership. She reported of Evita that "she took me by the hand, and submerged me in her gospel; and here I am, still following her footsteps" (Demitrópulos 1984:122).

It is evident that her influence had the virtue of changing lives, comparable to what happens during a religious conversion in a supernatural environment. In much the same way, Senator Justiniano de la Zerda started a discourse before the Chamber of Deputies by excusing himself for his poor health. He then begged for the power of healing that emanated from the figure of Evita, comparing it to that of the thaumaturgical kings and adding that he felt protected by the impression of her supernatural help (Subsecretaría de Informaciones 1952:446).

In the Catholic tradition, a life of saintliness is one characterized by a continuous dialogue with the divine, through which the saints go on discovering the outline of their mission, which is to concretize in their own temporal existence the eternal design of the Creator. As with all saints, Evita supposedly maintained fluent communication with God. For example, in *The Little Music Box*, a textbook by Nélida Picollo, there is a reading that tells of the occasion when Eva wanted to send a message of love but was not quite sure how to do so. In doubt, she turned to God, asking what she ought to do. God answered that her message would have the form of a train loaded with doctors and nurses, an obvious reference to the "hospital train" dispatched by the Eva Perón Foundation. Plotkin cites an obscure publication, *The Message of Light*, and finds the following is instructive: "[God decided] to end evil, and He sent His favorite angel [Evita] to the world . . . and on one day, God, seeing His desires fulfilled, ordered the return of the angel" (2003:129).

It becomes clear that Eva Perón represented the nature of lay sainthood, having all of the characteristics and functions of saints, including purity and martyrdom. Evita could also take care of petitions, tasks she handled while at Labor and Welfare. She was believed to have continued this after her death (J. M. Taylor 1979:107).

Martínez Estrada captures the symbolic relation between Evita and the Virgin Mary, recalling her title of "Mother of the People, the Virgin of the Wretched" (1956:251). Other titles that point to an identification with Mary include "Our Lady of Hope," "The Lady of Reality," and "Our Lady of Suffering" (Subsecretaría de Informaciones 1952:285, 287). Martínez Estrada also provides a magisterial description of the religious meaning of the regime, which reflects a reality that comprises all of the elements he understands to characterize new religions:

> By a natural metamorphosis, the locales of political proselytism had transformed the larvae of this type of sect into temples of an incipient religion of atheists and positivists. Meanwhile, the existence of [Eva's] mummy, removed from the gaze of the faithful while a monumental mausoleum was being built, augmented the prestige of the absent divinity. The construction of the temple, the pharaonic monument which would contain her remains, completed the picture of this religion of political sectarians. In sum,

> the Peronist religion contained fetishism, churches, unions, committees, a tabernacle (the mausoleum), a gospel (*The Reason for My Life*), catechists, missionaries and apostles. [Martínez Estrada 1956:251]

Certainly, this religion was not limited to treating the spontaneous impulses of humble village folk, as one might think, but also was a cult fostered by the same requests for power found in a true political religion.

At times official Peronism described Eva in only vaguely religious terms, but at other times she was referred to in specifically holy terms. The propagandists believed most of the Peronist public would be susceptible to the religiously charged terminology. They "formed a mystical cult around the party heroine" (J. M. Taylor 1979:106). Titles like "Our Lady of Hope" implied parallels to Christian hagiography and were used when opportunities arose. *Democracia* and other popular publications often used the term *saint* in describing Eva, though sometimes citing other sources, such as *Le Monde,* which had referred to Eva Perón as a madonna of poor Argentines. This was taken up in a book title shortly after: *Eva de América: Madonna de los Humildes* (J. M. Taylor 1979:107). And, as we have seen, in the schools the catechizing continued: "A first grade reader repeated, 'She was a saint. And for that reason, she flew to God.' . . . In still other books, Eva after death took her place by the side of God the Son, or at the right hand of God" (J. M. Taylor 1979:107).

Nonetheless, while there are elements of the Virgin Mary in the conceptualization of Eva, a more nuanced approach shows that the latter differs from the traditional figure of the Virgin in some ways, such as her "combativeness." Caimari finds that the parallels and comparisons made between Eva and the Virgin are ambivalent: "These images accompany not only her politically innocuous angelical image: they surround also the whole, integrated image of Eva Perón, which bespeaks the tension between the submissiveness and combativeness she embodied" (1995:226).

THE CANONIZATION

Of late, students of religious phenomena have given more attention to the theological-pastoral category referred to as "popular religiosity." In ecclesiastic circles, it is now customary to discuss the merits of such phenomena in relation to orthodox faith. By "popular religiosity" I refer to a form of understanding the Christian message and its living consequences within many sectors of Argentinian society, particularly those in the middle and lower economic strata. Thus, one might identify such phenomena with the religiosity of the poor or, in political terms, the working class, the majority of whom are considered to be Peronists. To the Church, this kind of religiosity reflects an "immaturity" in the faith and expresses a certain incapacity—individually and collectively—to live according to the "proper" content of the Gospels.

Popular religiosity is expressed in different ways and in different places from those of more formal Roman Catholicism—principally in sanctuaries, for example, and most of these are devoted to Mary. This is also seen in the *promesas* (vows) made to saints from whom one expects a favor in return, in the seeking of benedictions, and in the use of holy water. Having recourse to an extensive iconography is also important in popular religion. This need is filled by *estampitas,* medals, ex-votos, images, and various other material objects that are often given magico-religious significance.

In recent decades, an ill-advised pastoral perspective, perhaps inspired by a legitimate desire to preserve doctrinal purity, and perhaps also influenced by secular culture, has led many Catholic priests to disparage the use of religious images by the faithful. Paradoxically, the attempt to suppress such popular practices occasionally has had exactly the reverse effect from that sought by the clergy. Their rejection of such images, meant to purify the faith, overlooks that ours is precisely the oft-mentioned "civilization of the image." Nor does it take into account a human psychological need that responds to images.

Recognizing this important reality, the Peronist regime promoted the wide diffusion of an official iconography, some of which was coercively imposed on the public. In particular, a profusion of photographs of the smiling Perón and Evita—reproduced ad infinitum—were distributed, sparing no one's privacy, not even the homes of public functionaries. Here is the express instrumental use of religion, with the political and religious realms woven inextricably into the warp and woof of one plot (Abelardo Ramos 1966).

Latin America is a land prodigious in *caudillos* who enjoy strong popular roots and who often have converted their regimes into harsh dictatorships, in the manner of Anastasio Somoza in Nicaragua, Gustavo Rojas Pinilla in Colombia, and Castillo Armas in Guatemala, to cite only a few. On occasion, such strong political leaders were transformed into popular myths, always with religious trappings. Thus, one finds elements of a folkloric cult. One such example is Federico Cantoni, an Argentine provincial boss in the first decades of the 20th century. Although he was not anticlerical, he was not a believer either (P. Frías 1989:225). The regional historical chronicle records that near idolatrous admiration arose among the people for Cantoni, to such an extreme that women put his picture next to that of their preferred saint (Mansilla 1983:16). This politico-religious syncretism was so widespread in the *ranchos* (small farms) that one frequently saw a photograph of the leader together with many popular saints, all surrounded by candles and other liturgical paraphernalia (cf. J. M. Taylor 1979:115).

It is clear that the social reality described reflects an old phenomenon, one that characterizes many popular canonizations. Consider the privileged spot reserved in the Argentine imagination for the mythical figure of the singer famous for his espousal of the sad, nostalgic music of the tango, Carlos Gardel (1890–1935). Perón himself reportedly remarked that "in order to govern Argentina, we need the smile of Carlos Gardel." His cult has been popular for several decades in several American, European, and Far Eastern countries. Today, the details of Gardel's life can be found on many web sites, and *amazon.com* lists 34 volumes written about him, in several languages. Gardel died tragically in a plane crash in the Colombian city of Medellín, which contributed to the myth of his supernatural attributes. On occasion, such deaths have been associated with popular canonization. People leave written testimonies at the tomb of the singer, located in the cemetery of the Chacarita, the traditional *porteño* neighborhood. Such devotion attests to the popular canonization of the entertainer (Sánchez 1995).

The case of Elvis Presley perhaps may be taken as paradigmatic of the divinization of famous singers. His cult created the "First Presleyterian Church of Elvis the Divine." His "Basilica of St. Peter" is the Graceland mansion, converted since his death into a sanctuary for pilgrims. Some of his followers believe their idol will return, reincarnated, having discarded the supposition that he is still alive, but hidden, only to return one day to the scene. Argentina's Carlos Gardel provides similar data, as do many other influential figures in recent popular culture. Creators of Elvis Presley's new cult include Karl Edwards (aka Ed Karlin), its self-nominated theologist, and Mort Farndu (aka Marty Rush), who is considered to be a "reverend" ordained by Elvis (Doss 1999:104). Both are dedicated to writing the "Gospel According to Elvis," pray once a day with their gaze directed toward Las Vegas, and take "communion" with the favorite foods of their new god, such as hamburgers. Another case, perhaps less extensive in its social impact but no less significant, is that of the screen actor James Dean, who died young and tragically. One can speak of a "Deaner theology," blessed with its own beliefs, sentiments, and values (Hopgood 2000:342–345).

Within the Catholic tradition, the cult of the saints is a reverent tribute to outstanding people, now dead, who have been proposed for the veneration of the faithful because of the Christian perfection of their lives (Sauras 1972:14). This can happen by popular acclamation, by pontifical beatification, or by canonization. Such cults may be classified according to the kinds of beings they revere. A private cult is one that pays tribute to persons outstanding for their virtue, or for some special cause, but who have not been included in the official catalog of saints. In Catholic theology, respect paid angels and saints is referred to as *dulia,* in order to differentiate this attitude from *hiperdulia,* veneration granted only to the Virgin Mary, while the *latria* is homage reserved for God alone. The saint is one who, among many respected dead, supposedly has incarnated the evangelical virtues to a degree far superior (i.e., "heroically") to that of common Christian existence, so that he or she deserves to be called a "Servant of God."

The Church, at the request of the saint's devotees or admirers, examines the case by means of a rigorous procedure. After having determined the "correctness" of the person's saintly reputation, the proceeding evaluates proof of the heroic nature of theological, cardinal, and related virtues. The heroic level of the virtues must have been maintained for a notable period. A further very important point is that the candidate may not have fallen into any doctrinal errors, not even the smallest, in matters of faith (López Jordán 1985:12). Before canonization, beatification is declared, by which his or her cult is permitted only in some places or for some people. Canonization is a judgment of the Pontiff of Rome, a solemn declaration that the Servant of God now enjoys heavenly glory; consequently, it is recommended to *all* of the faithful that they now pay the homage of *dulia* in the saint's honor (de Echevarría 1972:859).

After the death of Eva, the CGT (General Confederation of Work) approved a "lay enthroning" of the image of Evita in all local syndicates. Although the Argentine government never got around to making any formal petition to the Holy See, it was clear that many humble people shared a profound conviction that Evita *was* a saint. Her death, long lamented by the people, spawned very strong feelings that there was a real chance for canonization. Devotion to Eva permeated the feelings of the working classes. Immediately after her death they adorned her images with all of the trappings of a martyr, the "lay altar" in the CGT being dedicated to her memory, and converted her into the "Martyr of the Workers" and "The Spiritual Head of the Peronist Movement" (Frigerio 1984:22).

Anti-Peronists accused Perón of wanting his own effigy and that of his wife enthroned on altars, as had the Argentine *caudillo* and dictator Juan Manuel de Rosas; they also noted that his ambition was analogous to that of the German Nazis, who replaced the cross as a symbol of faith with a picture of the Fuhrer (Garibaldi 1988:13).

Regardless of motivations, the point is that the government sacralized the cult of Evita (Floria and García Belsunce 1992:427). But that wasn't all. Her popular canonization rose above a vague, generic desire among ordinary people and took formal expression: the Pope received petitions urging that he canonize her (Main 1956:178). Although rumors of official canonization had circulated widely since the very moment of Evita's death, news of a concrete petition rose above the level of anonymous comments.

On July 31, 1952, the Syndicate of Food Workers sent a telegram to Pope Pious XII requesting the beatification and canonization of Doña María Eva Duarte de Perón (Page 1983:310). In reality, a request for canonization in itself does not amount to legitimacy. Under other circumstances, perhaps such a request would not have caused such a commotion, because the process is a traditional one within the Church. The causes of the saints, before the administrative reorganization advanced by Pope Paul VI, were transmitted by the Congregation of Rites created by Pope Sixtus V in 1588. Historically, the cult of a saint always started with a first beatification declared in the local environment, which was then promoted by a concrete request from the community of the faithful.

One cannot deny that many people believed the conditions traditionally demanded by the Church to open a cause for beatification had been carried out for Eva. Years later, and not without a certain dose of typical sarcastic arrogance, scornful of formalities, Perón exclaimed, "She is canonized in the hearts of the people, who maintain altars with her picture, and worship her" (Pavón Pereyra 1973:81). Perón boasted about this popular canonization, with megalomania, and considered it to be superior to being listed among official Christian saints: "At the entrance of each Peronist house, there is an altar dedicated to Evita; no saint of the Catholic Church can claim to have as many devotees as she. . . . Evita represents a new figure in history" (Luca de Tena et al. 1981:198).

An analysis of this personal reading of the phenomenon suggests the conclusion that through "*vox populi, vox Dei*" Juan Perón acquired the characteristic of infallibility, based on *sensus fidelium*, the consensus of the faithful. The leader's attitude—operating outside formal rules—is the context that permits an explanation of this interpretation. But here, the rules are essential. Whatever the popular consensus was it would not be sufficient to canonize Evita, for a technical and impartial declaration is necessary and must be so accepted. It becomes evident, then, that to arrive at a legitimate outcome, the commonsense opinion of the faithful must correspond to an "objective" determination of "heroic" saintliness, confirmed by the ecclesiastical hierarchy.

However, in the realm of popular religion, seen from the viewpoint of the majority in the working class at that time, nothing could have been more natural than recognizing the sanctity of one who so obviously had given her life for the poor. Never mind that this perception was not at all shared by those in other social strata. Frequently a mixture of nationalism and populism (*völkisch*) is connected with authoritarian institutions and accompanied by mystical fervor directed toward those in power (Chatelet and Kouchner 1981). It is not surprising, then, that among the poor Evita's image soon took on great significance or that their feelings inevitably mimicked the sentiments attached to supernatural beings. The devotion to Evita, present during her life, was consolidated by her early death (Caimari 1995:229). And, as is often observed, a premature death is many times a factor favoring popular canonizations.

Evita's tragic death raised her to a sphere of adoration like that of a saint. Since it served to legitimate the pretensions of his authoritarian rule, Perón used all means to keep alive the cult tied to her memory. As Robert McGeagh

(1987:89) observes, probably never before in Argentine history had the death of one person provoked an explosion of such feeling. Always the opportunist, Perón used the death of his wife as the first step in the creation of the mythical Evita, the immortal heroine of the Peronists.[4] The declaration of Representative Delia Degiulomini de Parodi, a prominent figure of the regime, says it all. Solemnly she intoned before the House, "She is our saint, our authentic saint" (Frigerio 1984:24), adding that "her presence emanated hope and modesty even to the level of saintliness" (Subsecretaría de Informaciones 1952:447). This belief was, of course, widely shared, especially among the poor.

Curing, the touchstone often needed by the Church to verify appropriateness of the process of canonization of a Servant of God, was also used to corroborate her saintly state. Caimari reports the views of her followers: "'Evita was a saint: I know, because she cured my mama.' . . . Many of the sick are healthy today; many of the destitute are happy today is a phrase repeated everywhere. . . . A Saint! A miraculous saint, because love always works miracles!" (1995:232).

The invocations of and references to her person always were couched in supernatural terms: for example, "the persuasive force of her luminous speech, daughter of inalterable, ordaining energy, wraps her in an air of wonder" (Subsecretaría de Informaciones 1952:447). The comparisons went so far as to include even Jesus, who, like her, threw the merchants from the temple and carried the cross. It was commonplace to see the image of Evita wearing a mystical halo (Figure 4.1). The official press soon began to sacralize her person, using religious elements, such as the poem "Nuestra Señora del Bien Hacer" (Our Lady of Good Works) published in the *Mundo Peronista* (Peronist World). The analogy was clear, especially for those who had always revered the image of the mother and her religious prototype, the Sainted Virgin, Mother of the Humble: "The *mise en scéne,* which surrounded her work, was never far from a comparison with biblical episodes. She replaced references taken from ancient Catholic sources with others inspiring justice, but which still were integrated effectively with biblical images" (Caimari 1995:225). It was not long before stories began to circulate among the people that lent facticity to the sacralizing. Testimonies from women who had worked with Eva in the feminine branch of the Peronist Party "corroborated the perception of her supernatural qualities, as they reconstructed the image of Evita: she was a 'saint,' 'the predestined one,' or even 'a second God'" (Caimari 1995:225–226).

The popular canonization of Evita began immediately after her death, and it continues today. Private altars have been erected in humble family homes, in the peripheries of great cities, and in the interior of the country. In those places one finds the smiling image of Evita, accompanied always by at least a pair of simple candles, giving eloquent testimony to the real adoration she aroused in a very considerable part of the Argentine population. She is "eternal in the soul of her

Figure 4.1. Evita with halo. (Courtesy of Archivo del Instituto Nacional Eva Perón—Museo Evita)

people," as one of the slightly tacky, but oft-cited, Peronist slogans declares. Another aspect of the mystical idolatry with which she is regarded can be found in the quantity of letters, often accompanied by family photographs, surrounding the altars where her smiling effigies are exhibited and watched over. These function like ex-votos, linking both word and image, the individual, the family, and the supernatural, validating the revered *estampitas* of the "Leader" (Perón) as well as those of the "Spiritual Leader" (Sánchez Zinny 1958:81).

J. M. Taylor (1979) observes that the regime manipulated authentic popular sentiment in the sacralization of Evita. He points out that during the weeks following her death, every edition of the official press published entire pages of photographs and texts, displaying the altars that were put up and printing the prayers offered in her honor. One regime article declared that those who could not "reach the room where the body lies in state . . . resignedly directed their steps toward the . . . [local offices] of the Woman's Branch of the Peronist Party," and before her portrait they kneeled, prayed, and left flowers as offerings. An altar was raised and crowned with Eva's photograph in the Plaza de Mayo (the main plaza in Buenos Aires), and an "unending line" of mourners passed by it. In many homes and in the offices of private and public associations candles were burned on altars erected for the glorification of "the woman who gave all for her people." Before the altar in the Plaza de Mayo, women prayed and called on Eva Perón as "*Regina Martirium*" (Queen of the Martyred) or as "Santa Evita" (J. M. Taylor 1979:109).

Toward the end of August, the coverage of the grief over her death began to diminish, introducing an important change. Without a single comment, the articles in *Democracia* began to designate the altars erected to the memory of Evita as "civic altars," where previously they had been labeled simply "altars." The change appeared to address the pressure being exerted on the journalists to modify the unqualifiedly religious image they had been promoting. Yet, the power of Eva's image was demonstrated in the continuation of a cult with altars for Eva, which endures among some Peronists today (J. M. Taylor 1979:109).

J. M. Taylor also observes that there is a difference between civic altars and traditional popular cults of the dead. By custom, families often place photographs of dead relatives on altars. They may offer prayers, but "generally they pray in memory *of* the dead, and not *to* them. . . . Members of the working classes do mention the custom of addressing prayers to a dead person, but they describe such prayers in terms of requests for favours and not cult rendered to the person addressed" (J. M. Taylor 1979:109–110). Due to ignorance or bias, then, Peronist propagandists may have consciously distorted or unintentionally misinterpreted the practice of making altars to the memory of Evita (J. M. Taylor 1979:110).

DISCUSSION AND CONCLUSIONS

There are saintly antecedents to be found among politicians. Thomas More of England provides an example, as does Nicolas Flue, venerated as the patron of Switzerland. Even some heads of state, such as St. Louis of France and St. Isabel of Hungary, have achieved this status. The process of beatification has been initiated for some of today's European statesmen, such as Alcides de Gasperi, Robert Schuman, and the Florentine politician Giorgio La Pira. In the Germanic Holy Roman Empire, the Emperor Frederick I Barbarosa petitioned the antipope Paschal III to canonize Charlemagne, which of course makes his sainthood illegitimate (Eguía 1974:652). Nevertheless, even today in Trier, the Christian emperor, adopted as patron and protector by the French monarchy, receives a cult of *dulia*.

These differ from popular canonizations, which are often doctrinally doubtful—some being of distinctly pagan origin as well. The search for popular folk saints occurs widely in many Latin American Catholic countries. These are people to whom the possession of supernatural or paranormal gifts has been attributed, or they are individuals famous for their abilities to cure or for living a saint's life during their earthly existence. Occasionally "innocent" creatures who died tragically (as in the case of Evita) are so regarded.

The particular case of Brazilian President Tancredo Neves may be taken as paradigmatic of those political figures or heads of state who have been sacralized. Suffering from a fatal disease, he became the focus of a profound, syncretic popular religiosity that exploded throughout the country. Brazilian civic content, which already sacralized the idea of the country by means of nationalist symbols, including the national hymn, became markedly religious. At the entrances of the hospital where Tancredo's operation occurred, processions showed up almost daily, giving evidence of authentic and widespread popular fervor. People built crude syncretic Catholic altars, some with a photograph of the president alongside images of various gods and saints, including Umbanda and Candomble congas. It seemed inevitable that Tancredo would be seen as approximating Biblical figures, such as Moses. He was even compared to Jesus Christ. Some people asked that he be declared a saint by the Catholic Church (Rodrígues Brandào 1988:398).

Martínez Estrada sees in the figure of Evita the sacralization of the functions of mother and virgin: "Had she been canonized by the Vatican . . . the people would have adored in her the Mother and the Virgin together, since for many centuries they had not reflected on the meaning of these two words" (1956: 257). Among the humble, the figure of Evita, resplendent on her "way to immortality," inevitably would have become a sanctified virgin: "nothing existed which could compare with her, not even remotely"; followers would soon be "reverencing that golden head and that luminous smile, even as they reverenced the little virgin of the ancient church of adobe" (Main 1956:66).

The government that followed the Peronist regime wished to discredit her, but this did no harm among her followers, because once the myth had settled into the culture, it was unshakable. On the contrary, exposing her presumed loss of reputation resulted in a procession of her supporters: "When they contemplated in astonishment how many 'riches' she had stored up, the truth is that they paraded through the streets with images of Evita as if in a process of both popular and national beatification" (Llorca 1978:303). With the passage of time the most exaggerated expressions and excessiveness of the myth have moderated, perhaps acquiring for her a final consolidation as the "delirium became attenuated": "The myth of Eva resumed a course of common sense, abandoned the streets, the enthusiasm of the multitudes, and withdrew into the prayers of her devotees. A respectable fervor returned to the breast of democratic pluralism, where diverse—and even opposed—myths and idols, cohabit without exterminating each other" (Massuh 1995).

In conclusion, it is appropriate to seek a nuanced analysis of popular canonization following the death of an eminent person, even though the details in themselves may admit diverse readings and interpretations. Still, the facts of Evita's case offer a number of unique characteristics that exceed the mere veneration of her memory. The details of her popular adoration and veneration by the Argentinian people permit her elevation to a political, if not a religious, icon.

NOTES

1. "Evita lives" is a traditional political slogan that is tirelessly repeated, even today, by Evita's fanatical supporters. A similar expression, "el Che vive" (Che lives), is used for the Argentine guerrilla Ernesto "Che" Guevara, who represents another case of popular canonization.

2. Nevertheless, it should be noted that *Tonantzin* in Nahuatl means "little mother," which refers to her role as the benevolent mother of humankind.—ED.

3. In this context, the "rainbow" of love is significant and is interpreted as a symbol of the union and forgiveness given by God to humankind after the Biblical flood.

4. Popular opinion, according to McGeagh (1987:214), considers her to be sacrosanct, and as used by Perón she appears to be the holy inspiration for his politics. Martínez Estrada (1956:250) says that Eva's death offered Perón the fortunate circumstance for finalizing the sentiments of adoration among her followers and for converting himself into a prophet and a legislator who would receive inspiration from her intercession with God.

5

Desperately Seeking *Something*

Che Guevara as Secular Saint

Phyllis Passariello

Though human beings are always social and collective, individuals often emerge as leaders, guides, or organizers for a group. Similarly, but not in an exactly parallel manner, heroes emerge from human groups and subgroups. These heroes, who may become icons, or perhaps saints, must in some way express a part of an ethos or value system or template for a code of conduct for the group they represent. Why are some of the icons at best unrealistic, even quixotic in their goals, and sometimes downright dangerous, high-risk role models? Why do some iconic figures, in fact, embody expressions of human extremes? (Examples include St. Francis's zeal, Joan of Arc's stubbornness, the Blessed Virgin Mary's suffering, and Jesus Christ's self-sacrifice.) These culture heroes lived lives in the extreme, as though in high relief, even unto tragedy and death. How is the social construction of icons and the related human attraction to such representations of the extreme, at the edge of human experience, indicative of a particular moment in a particular culture? What do these behaviors, of the heroes and of the devotees, reveal about the human condition? How do saints, sainthood, and the making of saints fit into this puzzle?

Whereas a *hero,* and sometimes an antihero, is remembered as someone endowed with special traits of courage and strength and is respected for his or her noble pursuits, an *icon* is a person whose being becomes an enduring symbol of cultural specialness, often with a tinge of religion-like awe. To complete the related trio, a *saint* is an officially recognized, often institutionalized person who is entitled to public veneration beyond simple respect and admiration and who also may be someone who is capable of interceding with the cosmos—someone with not only special status but perhaps even special power. Where and how does Ernesto "Che" Guevara qualify and belong?

Two scholars seemingly divided by discipline, background, era, and intention help coalesce an understanding of the cultural process of producing heroes and icons, which parallels, overlaps, and envelops the process of the making of saints. In 1934, Lord Raglan (aka Fitzroy Richard Somerset, the Fourth Baron Raglan) published in the British journal *Folklore* an essay entitled "The Hero of Tradition" (Raglan 1934), in which he outlines a general pattern with 22 specific traits he suggests appear cross-culturally in the life stories of culture heroes. This article has become a classic of folklore literature. To form as well as to test his hypothesis, Lord Raglan derives and applies his pattern of traits from and to the lives of many heroes from Oedipus to Jason to Moses to Siegfried (and they can be applied to Jesus and Che Guevara, I would add). Once noted, his pattern of traits appears obvious and certainly familiar, even though *every* hero's story or narrative does not include *every* trait. Raglan's pattern includes the following: the hero's mother is a royal virgin, his father is a king, the conditions of his conception are unusual, he is often reputed to be divine, he is often reared far away by foster parents, we know little of his childhood but he returns to his kingdom at manhood, he has to face terrible trials and dangers like dragons and other wild beasts, he often encounters or marries a princess who may be a rival's daughter, he loses favor with his kingdom somehow and is driven from the throne, he meets a mysterious death, often on top of a hill, and if there are children, they do not succeed him, and though his body is not buried, he has at least one holy sepulcher (Raglan 1934). Certainly hero stories have some clear commonalities.

A young American biological anthropologist from Yale, Misia Landau, wrote an extraordinary book, *Narratives of Human Evolution* (1991), in which she identified and examined a distinct pattern that appeared in several competing theories of human evolution. Landau says: "I suggest that all these paleoanthropological narratives approximate the structure of the hero tale, along the lines proposed by Vladimir Propp [1968 (1928)] in his classic *Morphology of the Folktale*. . . . They feature a humble hero who departs on a journey, receives essential equipment from a helper or donor figure, goes through tests and transformations, and finally arrives at a higher state" (Landau 1991:x). Again, it is in the particulars of the narrative and how it builds that a hero grows and, perhaps, how the saint is made. And, cross-culturally, we can find repetition and constancy to the patterns of the structure and of the morphology of the stories, even if the details expressed, the culturally specific values, change with time, place, and culture.

If Arnold van Gennep's (1960) typology of the structure of a rite of passage—separation, initiation/transition, and reintegration—is added to the hero's narrative and then connected with how heroes often play with Victor Turner's (1969) boundary-flexing concept of *liminality* as well as his socially coalescing concept of *communitas*, the stories become simultaneously more complex and compelling.

Comparative mythologist Wendy Doniger (1998) adds an interesting political dimension to the analysis of hero narratives. Myth, according to Doniger, is a narrative that encourages, even demands, double vision, the microscope and the telescope, the magnifying lens, and the wide-angle lens. Referring to Roland Barthes, Doniger (1998:9) notes that when you look out a car window, you can focus at one moment on the scenery outside while at another moment on the glass of the window. Barthes implies that a mythical narrative is the same way, and thus through its multiple points of view, myth becomes "depoliticized speech" since it does not maintain a constant point of view (Doniger 1998:101). Doniger disagrees and points out that the double vision of a mythical narrative "enables us to do what the bumper sticker urges: think globally, act locally" (1998:19). In fact, Doniger feels that an effective mythical narrative *demands* political action just as it demands radical shifts in perspective. Importantly, then, Doniger sees the elaborate, fantastic, superhuman, compelling stories of culture heroes and saints as "key" to finding "our place in the world" (1998:23). She goes further by noting David Tracy's assertion that particularly "revolutionary myths" express "not the status quo but the fluxus quo" (Doniger 1998:107). So, in a way, the myths, the power narratives, belong to the winners, whether they win or not! The narratives define the winners.

Saints are a type of culture hero, and, as such, the ideas of Lord Raglan, Vladimir Propp, Misia Landau, Victor Turner, and Wendy Doniger certainly may apply to saints' stories as well. Female heroes and female saints present an analytical dilemma at this point. Femaleness may have a somewhat different narrative or at least a variation of the largely male hero pattern charted above. This would be a topic of considerable interest for another time.

CONSTRUCTING CHE: "LIKE SOMETHING OUT OF A TANGO"

After several visits to Mexico, South America, and most recently Cuba, I noticed how Ernesto "Che" Guevara has come forward clearly as a pan–Latin American hero, a pan–youth culture hero—not only a hero of Cuban communism but also of the almost generic concept of "revolution." El Che, or simply Che, is a "hero of tradition," with a life story or narrative that follows the "morphology of the folktale" and dips into the realms of liminality and communitas. His life story and its propagation have helped to make him not only a hero but also a secular saint, a sacred figure, someone to be revered, emulated, and even beseeched.

To find an explanatory path to the questions raised by the making of heroes, icons, and saints, a variety of ethnographic contexts are relevant. The making of heroes, icons, and saints is a process, of course, and the active components of this process involve human behaviors that potentially can be observed and documented. With an understanding of how a hero's narrative is structured, it is possible to examine how it becomes "popular" and how sometimes a story told again and again accrues "success" with almost sacred power, ushering the hero on the path to possible sainthood. What are the means taken by this process of popularization?

The construction of Che Guevara as a culture hero in Latin America, and especially in Cuba, provides a vivid, ethnographic example. In several ways, the literal *image* of Che—whether in a photograph, in a drawing, or on a poster, billboard, or T-shirt—is itself a powerful ethnographic fact (Figure 5.1). An image can be dynamic and processual, not only culture-bearing but also culture-generating. In this study, the issue revolves around how the image is key to the process of Che's journey to secular sainthood.

Semiotically, the concepts of the *icon* and the *saint* are paradoxical—each icon/saint teeters between being a *keeper* and a *validator* of tradition and being a *transformer, breaker,* or even *iconoclastic changer* of tradition. The icon often reinvents tradition, redirects it, or even institutionalizes a new, invented tradition. A saint reiterates but also may create a new holy way. Of course, all "tradition" at some point is invented (Hobsbawm 1983:1–4) and it is never static. The traditional icons of Cuba and of Cuban culture might range from Ricky Ricardo to Batista to Fidel to José Ferrar to Elian González, depending on your point of view. And, of course, there is Che Guevara.

Che Guevara is perhaps the most prevalent contemporary pan–Latin American hero, icon, and, I suggest, secular saint. "Che por las Américas" is a common slogan throughout the Americas, documented by ubiquitous images of Che, from walls to T-shirts. During 25 years of travel and residence in several parts of Latin America, I have noticed a growing interest in Che Guevara and maybe even a revival in the past 10 years. Even in the United States, Che as image and as concept is part of youth culture. Anecdotally but not unusually, Che deeply interests my young teenage daughter, and images of Che have a place of honor on her bedroom wall along with Bob Dylan, Janis Joplin, the two Jimmies (Hendrix and Morrison), and Bob Marley—all arguably revolutionary heroes/icons.

Che Guevara was born in Argentina to a middle-class family in 1928, was educated in medicine, practicing somewhat as a dentist, and then took off on a personal journey, a quest across Latin America on a motorcycle, seeking a vocation. From the start, he documented his own quest, beginning with his early "motorcycle diaries," building his own story (Guevara 1995). Finding revolution, he devoted the rest of his life to proselytizing on justice and freedom and inciting violent revolution as the road to justice around Latin America, starting the Cuban revolution with Fidel Castro, and dying by assassination in Bolivia in 1967 at the age of 38. Only recently, in 1997, were most of his bones recovered and moved to Cuba, where they are ensconced in a mausoleum and vener-

Figure 5.1. Author with Che images based on Korda's "Guerrillero Heroico" (Photograph by James F. Hopgood)

ated as though they were the tongue of St. Anthony of Padua or pieces of the True Cross.

Ernesto Guevara de la Serna, the man, was born middle class and intelligent; he became a well-educated, well-read, trained physician and dentist, and, by choice, an adventurer. From Mexico when he was only beginning his serious questing, he wrote to his mother in Argentina, "I feel like something out of a tango" (Taibo 1997:53). Che knew that he danced to his own tune and needed to find his proper steps. As noted above, it was his coming-of-age motorcycle rides around Latin America in 1951–1952 and again in 1953–1956 (Guevara 2001) that incited his passion for revolution along with his reading of Jean-Paul Sartre, Pablo Neruda, and, of course, Karl Marx. His lifelong severe asthma (his inhaler is now a relic at his death shrine in Cuba) simply spurred him on to try harder. And, like most heroes who make it to iconic status, he was very handsome, a compellingly attractive and charming man. He was masculine, sexy, charismatic, well-spoken, tough, and thoroughly committed to overthrowing imperialism and thus bettering the lot of the poor and oppressed. He professed convincingly for *moral* versus *material* work incentives and emphasized what he called "The New Socialist Man," someone whose socialistic, other-directed, equalizing morality was a core belief and incentive to action. "The Harsh Angel," as Alma Guillermoprieto said of Che, was "a living banner" who would "change the world by example" (2001:73).

Che, the future revolutionary, was also a macho womanizer, not unaware of his appeal to women. In a diary entry about his first wife, Hilda, he coldly comments: "Hilda declared her love. . . . I was with a lot of asthma, if not, I might have fucked her. . . . The little letter she left me upon leaving is very good, too bad she is so ugly" (Guillermoprieto 2001:77–78). Che married Hilda in 1955, fathered her child, left her, and then got married again in 1958 to a young, pretty revolutionary, Aleida March.

Che lived life as an unbending radical who never even considered any alternatives to violence and revolution. These were his remedies for all social ills. In 1953, he was in Guatemala and witnessed the CIA-sponsored invasion that unleashed unrelenting repression still evident today. In 1955, he had to flee to Mexico City, where he first met Fidel Castro, and he was among the first to join up with Castro's revolutionary mission. In 1956, he was with Fidel on the ill-fated voyage of the yacht *Granma*, and he remained at his right hand throughout the fight to overthrow Batista's dictatorship.

The Cuban rebels nicknamed Ernesto "Che," for his Argentinian habit of frequently interjecting the word *che*, similar to "hey!" or "say!," in his conversations. Though most of the men in the first onslaught on Batista's troops were killed, Che, injured, escaped with Fidel into the rugged mountains of eastern Cuba, the Sierra Maestra. In 1957, Che was made a *commandante* of a group of rebel fighters, nicknamed "*los barbudos*" (the bearded ones). In August 1958 Che and his *barbudos* made a successful, epic march to bring the revolution to central Cuba and by December 1958 Che and his troops had essentially cut Cuba in two. On December 28, the Battle of Santa Clara began and was quickly won, causing Batista to flee into exile, allowing Che and his guerrillas to march triumphantly into Havana.

Fidel made Che a Cuban citizen in 1959 as well as his cabinet minister, trade advisor, and informal foreign ambassador. For years, Che traveled around the world speaking of the Cuban mission and professing his faith in revolution as the way to overcome poverty. In 1965, Che became restless and secretly traveled to the Congo to fight in their revolution. Returning to Cuba after several months, Che then decided to travel back to South America and help organize the revolution in Bolivia. In March 1967, he led a successful antigovernment ambush in Bolivia and alarmed the U.S. government with his boasts about how he and his men were calling for "two, three, many Vietnams" (Stanley 1997:271). The U.S. government sent military advisors to Bolivia to organize thousands of troops to comb the mountains for Che's small band, and "on October 8, 1967, Guevara was captured by the Bolivian army, and after consultation with military leaders in La Paz and Washington, D.C., he was murdered before the eyes of U.S. advisors" (Stanley 1997:271).

Che's devotion to the Cuban cause and his blood-brotherly relationship with Fidel were fanatical, even a bit curious considering his decidedly South American heritage, but he was beloved by Cubans as a hero even during his lifetime—as el Che, The Argentine, the foreigner who adopted their revolution. Che was irreligious, not unspiritual. Yet, he was a wholly troubled soul who recounts in his so-called motorcycle diaries his meeting with a "prophet" who tells him that revolution *will* come to Latin America. Che says, "I knew that when the great guiding spirit cleaves humanity into two antagonistic halves, *I* will be with the people, howling like a man possessed." Well, he *was* a man possessed; he was a fanatic, he was desperate, and he was seeking—something. Like Joan of Arc, like Francis of Assisi, like Jesus in the desert, he was desperately seeking *something*—a cause, his essential self. He found the revolutionary faith, and of course, he was and still is, certainly in Cuba, the peoples' savior, a Marxist saint. This evolved even before his death. Che himself was aware of the place he held in the eyes of some: "Returning from a visit to rural eastern Cuba, Che told a friend of a visit he had made to a peasant's home. Inside on an altar complete with candles, was his own portrait—placed there like an image of Christ" (J. Anderson 1997:23). Che, apparently, shook his head in wry amazement as he told the story. Che inspired, personified, and literally became a powerful narrative and an image of hope for the people.

In Cuba, the state, under Fidel Castro's tight control, has used the opportunity to consciously construct a national saint-hero, Che. Ironically a foreigner, Che, as Fidel's friend and compatriot, is a *historical* figure who became very large quickly, "iconizing" with alacrity like James Dean, John Kennedy, and John Lennon and becoming sainted within what would have been his natural life span.

All over Cuba, there are memorial stops along the pilgrimage path that I think of as "The Way of Che." In Havana, encased in glass, is the modest yacht, *Granma,* in which Fidel and Che first traveled together to Cuba in the budding days of their friendship and their revolution. All over Havana, instead of commercial advertising, the government-controlled billboards and street murals sport quotations from Che and Fidel and, importantly, *images.* Then, there is the Plaza of the Revolution. Formerly known as the Plaza of the Republic, the Plaza of the Revolution dominates a large expanse of downtown Havana. Mostly the plaza is empty concrete-paved space, with a perimeter of 1950s uninteresting government buildings. The plaza is the place where Fidel Castro has always given his important speeches to the Cuban people. At one end of the plaza, there is a large marble statue and an almost 500-foot obelisk in memory of José Martí, Cuba's poet-journalist-intellectual and first fighter for independence, who died in the 1890s. And then there is a huge three-dimensional silhouette of Che's face on an almost 200-foot wall of the Ministry of Industry building at the other end of the empty plaza. One of the best current guidebooks to Cuba, *The Rough Guide to Cuba,* characterizes the monument eloquently:

> The ultimate Cuban photo opportunity is presented by the *Memorial Ernesto Che Guevara,* a stylized steel frieze replica of Alberto "Korda" [Díaz] Gutiérrez' famous photo of Guevara—the most widely recognized image of Guevara in existence. Taken during a speech on Calle 23 in 1960, the photo, with Guevara's messianic gaze fixed on some distant horizon and hair flowing out from beneath his army beret, embodies the unwavering, zealous spirit of the revolution. [McAuslan and Norman 2000:107]

Though the photo-frieze itself dates to 1993, a gift to Cuba from France, the Korda image was first displayed on that wall in 1967, right after Che's assassination. At that time, the image was printed on a huge piece of cloth that was draped over the wall, and the space in front of the image, the expanse of the plaza, served as a gathering place for millions of Cubans to pay their last respects to their hero. In effect, the iconic image has operated efficiently over the past 40 years since its creation to help along the Che legend, and now its revival, and what is the sanctification process for Che.

In my trip across Cuba in August 2000, I was an informed tourist/pilgrim and knew to go to central Cuba, to the small town of Santa Clara, to see the original Korda photograph and much more. Santa Clara is where Che fought and won the decisive battle that solidified rebel control of Cuba and forced Batista to flee. Consequently, Santa Clara is important in Che iconography and hagiography. In 1987, a huge statue of Che was erected in Santa Clara in another massive open space created to be a Plaza of the Revolution, commemorating the 20-year anniversary of Che's assassination. Ultimately, Santa Clara was chosen as the place to enshrine Che's remains. And Santa Clara is where the original Korda photograph of Che, the crown of Che hagiography, is found.

BIOGRAPHY OF AN IMAGE

The renown of the most famous image of Che evolved along with Che's legend, and its genesis from photograph to icon deserves special consideration. Its maker, Alberto Díaz Gutiérrez, known professionally as "Korda," was born in Havana, the son of a railway worker. He began working as a fashion photographer in 1956, during the regime of Batista, a time of glamour and plenty for some. Díaz Gutiérrez thrived in this career, living a life of material success, full of beautiful women, sports cars, and a fancy studio in the heart of Havana's hotel district. He changed his name to Korda early in his career—some say because it sounded like "Kodak" and others say after the Hungarian filmmaker Alexander Korda. During and after the success of the Cuban revolution, Korda's life changed dramatically along with his country's. Korda became an adamant supporter of communism and the new Cuban way of thinking. He abandoned his lucrative photography to become a photojournalist and eventually became Fidel Castro's personal photographer.

Korda, even in his early prerevolutionary career, was recognized as a noteworthy artist. A photo historian, Bill Lasarow, comments that Korda seems to have been able to capture something special about his subjects, such that presumably "a simple society shot ends up seducing you into considering the model's individual inner life" (2002 [1998]). This observation raises the interesting question of the role of the artist/photographer in the creation of an icon. With his sympathy to the revolution, and already an established artist, Korda's position as Castro's "court photographer" for ten years is not surprising. The leaders of the revolution were all dynamic men in their twenties and thirties, shaping history, and Korda perhaps saw his chance to be part of the equation. Korda photographed Castro and Che in many settings: informally, smoking cigars, and, amusingly and famously, playing golf. Korda helped to shape their personae for the public—a powerful position. Korda served as Castro's personal photographer until 1968 and they remained personal friends until his death in 2001. He continues to be revered as a great artist of the revolution.

There is, of course, the most famous Korda photo, the iconic photo of Che, gazing sternly and messiah-like into the cosmos. The photo was taken by Korda in 1960 and was entitled "*Guerrillero Heroico*" ("Heroic Guerrilla") by Korda (Figure 5.1). Though it was favored by the artist, it languished in his studio for years. The incident that the photo indirectly documents involved the funeral in March 1960 of 136 victims of a sabotaged steamboat, a Belgian arms transport, which exploded in the port of Havana. Several famous people, chic, intellectual, foreign supporters of the revolution, were among the mourners, including Simone de Beauvoir and Jean-Paul Sartre. They were listening to Fidel Castro giving one of his infamously long speeches when Che very briefly wandered onto the stage for a matter of seconds. Korda snapped two photos before Che wandered off again. Korda later said that he was aware he had captured an excellent picture (negative #40, 3/5/60). Later that day, Korda printed two of his negatives from the roll, one of Che and another of Fidel, but an editor for the Havana newspaper, *Revolución*, chose the Castro shot instead of the Che photo to run in the paper. Korda stuck the Che picture on the wall of his studio because he liked it. It remained there for the next seven years.

In 1967, an established Italian publisher named Feltrinelli, at the time unknown to Korda, arrived in Cuba looking for a Che photo. Feltrinelli was famous in Europe for having smuggled the manuscript of *Dr. Zhivago* out of the Soviet Union and profiting from it. When asked by Feltrinelli about a Che photo, Korda apparently pointed to the picture on the wall and said, "This is my best Che picture" (Harder 2002:2). Korda made two prints of the photo for him without charge, since Feltrinelli was a friend of the revolution.

Feltrinelli had traveled to Cuba because of inside information on the impending assassination of Che in Bolivia; he saw a possible business opportunity. Copies of the Korda photograph began showing up all over the world after Che's death and some say that Korda also profited from the sale of his photo. In fact, Korda continued to make a good living largely because of that one photo (*Los Angeles Times* 2001). However, in an "as told to" story in 1993, Korda claimed that he never made a peso from his photo, but many others did, and many still do today. Historically, in tune with the revolutionary spirit, Korda pointed out that Cuba had never signed the Berne Convention protecting the rights of artists and that Fidel Castro himself described intellectual property rights as imperialistic "bullshit" (Harder 2002:3).

Korda died in 2001 at age 72 but not before winning a lawsuit in the United Kingdom against two British advertising agencies, Rex Features, Ltd., and Lowe, Ltd., because of their unauthorized use of the Che image in a Smirnoff Vodka advertisement. Korda distinctly said that he did not push forward the suit because he objected to the use of the image per se as long as the purpose was somehow in the cause of social justice; rather, he objected because of the *specific* use of the image by the liquor company. He said, "I am categorically against the exploitation of Che's image for the promotion of products such as alcohol, or for any purpose that denigrates the reputation of Che" (Vallen 2004). Korda won the suit for an unspecified amount of money, which he donated toward medical assistance for children in Cuba. The roles of art, the artist, and artistic integrity remain intriguing in the evolution of Che as an icon.

When biographer Jon Anderson questioned Che's second wife, Aleida, in the mid-1990s about the "rampant consumer industry" surrounding her dead husband (much of it, of course, centered on the photograph) she reacted, he says, by blanching and rationalizing her feelings, saying, "Well, we live surrounded by a consumer world. If it takes a T-shirt for a young European or American to be introduced to Che and the ideas he stood for, then it is something we must live with" (J. Anderson 1997:25). And some would say that a T-shirt, after all, is not a liquor ad. Others would say that all publicity is positive and fodder for the cause. Commercialism, arguably, has its interactive role as well in the evolution of an icon or the making of a saint.

Of course, there are many other photographs of Che and many are by Korda himself. Some are excellent, powerful photographs. For example, consider Che's death photo: his body on a slab in a small hospital in Bolivia presents a powerful portrait and is a direct analogue in some ways to Korda's messiah portrait, and it is well known to devotees, historians, and students of politics. But no image comes near to carrying the weight of renown or of power of the Korda photograph.

FIELD OBSERVATIONS

During the summer of 2001, I traveled to Cuba, spending time in Havana but also in the central and south-central parts of the island, specifically targeting "Che sites" for my tour. All over Cuba, there are memorial stops along a pilgrimage path, well known to Cubans, somewhat known to Europeans and some Americans, representing a quasi-institutionalized "Way of Che."

In my pilgrimage, besides Havana and the Bay of Pigs, I went to Santa Clara again to see the monument and mausoleum that contain Che's remains. The grandeur of the site was carefully constructed and its impact clearly intentional. In what can be described as a spectacular but minimalist assault, somehow reminiscent of the bold aesthetic integrity of the Third Reich, the Hagia Sophia in Istanbul, or the Temple of Karnak in Luxor, the monument of Che, his "holy sepulcher," creates an unforgettable experience.

Like Priscilla Presley studying the success of Monticello's appeal before designing the Graceland experience, the Cuban government, perhaps Castro himself, orchestrated for Che's mausoleum an experiential totality—a transcendent space, a hallowed ground, reiterating and reinforcing the sanctification of Che. Broad expanses of lawn surround and encircle the low, rather modest exterior of the main building. Here it is the empty expanses that impress. Even the huge parking lots are of such a gigantic scale that they can never be full, somehow increasing Che's grandeur in proportion to the pilgrim's humility. A narrow path leads to the shrine's entrance; walking off the path is not tolerated. Armed soldiers solemnly and seriously guard against any visitor's possible disruptive behavior. Pilgrims are stopped at the door; cameras are taken away and everyone is instructed to maintain silence from that point on. Visitors must wait at the entrance until another leaves and only then will be allowed by a guard to enter.

Once inside the actual monument, the first enclosed space encountered is an empty anteroom with a very few silent visitors waiting their turn to enter the inner sanctum. Finally, the pilgrim is escorted to the door of the sanctum and admitted. There are no windows, no natural light, no sounds except the trickle of a modest fountain in a simple rock garden off to the side. Che's sepulcher, communistically yet ironically, considering the required preamble, is simply one of 12 plaques set in the wall for the 12 heroes—Che and the 11 others with whom he died in Bolivia. The inner area is approximately 20 by 20 feet. After reading the 12 names and a very brief tribute on a central plaque, the visitor can walk to the garden and fountain on the edge of the room, which seems to disappear into dark nonspace beyond. Then, silently "encouraged" to leave by the guard, who holds open the door, the visitor exits quietly back into the first room, then back outside, and the visit is over.

Back in the parking lot, visitors gaze up at several seemingly small statues dwarfed by a major, large statue of an armed Che, much larger than life. Politically didactic billboards ring the outer limits of the parking lot, and somehow the state of compulsory silence continues even there. There are no vendors, no food, no souvenirs, not here. The experience is programmed to be "sacralizing" of Che's status as saint.

Nearby is the separate and more secular Che museum, which perhaps serves the prurient needs of Che's devotees. Che's clothes, dental tools, old letters, old and used shaving kit, more minor toilet articles, and even things, curiously, from his immediate family members are displayed. Poignantly, enshrined in glass, is Che's old-fashioned, beat-up inhaler. And almost unexpectedly, there is *the* actual hat and *the* actual jacket in which Che is seen in Korda's famous photograph. The original photograph itself is also unobtrusively on display, almost as an afterthought compared to its fame and its iconic status.

"VISUAL PIETY": THE INSTITUTIONALIZATION AND SANCTIFICATION OF CHE'S IMAGE

Popular religious imagery abounds in Latin America, as in most of the world. In Mexico, for example, the image of the Virgin of Guadalupe (a black Madonna who appeared to an Aztec Indian following the Spanish Conquest and has become the *mestiza* patroness of Mexico) appears everywhere from banners to roadside shrines, murals, taxi stands, and individual tattoos. And, as I am arguing, the *image* itself is dynamic and generates even more interest and involvement than mere representation and display. Dean MacCannell (1976) in his groundbreaking work on tourism introduces the ideas of the conjunction between sites (sights, in his terms) and their "markers" (marking the sight or site) and, then, what he discusses as "sight→marker→sight transformations" (1976: 121). He points out how a site, such as the Eiffel Tower, is *so* seriously represented by its marker—the photo of the Eiffel Tower or the little metal replica of the tower on one's desk—that in some ways, the *marker* may even overtake the actual site in specific cultural meaning. That is, if the Eiffel Tower exists but no one can prove they have seen it, does it really exist? But with a photo (preferably with the viewer *in* the photo) or a replica of the tower there is material evidence of the specialness and the personal access of the viewer to the meaning of the site. Sometimes, MacCannell notes, the marker itself is transformed into a kind of site, and so the conjunctions and transformations progress. A tattoo of the Virgin of Guadalupe carries the weight of her sainthood with it, even though it is "only" an image.

The power of the ritual uses of religious imagery is examined by David Morgan (1998) and is capsulized in what he calls "visual piety." Morgan sees religious images as part of the "visual formation and practice of religious belief" and also highlights "the role of mass-produced religious images in the social construction of reality by those who exchange and display them." Further, he argues that "the act of looking itself contributes to religious formation and . . . constitutes a powerful practice of belief" (1998:1, 2, 3).

Ethnographically then, the image of Che itself has the potential not only to display devotion but also to legitimize and actually generate and intensify devotion. An image of Christ on the cross, especially a bloody Christ on the cross, provides a powerful incentive for belief in the historical Jesus or at least culturally legitimates the possibility. As Morgan notes, "Proponents of religious imagery have not failed to underscore the unique capacity of images to make real what they depict" (1998:8). Religious imagery and, I would add, heroic and iconic images also serve as very special, powerful objects in this creation of identity.

Turning specifically to photographs, we see an even more literal connection between object and a past reality. Roland Barthes (1978) has explored deeply the significance of photographs. He points out how the photograph represents "an anthropological revolution," because "the type of consciousness the photograph involves is indeed truly unprecedented, since it establishes not a consciousness of the *being-there* of the thing (which any copy could provoke) but an awareness of its *having-been-there*" (1978:44). The photograph makes the past concrete so that it reaches into and has an impact in the present. The photographic image of the "messianic gaze" of a noble, young, handsome, uniformed

Che moves us emotionally but impresses us rationally as well because we know that the very moment of that gaze existed; it really happened. So the photograph itself becomes an icon, to be reproduced in many forms, many media, and many places. The image has performed a site/marker transformation and has become an active, dynamic instrument in the creation, maintenance, and perpetuation of the cult of Che.

In any discussion of the power of images in popular culture, the concept of media as a "Draconian monster" naturally arises. Of course, from the photocopy machine to the satellite dish to the internet, contemporary communications technology is instrumental in making and maintaining Che's secular sainthood, just as it is involved in creating the rest of public "reality." John Hartley puts forth a new area of analysis he calls "the politics of pictures," wherein he widens the power of the image to include not only the construction of the reality perceived by the "public" but also "the public itself," which he sees as "part of the popular reality that visualization helps to create" (1992:5). With a bit of a twisted application of theoretical constructs, we might say that Hartley's conception of the relationship between the media (the picture becomes reality) and the public (the audience becomes reality) is somewhat analogous to, or at least in the same trope domain as, MacCannell's site (sight)/marker transformation. In any case, "reality," including the humans involved, is thoroughly *mediated* by the media. However, to understand these connections, the power of the *image* remains key.

CONCLUSIONS

Finally, when we *look* at a saint, when we *see* how a saint might be "made," what themes emerge? Initially, we can turn to the specific role of the "saint" and the relevance of the saint's viewpoint about his or her own *re*-construction. Che consciously led his life as a revolutionary, an iconoclast, a person operating above the common fray. Born an Argentine, reborn a Cuban, and fighting for the people in Cuba, in South Africa, and ultimately in Bolivia, Che could portray himself as a soldier of freedom, similar to how Joan of Arc saw herself as a soldier of Christ (albeit a Francophile Christ). Then, Che was assassinated, killed, or executed, depending, again, upon point of view. Although we can never know with certainty, we may surmise that Che felt like a martyr facing his death. He was fully aware of the dangers he faced in fighting the "good fight." Again, we can never know, but we may suspect that Che self-identified as a hero. But as a saint?

Che was a hero in his own lifetime and the seeds of his budding sainthood were sown during his lifetime. But it was his untimely and gravely melodramatic death that set his popular "canonization" into full-blown fast-forward. *Canonization*, the word itself, nicely crystallizes the process of saint-making because it emphasizes how the process of becoming a saint is actually a progression of the idea of an ordinary person developing into a special person, then influencing and altering the mainstream, and thus becoming part of a transformed cultural canon. In Che's case, his canonization required his movement from iconoclast to icon, from someone outside the system to one who has not only become an insider but in fact has helped to redefine and to transform the system and now represents or even epitomizes the glorified "everyman," the hero of the system.

Ironically, the living Che became an icon in his lifetime because he was a charismatic good-looking iconoclast, searching for a cause, which for him was found and ended in revolution. Revolution breaks as it creates, allowing the dead Che to become an idealized hero cast in a hyper-real context of idealized characters, idealized emotions, idealized shared goals. In a way, an underlying condition necessary to becoming an icon or a saint is being something of a freak, different in every way, an iconoclast almost to the point of denial—a necessary denial, perhaps, of the normal, ordinary, daily tasks of being an imperfect and frail human being. What is remembered of Che? Do we remember Che sucking on his inhaler? No, we remember Che at the height of his glory, in Korda's larger-than-life photograph where he embodies larger-than-life emotions and aspirations and displays a larger-than-life, transcendent essence. Like a saint.

In a final very human irony, Che, who was of course desperately seeking something—like heroes, like saints—ultimately found a vocation, a mission, that vitalized him to death. His was a death to become saturated with meaning. There is something very attractive about a constructed, tragic, and beautiful hero/saint, swollen with meaning. There is the attraction to Korda's iconic image of Che, whether or not his cause is known or understood. It is clear the *image* itself has been transformed semiotically into a sign, an icon, and more. The image itself has become that which is "signified." In other words, the image itself has become "real" with a life of its own. The Che image connects the sympathetic viewer to his massive heroic angst. He elevates a bothersome mini-angst into heroic angst, the martyr's angst, the saint's angst.

The young Che died still desperately seeking something—he was not complete nor fulfilled. He had not found all of the answers. But what he lacked, he lacked grandly. And he died pursuing, questing to fill a void. Yet his quest and the void are part of what continues to attract devotees and a following. His image sustains people everywhere, just as it sustains his memory. The very human narrative of Che sanctified in conjunction with the sacralized image of Che has made him a hero for the people, a secular saint for the masses. The *narrative* and the *image* interact, interweave, and cooperate to create, build, codify, and finally sustain Che in a sacred status. It is interaction of hagiography and iconography. Because of the power of narrative and image and because of the needs and tendencies of a common human condition, Che has become, for some, a special human being to be revered, emulated, and perhaps even beseeched: a saint.

6
Teresa Urrea, Santa de Cabora and Early Chicana?

The Politics of Representation, Identity, and Social Memory

Gillian E. Newell

> Teresa Urrea . . . precursor not only of the Mexican revolution but of Chicano political movements . . . remains a symbol of resistence to oppression for contemporary Chicanos. She is thereby a Chicana counterpart to La Virgin de Guadalupe, a symbol of warmth, succor, and hope for the poor, destitute, and exploited.
>
> Mirandé and Enríquez 1982:178

The Chicano movement developed in the 1960s from an extremely varied, temporally and spatially, Mexican American experience.[1] Teresa Urrea, a Mexican healer and popular saint of the 19th century, was one of many figures who appealed to Chicano writers during the emergence of the movement. Parts of her life story were taken and re-presented to construct a history and social memory by an emerging Chicano ideology.

The above quotation portrays Teresa as a fundamental personage in Chicano history and as a counterpart of the Virgin of Guadalupe, calling her a highly significant, historical, diverse symbolic figure. In spite of these seemingly unequivocal representations, Chicanos today, roughly 40 years after the emergence of the Chicano movement, have little knowledge of her. Did Teresa ever achieve a saintly status equivalent to Guadalupe for Chicanos? How did Chicano writers appropriate her into Chicano history and with what symbols was she inscribed? Why did Teresa appeal to Chicano writers whereas other Mexican folk saints, such as El Niño Fidencio, did not? Why have other figures appropriated by Chicanos, such as la Malinche, continued in importance, when Teresa has not?

Examining how Teresa was re-presented and associated with *Chicanismo* reveals the process of constructing a particular historical figure, who served an emerging general Chicano history, social memory, and desired nationalistic identity. I use the term *history* to refer to the official and formally constructed body of knowledge, whereas *social memory* corresponds to a reservoir of lived experiences maintained by a collective (Connerton 1989; Hutton 1993). These queries serve to explain an apparent contradiction between how Chicanos write about Teresa and how today Chicanos on the whole have forgotten her. Hence, this study shows how the construction of Teresa Urrea, and of any historical figure such as a saint, has a particular purpose and may be unmade—a useful contribution to a volume discussing the making of saints.

TERESA URREA, LA SANTA DE CABORA

Teresa Urrea, an illegitimate child, was born in Ocoroni, Sinaloa, Mexico, on October 15, 1873.[2] Her father, Tomás Urrea, a prosperous hacienda owner, had forced himself upon her mother, Cayenta Chavez, a 14-year-old girl who worked at his hacienda. Most references emphasize that Teresa's mother was indigenous. Some suggest her mother was Yaqui (McWilliams 1968; Mirandé and Enríquez 1982; Rodriguez and Rodriguez 1972), while others say she was a Tehueco Indian of Sinaloa (Holden 1978; Meier 1997). Luis Pérez, a retired history and journalism professor, doubts Chavez was Indian; on the basis of a photograph, he suggests she was a mestizo peasant (interview by author, June 27, 1998).

At the age of 16, Teresa came to live with her father at his ranch of Cabora, near Alamos, Sonora, Mexico. At the ranch, a servant named "La Huila" taught Teresa how to heal various diseases with different herbs, a well-established tradition and profession in that area and time. Suffering a cataleptic attack, Teresa went into a deep trance for two weeks; her family thought she had died. While the family prepared her funeral, she awoke, miraculously, and told the family to use the coffin for La Huila, who indeed died that night. Besides having visions that accurately predicted the future, Teresa had developed healing powers as a result of the attack (Figure 6.1). She saw people's afflictions and cured patients through combinations of laying of hands, rubbing the afflicted area with a mixture of earth and her saliva, sometimes with a drop of her blood, and the use of herbal remedies. Teresa was also said to have emitted the soothing aroma of roses, and some people attempted to collect her sweat or tears to use as perfume.

After she awoke from her comatose state, she remained in a lighter trance for three months and is reported to have spoken frequently of God (*La Ilustración Espirita* 1892). Several years later, she explained to the *San Francisco Examiner* that she had received her abilities from God, who had visited her during her trance, as had the Virgin Mary: "I believe God has placed me here as one of his instruments to do good" (Dare 1900).

Macklin and Crumrine (1973) note that such features as the trance, the near-death experience, the seemingly miraculous awakening, and the visitation by God or other religious figures are the commonly observed and recognized aspects in the acquisition of healing powers and the transformation into a holy, saintly figure. These events legitimized Teresa's new status as a healer. Since these powers were gifts of God and the Virgin, she chose not to charge for her

Figure 6.1. Teresa healing in El Paso, Texas. (Courtesy of Fototeca de la Dirección General del Acervo Históric Diplomático de la Secretaría de Relaciones Exteriores, México, D.F.)

healing gifts, which added to her charisma as a spiritual person. Within months, thousands of people from northern Mexico traveled to the ranch to be cured by Teresa; she rapidly gained fame and people named her "La Santa de Cabora" or, more endearingly, "La Niña de Cabora."

Teresa, however, did more than heal poor peasants and Indians without charge. During Porfirio Díaz's dictatorship (1876–1911), these people provided the labor for the country's development while living in extreme poverty (MacLachlan and Beezley 1999). The intolerant Porfirian government viewed Teresa's popularity with suspicion. Whether or not she spoke out directly against the government is unclear. She did criticize the Church for its corruption, assuring people they could love God directly without having to pay for "guidance" from the Church. As the Church was aligned with the government during the Porfiriato, she spoke treason as well as heresy.

Two different groups, the Mayo Indians and the *gente de razón* (non-Indians) of Tomochic, Chihuahua, invoked her name and identity as healer in their protests against the government's oppression. Mayo Indians attacked the town of Navajoa and killed several officials (Troncoso 1905; Vanderwood 1998:196). The Tomochic rebellion consisted of several small skirmishes over the period of a year between the *gente de razón* and the federal army (H. Frías 1911; Illades Aguiar 1993). This rebellion has been attributed to several causes, including Teresa's influence and instigation. The Tomochic people, however, turned to Teresa after their problems with the government had begun. They primarily wished to arrest the totalizing power of the nation (Almada 1938; Nugent 1993; Osorio 1995). After the first skirmish in December 1891, the Tomochics made a pilgrimage to the ranch of Cabora to get Teresa's blessing, involving her indirectly in their struggle. In December 1892, after a long battle, the army massacred most villagers and burned Tomochic to the ground.

After Teresa became associated with Tomochic, Díaz felt so threatened he had her arrested on May 19, 1892, and exiled her without trial to the United States. She initially resided in Nogales, Arizona, in a house provided by her followers, where she cured many people, mostly Mexicans and Mexican Americans. More than a few were likely grandparents to the Chicanos of the 1960s (Arias 1995).

In spite of her exile, Teresa's influence continued. In 1896, Teresa again became associated with a rebellion in Sonora when Yaqui Indians raided the customs house in Nogales, Mexico, protesting "*el mal gobierno*" (bad government). Photographs of Teresa were found on some Yaquis killed in the attack, and during the raid the *grito* "*¡Viva la Santa de Cabora!*" had been heard. Several copies of antigovernment, revolutionary newspaper articles written by Lauro Aguirre, a family friend also living in exile due to Díaz, were also found. Some newspapers interpreted the raid as the start of a larger national revolution, planned by Lauro Aguirre. Teresa's association with him added significant weight to her public image as a revolutionary (*La Constitución* 1896; *El Imparcial* 1896; *Oasis* 1896[3]). Although Teresa used her skills for the sacred purpose of healing, the media now portrayed her as using them to bewitch these fearsome Yaquis to attack the establishment and law-abiding citizens of both countries. She earned the name "*bruja*" (witch) of Nogales (*San Francisco Call* 1896; *San Francisco Examiner* 1896; *La Voz del Estado* 1896).

Following this, Teresa moved to the mining town of Clifton, Arizona. In 1900, she married a Yaqui mine worker, Guadalupe Rodríguez, but the marriage ended the next day; Guadalupe, under command of the Mexican government, attempted to kill her. Having upset her father with her rash marriage, Teresa left Clifton and moved to California to heal a friend's child. There, Teresa was contracted by a so-called medical company to travel across the United States on a healing tour. On the tour, she married an Anglo and had their first daughter in New York in 1902. She had a second in Solomonville, Arizona, in 1904. Although the tour enjoyed a successful start, once they left the Southwest her appeal foundered. Bankrupt, the entire entourage returned to Los Angeles, where Teresa ended her contract. She moved back to Clifton, built a hospital with the money from the bankruptcy settlement, and spent her last years healing the people of Clifton. In 1906, she died at the age of 33 from tuberculosis. The people she healed, or were affected by her words, beauty, or disposition, agreed she had worn out her spirit.

CHICANO: MOVEMENT, IDENTITY, AND IMAGINED COMMUNITY

After a century of being treated as second-class citizens, if as citizens at all, people of Mexican descent in the United States began to assert their identity in the 1950s and 1960s (Acuña 1988; García 1997; Muñoz 1989). The older pre–World War II Mexican American generation had advanced a middle-class reformist, Americanist agenda. The younger generation—many already war veterans—questioned their parents' reformist ideology. They realized, aided by a college education pushed by the G.I. Bill, that Americanization had not improved Mexican Americans' position in society. In fact, they felt that they were losing their identity. Speaking Spanish and maintaining Mexican culture had been de-emphasized or even regulated by discriminatory Jim Crow–type legislation. More Mexican Americans turned to their own history and traditions and away from Anglo America as the model of the ideal way of life.

The Chicano, or "Brown Power," movement emerged through the actions and words of many people and must be understood as tremendously diverse. This social movement was "agitating for social and political change and promoting a militant version of self-help and racial solidarity" (García 1997:3). To understand what being Mexican American meant and to recognize the causes of their poverty and second-class status, Mexican American students, professors, and artists turned to history for "a reinterpretation of their existence that would uncover the myths and legends of the struggle for survival and provide the basis for a cultural and political renaissance" (García 1997:48–49).

Leaders like Chávez, López Tijerina, and "Corky" Gonzales provided historicity by drawing parallels to the Mexican Revolution and its heroes (Acuña 1988; Muñoz 1989). Chicanos also used religious symbolism, especially the Virgin de Guadalupe, in their construction of a collective nationalist identity and image. Employing the Mexican Revolution and Guadalupe provided the Chicano movement with historical continuity while acknowledging and legitimizing their Mexicanness and their militant acts (García 1997). Collective experiences like the discrimination based on their darker, bronze skin functioned as "selective traditions" for the Chicano people and as "structural feelings" creating a sense of "imagined community" (B. Anderson 1991; R. Williams 1977). Chicanos fully realized that "memory is history-in-action" (Bauman 1982:1). By evoking history and drawing from a diverse and extensive social memory and heritage, the Chicano movement appeared, legitimized itself, and provided the broad historical and cultural basis to which all could relate and through which they could feel a sense of imagined community. These developments demonstrate that Chicanos recognized that the past is manipulated politically and strategically in order to build and legitimize a particular collective hegemonic identity, history, present, and future (Alonso 1994; cf. Alonso 1988:50).

"Selective traditions" are of course inherently vulnerable: the past may just as easily be re-presented by composing counter histories that empower subalterns in forging a renegotiated social reality. The turn to their own experiences and memories enabled Chicanos to construct a movement, an identity, and a re-presented history based on indigenous roots, the cultural survival of what was Mexican, and the rejection of Anglo oppression. Their social memory of more than a century of oppression, hardship, and denied opportunities provided the substance and historical roots, the "structures of feeling," for a new "selective tradition" (R. Williams 1977).

TERESA URREA: SANTA DE CABORA AND REVOLUTIONARY HEROINE?

In rewriting their history, Chicanos drew upon a large body of personal and collective memories and experiences as Mexican Americans and re-presented Anglo history. Teresa Urrea was one of many figures whom Chicano writers discovered and deemed suitable for integration into a developing Chicano history and identity (Larralde 1976; Rodriguez and Rodriguez 1972). Teresa appears in many encyclopedias and dictionaries on Mexican American and Latino history (Chabrán and Chabrán 1996:1666–1667; Meier 1997; Meier and Rivera 1981; Telgen and Kamp 1993:405–406) and in historical works and journals on Chicanismo (Acuña 1988:99; Gomez-Quiñones 1994:288–289; Larralde 1976; McWilliams 1968:200; Mirandé and Enríquez 1982:173–178; Rodriguez and Rodriguez 1972). These authors first identify Teresa as a *curandera,* herbalist, and faith healer and, then, like those she healed, as "La Santa" or "La Niña de Cabora." They describe how and whom she healed and note the large numbers of people who streamed to Cabora for physical healing. Notably, these sources emphasize the social healing Santa Teresa performed for the poor, oppressed, and destitute: "Even more significant than her healing powers were her social pronouncements against the Church and the government. . . . She was also extremely critical of the government and its treatment of the Indian" (Mirandé and Enríquez 1982:173). In *Roots of Chicano Politics*, Gomez-Quiñones underscores this emphasis as he assesses her as a healer "who made social pronouncements against the . . . Church and the Díaz government. . . . Her denunciations transformed her into a symbol of resistance to oppression" (1994:288). This statement further illustrates the symbolic value ascribed to Santa Teresa because of her healing activities, as supported by Mirandé and Enríquez: "she became a symbol of the Indian resistance against the dictatorship of Porfirio Díaz" (1982:174).

All Chicano sources relate her association with various revolts against the government. While detail is scant and facts have been confused, several common threads appear, such as a concern for Teresa's degree of involvement. Rodriguez and Rodriguez show that evidence is lacking for Teresa to have inspired these rebellions: "even though delegations from the Tarahumaras, Mayos, and Yaquis visited and sought her approval . . . Teresa would only answer, 'God intended for you to have the lands, or He would not have given them to you'" (1972:57). Most sources confirm a more benign depiction. Gomez-Quiñones writes that Teresa "became a *symbol* of mountain discontent in northern Mexico, witnessing local uprisings in 1892 even though her advocacy did not have any explicit progressive character politically" (1994:288). Larralde (1976) and Acuña (1988) suggest a more active role and explain that while the evidence fails to associate Teresa with the revolutionary activity, her father, stepmother, and friend, Lauro Aguirre, certainly were directly involved. Larralde (1976:64) identifies Teresa as a revolutionary with a rather suggestive image of active political protest. Mirandé and Enríquez (1982:177–178) astutely characterize the ambiguity resulting from a lack of conclusive information.

No matter the extent of her activity, all sources agree that Teresa played an important historical role as heroine and advocate for the oppressed and exploited. Gomez-Quiñones sums up: "Whether she was an authentic rural charismatic, a nonconformist, another 'holy woman,' or a 'loca,' Teresa Urrea suggested an as yet unraveled amalgamation of women's discontent. But she also addressed issues of economic inequities, as well as gender and ethnic discrimination, and clearly, she symbolized a people's discontent" (1994:288).

Besides tying her to important historical events, some Chicano authors relate her directly to Guadalupe (Mirandé and Enríquez 1982:178). McWilliams notes that to Mexican copper miners, "La Niña was a saint whose prayers and intercessions could heal the sick and restore sight to the blind . . . she was loved and worshiped as a miraculous border-counterpart of the Virgin of Guadalupe" (1968:200). Others refrain from likening Teresa to Guadalupe but present her as a saint: under a photograph of Teresa surrounded by angels and crowns the caption reads, "Symbol of an era, Teresa Urrea was a saint to many Chicanos. To the end, she retained the devotion and admiration of her people" (Larralde 1976:60). Either way, Teresa's physical and social healing formed the basis of her sanctity.

TERESA URREA: EARLY CHICANA?

Teresa's representations in Chicano literature relate to Mexican American and Chicano core values and experiences; these accordances help explain Teresa's appeal to Chicano authors over other figures, such as El Niño Fidencio.

Chicanos struggle for "*la causa*," rejecting their lives of poverty, discrimination, and injustice. Society's oppression is economic, political, cultural, linguistic (English versus Spanish), and religious (Protestantism versus Roman Catholicism) (Acuña 1988; Muñoz 1989; Rosaldo et al. 1973). While the Chicano movement emerged from and against the experienced oppression based on origin, color, and class, Chicanas ensured that the movement also addressed gender oppression. Teresa strove for the same, whether directly through revolutionary activity or indirectly by providing inspiration, healing, and comfort. She selflessly aimed to create a better future for the oppressed and exploited by advocating indigenous and peasant rights and by speaking out against the Church and government.

Teresa's mixed ethnic background, either inherently as Mexican or through an indigenous mother and lighter skinned Mexican father, and her childhood in poverty correspond with membership in *la raza*. Proud of their bronze skin color, Chicanos consider themselves a distinct social and ethnic group they call *la raza*. Emphasizing their Native American roots, they consider themselves indigenous to the U.S. Southwest, an area they call "Aztlán" (the mythical homeland of the Aztecs before they moved south to settle in central Mexico). Their great-grandparents owned this land before the Americans invaded and conquered the area during the 1846 Mexican-American War. Being Chicano, *raza*, also entails living a borderland experience in terms of geographic location and in the construction of self. Anzaldúa describes this negotiated and contradictory reality: "the *india* in you, betrayed for 500 years, is no longer speaking to you . . . *mexicanos* call you *rajetas* . . . den[y]ing the Anglo inside you is as bad as having denied the Indian or Black" (1987:194). Being *raza* further means that even if one rises above working-class status, one returns to the *barrios* to help the community. To deny one's working-class roots and community results in the loss of identity, in becoming a "sell-out" (Acuña 1988; Tomás Martinez, personal communication, 1999).

Although Teresa rose in status when she moved in with her father, she never forgot her humble origins. When she developed healing powers, she offered her skills to lower-class people free of charge and devoted her life to this task. While expatriated, "she concentrated on the healing of people, but voiced the grievances of workers, mine and track laborers among them" (Gomez-Quiñones 1994:288). After her deportation, Teresa still cured among the lower classes, becoming "idolized by Chicano miners [in Clifton] as a saint capable of curing the sick and restoring sight to the blind" (Mirandé and Enríquez 1982:176).

Teresa also reflected Mexican American and Chicano religiosity. People had considered Teresa a saint during her life, thus facilitating such representation. The comparisons of Teresa with Guadalupe, while forced, are not without foundation. Guadalupe symbolizes resistance against oppression, revolution, liberation, native rights, empowerment, hope, and protection. In the Mexican War of Independence of 1821, the *criollos* carried the image of Guadalupe into battle while fighting for land and liberty. Almost a century later in the Mexican Revolution of 1910, the revolutionary Emiliano Zapata again brought Guadalupe's image to the battlefields in search of land, liberty, and native rights (Poole 1995; Wolf 1959). Only a few years earlier, some of those peasants and Indians had carried Teresa's image and name into their localized rebellions. Teresa was to play a similar role for Chicanos.

Additionally, Guadalupe denotes *mestizaje* and celebrates mixed heritage, ethnicity, and color, qualities also associated with Teresa. Although the Spanish colonists brought Guadalupe to New Spain, she enjoyed growing popularity among the *criollos* and subsequently among the indigenous peoples during the colonial period. Poole (1995) explains that Guadalupe, associated with complex pre-Hispanic roots, brought comfort, hope, submission, and liberation to the indigenous and *criollo* people in a period of major native cultural disruption (Rodriguez 1994; Wolf 1959). Teresa likewise drew on a syncretic religious heritage. Gomez-Quiñones explains that she, as a "public healer incorporated . . . the functions of the Indian curandera, but with Christian and communitarian political overtones that were more likely to be effective among rural mestizos" (1994:288). Teresa's mixed practice—*curanderismo* and herbal healing with Catholic trappings—was a familiar combination to Mexican Americans.

Teresa and Guadalupe symbolize a particular version of femininity as well: motherhood and virginity, two highly valued qualities in Catholicism and in Mexican/Mexican American culture. As a provider of hope, health, continuing life, and salvation from oppression, Guadalupe is the archetype of the Mother, who cares deeply for her children, her people. Teresa was a virgin when she started healing. Her ability to heal enabled Teresa to cleanse the afflicted of disease, which was in part attributed to her virginal purity. The anger some people expressed when she married underscores the importance of this holy status (Larralde 1976): "When La Niña married a Yaqui Indian, she was separated from her husband by a mob of irate miners who looked upon the marriage as a sacrilege" (McWilliams 1968:200).

Teresa's selfless dedication is reminiscent of the ideal mother. By comparing Teresa with Guadalupe, and by extension the Virgin, Chicano writers inscribed her with the same attributes and connotations and strengthened her representation as a Chicana saint of equal symbolic import.

TECHNIQUES AND STRATEGIES FOR MAKING LA SANTA DE CABORA

Seeing Teresa's representation in the context of Chicanismo makes clear how her association with particular aspects of the Chicano experience and identity were forged and emphasized for particular purposes. Selected parts of Teresa's life story were re-presented in certain ways to construct a specific social memory for an emerging Chicano ideology. This process is strategically masked because, as Alonso (1988) explains, the hermeneutics of history and social memory are usually hidden to lend "truth" authority. To understand these processes, the act of building a collective history and identity from an existing reservoir of social memory must itself be treated as historical process in order to "untangle the subtle dialectical interaction between the future orientation and the past determination, Utopia and tradition" (Bauman 1982:3). As "historians of the present too" (Popular Memory Group 1982:205), we look not at what history is, but at how it works (Trouillot 1995).

Drawing on Goffman's idea of "framing" in social situations, Irwin-Zarecka (1994) suggests that memories must be read as texts to discover how their public articulation influences private reasoning. Yet, how do memories depend on socially shared framing strategies and devices? Alonso (1988) discusses three strategies that produce effects of truth: the employment of framing devices to define and categorize the event, the manipulation of voice, and the use of iconicism to structure the re-presentation of the past. Alonso shows how images and symbolic icons function as mnemonic markers of certain experiences and operate as signifiers in and of themselves by contributing particular symbolic content and meaning to memory and history.

Teresa's comparison to Guadalupe is a suitable case in point. Although the likening is not entirely without basis, a clear divergent order of magnitude exists. Guadalupe is an icon with greater symbolism, historicity, religious power, cultural significance, political participation, and national import. Guadalupe is recognized by the Church, while Teresa, not surprisingly considering her anticlerical pronouncements, is not; she is a popular saint of the people. The iconicism framing Teresa as counterpart ascribes her with some of Guadalupe's importance, therefore legitimizing Teresa and giving the Chicanos their own saint and virgin. The association with Guadalupe creates a Teresa as a mnemonic marker for the two ideal images of a female, virgin and mother, and unambiguously confirms the prescribed norm for the Chicana as defined by their Mexican American culture and heritage. Teresa's voice is manipulated and aggrandized, creating a re-presentation that reflects as mnemonic marker and legitimizes an idealized and naturalized moral definition of a unique self. This Chicano self, though influenced by Mexican and Anglo, can still claim its own saint.

Before re-presenting Teresa by using framing devices, iconicism, and the manipulation of voice, other strategies are employed to convert such a localized figure and memory into an acceptable saint representative of a collective history (Alonso 1988). Teresa's persona and the events that shaped her needed to be departicularized, or separated from their local, regional context. Figuratively emptying out these receptacles of meaning enables nations and groups, such as the Chicano intellectuals, to construct a more appropriate image that reflects their definition of self. Certain aspects are then idealized, purified, and made manifest according to current expectations and interpretations of the past. Finally, these hermeneutics are hidden through naturalization, the transformation of constructions into facts. By cleverly drawing upon past and present, the newest re-presentation or invented tradition (Hobsbawm and Ranger 1983) is legitimized, naturalized, and historicized.

Chicano writers exemplify the processes of idealization and departicularization through the poetic license they often take in recounting Teresa's life story. Her re-presented involvement with Mexican Americans is illustrative. As Teresa crossed the border, she obviously became familiar with the Mexican American experience of oppression firsthand, but little information exists about her feelings or actions in this regard; this lack obviously facilitates departicularization. Teresa continued healing after her exile and most of her clients continued to be Mexicans or Mexican Americans.

Chicano history writer Larralde uses several events to exemplify Teresa's familiarity, concern, and action regarding the problems of the Mexicans and Mexican Americans. He depicts Teresa as having led a strike to protest Pacific Electric paying Mexican and Mexican American workers according to a lower pay scale (Larralde 1976:68). Actually, only the strike is documented (*Los Angeles Record* 1903; Wollenberg 1973:365). Through a process of departicularization, idealization, and naturalization, Larralde re-presents Teresa as more of an advocate for early Mexican Americans than the documentary record confirms. Since his portrayal contributes to the making of Teresa as a saint, these hermeneutics are important to uncover.

Chicano writers also draw upon an existing reservoir of social memory that entails more than mere recollection of past experiences. Connerton (1989) argues that to explain how collective or social memories are transmitted within a group the cognitive act of recollection and sensory bodily practices must be related (cf. Hutton 1993; Seremetakis 1994). Cognitive recollection alone fails to account for the affective and sensory response memories generated on the everyday level. Especially in matters of belief, sensory memory is of particular importance; belief is also a felt, affective experience. Connerton's notion of "habit-memory," similar to Bourdieu's (1977) "habitus," indicates that memory in part takes place through the body. The body is inscribed with mnemonic markers of group identity and history. Habit-memory sustains social memory through commemorative ceremonies and bodily practices. Through such enactment, repetition, and practice, "the past is sedimented in the body" (Connerton 1989:72).

Habit-memory celebrates not only the past in the present but also the continuity of this relation. So, the body in the formation, maintenance, and, especially, reproduction of habit-memory is a central conduit for social memory and collective identity. Bodily practices and sensory experience operate to produce an experience of imagined community. These constructions are further naturalized through incorporation and objectification by institutions (Bourdieu 1977). By appealing to this sensory, sedimented, bodily memory, Chicano writers attempt to produce an experience of an imagined Chicano community. An analysis of Teresa's life story in terms of the sensory aspects of Chicanismo illustrates how both cognitive and sensory memories are required for the making of a saint.

Teresa's ethnicity and the poverty of Teresa's childhood correspond to the experience many Chicanos were forced to endure. The association with *la raza* not only is made on a cognitive level but also corresponds to sensory experiences. Chicanos reading about Teresa's background can instantly relate to her. As have many generations of Mexican Americans, Teresa worked, experienced discrimination, married, had children, died, and was buried in Aztlán. Another parallel is found in the oppression to which Mexico's powerful elites subjected Teresa and the powerless peasants and Indians: it resembles the Chicano experience with Anglo oppression in content, structure, and color.

Finally, Teresa's healing appeals to the affective senses. "*Curanderas* have been part of Mexican and Chicano/a societies since the days of the conquistadors. They are the medicine women or healers of these communities" (Arias 1995:1). Many Mexicans and Mexican Americans Teresa healed were likely the grandparents of the Chicano generation. In a Chicano history class paper, a student narrates Teresa's healing of his grandfather, who had been given up to die by the local Clifton Anglo doctor in 1904:

> My grandfather, and I, will never forget her because of the great gift she gave my *Tata*. He will be ninety-nine years old next month in November. His eyesight is bad but other than that he is 100%. No heart condition, cholesterol, high blood pressure, or anything. In addition, in his long life he has escaped death many times. He fought in the revolution in Mexico, was a law man in Agua Prieta, and was a bootlegger for a short time. Needless to say, many people tried to kill him at one time or another. Nevertheless, he has lived this long with out a scratch. For this he will always remember *La Santa de Cabora*. For she gave him a second life and maybe a bit more. [Arias 1995:9]

The writer's appreciation includes admiration for what Teresa gave his beloved grandfather. He also verbalizes his own, his grandfather's, and his whole family's sensory memory of Teresa.

This analysis suggests that Teresa's persona and life story gave the Chicanos sufficient material from which to construct a saint. The ease with which they applied several techniques and strategies and drew upon cognitive memory and sensory memory suggests that Teresa could have become a powerful Chicana saint.

THE UNMAKING OF LA SANTA DE CABORA

After Teresa had been written about by so many Chicanos and with such apparent import, this observation by Arias appears surprising:

> What is intriguing to me is that, for the most part, Teresa Urrea was almost ignored . . . There is [*sic*] only two full books about her in Tucson one of which is written in Spanish by a Mexican author. Therefore, this leads me to believe that mainstream America is not aware of this Mexican/ Chicana woman's accomplishments. When I come to think of it, Teresita is not well known within the Chicano community. Some how we have forgotten her. It is only through courses that deal with Chicano/Chicana issues can Teresa Urrea be found. [Arias 1995:9]

Forgotten, it appears that Teresa, La Santa de Cabora, was unmade, and this raises several important issues.

Alonso (1988) encourages an analysis of the way personal and local memories are departicularized and, then, applied to a wider collective history and identity. In contemplating the making of a saint or any figure based on social memory, it is necessary to consider the issues of power of those who participated in the process. While many quotations from Chicano writers suggest that Teresa was important to the Chicano movement, it is difficult to reconstruct who rediscovered and resurrected Teresa. Still, based on primary and secondary sources several observations can be made regarding the formation and incorporation of Teresa into Chicano history: (1) California universities formed important producers of Chicano knowledge and organization; and (2) this academic realm actively built a legacy for Teresa, and her importance was at least academic in nature.

As amply illustrated above, through her healing and visions, Teresa played a personal and saintly role for many families. Curiously, as Arias reveals, such memories have remained familiar and geographically localized, different and largely disconnected from the inspirational role Chicano intellectuals constructed for her academically to serve all of Aztlán. Chicano writers appealed to Chicano sensory memory by writing about the parallels between Teresa's past and Chicano peoples' sedimented history. Still, few Chicanos have knowledge of Teresa. Those who are familiar with her story learned it in college classes or academic references (Arias 1995; Salomon Baldenegro, personal communication, 1999; Tomás Martinez, personal communication, 1999; Raquel Rubio-Goldsmith, personal communication, 1999). Chicano students cognitively mastered this tidbit of information, rather than reliving it through family memories and experiences. Even in the academic realm knowledge of Teresa is limited to those having an interest in Chicano history.

In the academic sphere cognitive memory was transformed into history, but, significantly, it developed disconnected from popular, personal, affective, and habit memory. Cognitive recollection failed to integrate with the sensory, personal, familiar social memory, affecting the unmaking of La Santa de Cabora. For Chicanos, La Santa de Cabora now lives on mainly in libraries, in archives, and in the curious minds of those who enjoy and seek historical knowledge. Why Teresa failed as a saint requires additional discussion of the level of her popular appropriation by Chicanos when the movement emerged.

DISCUSSION

The Chicano movement developed because of a strong desire by Chicanos to return to their own memories and to construct their own history. The literature confirms that the separation and inequality between official Anglo-American history and Mexican American social memory motivated the search for a Chicano history. While Mexican immigrants labored, the U.S. government's policies advocated assimilation and Americanization, intent on erasing Mexican "traits." After decades of education programs designed to teach immigrant children an official Anglo-American history, little Mexican American social memory survived to be appropriated by Chicanos. They had to rely on an academic literature rich in the history and traditions of Mexico that included Guadalupe, la Malinche, and Cinco de Mayo.

These sociohistorical considerations show that Teresa was essentially forgotten for several decades before the Chicano movement arose and suggest why her appropriation could only emerge from the academic world. Another possible reason for her unmaking lies in the historiography and construction of an imagined Chicano community.

Benedict Anderson's (1991:5–7) concept of "imaged community" is applicable where there exists a group of people connected by the way they collectively remember the same traditions, events, and experiences. When the Chicano movement emerged, however, multiple differences divided the Mexican Americans, such as lower versus middle class, worker versus intellectual, and rural versus urban. The movement never successfully bridged these differences to create a *raza unida*, or "united race" (García 1989), of Chicanos and Mexican Americans. In fact, many Mexican Americans today still refuse to be identified as Chicanos. This ambivalent relationship impeded the construction of an "official," popularly accepted Chicano history. From this fragmented reality only the most outstanding figures with the greatest historical or geographical relevance were accepted, remembered, or revered as important, exemplary cultural icons. Compared with Guadalupe, César Chávez, Reies López Tijerina, and Rudolfo "Corky" Gonzales, Chicanos felt Teresa Urrea to be a figure of less relevance.

CONCLUSIONS

This analysis of the re-presentation of Teresa, La Santa de Cabora, as early Chicana and saint clarifies that a distinct, intellectual memory was purposefully reconstructed to serve a particular political purpose. That purpose was to provide historical depth, legitimacy, and a sense of community to the Chicano movement. In the reconstruction, aspects of Teresa's persona and life story were departicularized and idealized but were never naturalized and integrated at a popular, nonacademic level. Consequently, a once popular saint was resurrected and re-produced, only to be stillborn.

The re-presentation of Teresa Urrea provides several productive insights regarding key characteristics that played a role in the making of La Santa de Cabora. Virginity with physical and spiritual purity are presented as essential qualities. Likewise, personal suffering associated with a physical, debilitating episode legitimizes the development of healing and visionary powers. A visitation by divine beings also is a common theme. Finally, selfless devotion and dedication, reminiscent of the mother figure, exemplified by actively helping the downtrodden and oppressed, function as key characteristics contributing to Teresa's sanctity and potential popular sainthood. Such particulars explain why Teresa appealed on both cognitive and sensory levels to the architects of the Chicano movement.

This analysis of the remaking of Teresa Urrea as a Chicana counterpart to Guadalupe confirms that saints are the products of ongoing processes of selective traditions and illustrates how the construction of social memory and of a saint reflects present interpretations, needs, and political practices. The authoring of the representations of Teresa drew upon a set of techniques and strategies along with an appeal to both cognitive and sensory memory in order to produce a true Chicana saint. How Teresa failed to function as Chicana saint demonstrates the complex and multifaceted mechanics of selecting and constructing traditions and mnemonic figures. The fragmented, diverse, and to some degree erased or incomplete historical experiences of the Chicanos and Mexican Americans on their individual and collective levels obstructed the full formation of a Chicano imagined community. Consequently, La Santa de Cabora, reconstructed cognitively in academia to serve the Chicano community as Chicana saint, had no audience to receive, appreciate, or celebrate her. Without this felt and understood collective sense, she could not be connected to a popular, public domain. This selective, mnemonic figure fell on deaf ears, unmade. The unmaking of Teresa as Chicana saint is only one example, of course, of many failed efforts to develop an imagined community and a strong ethnic identity. This case further underscores how existing societal structures in an intended community may obstruct the process of formation of broader, more inclusive traditions, including the making of saints.

In the instance of the Chicano movement, and of Teresa, this investigation underscores that history and social memory are essential to drawing and maintaining boundaries of ethnic and national entities. It shows the integral role history and social memory play in the definition of self and other, the interplay between personal and collective identity, and the dialectic between the subaltern and the hegemonic state. Producing religious symbols and icons, such as saints, to reflect a collective history and memory will continue to serve the strategy of nation and ethnic formation and boundary maintenance. Given the power religious symbols wield in human behavior, the making and unmaking of saints is unlikely to disappear under conditions of either modernity or postmodernity.

NOTES

This chapter is dedicated to the memory of Daniel Nugent, who introduced me to Teresa but regrettably passed away too soon to see my writings. I am grateful to my M.A. committee (Newell 1999), Dr. Ana Alonso, Dr. Raquel Rubio-Goldsmith, and Dr. Thomas Sheridan, and thank Salomón Baldenegro, Tomás Martínez, Luis Pérez, Emiliano Gallaga, James Hopgood, Steven Striffler, and June Macklin. Two Edward Spicer Grants (Anthropology Department, University of Arizona) facilitated this research.

1. *Chicano* refers to Mexican American men and women who have purposefully adopted the militant political ideology of the movement. The term carries the connotation of activism for Chicano national consciousness. Some Mexican Americans identify as Chicanos, while others do not.

2. This section is based on Holden 1978, Putnam 1963, and Rodriguez and Rodriguez 1972.

3. See Archivo General de la Nación-Manuel González Ramírez; Archivo Histórico de la Secretaría de Relaciones Exteriores, Exp. L.E. 730(I), 1-3-670(I)+(II), 9-15-14, 9-15-15, 11-19-11.

7
Spirits of a Holy Land
Place and Time in a Modern Mexican Religious Movement

William Breen Murray

Followers of the popular folk saint El Niño Fidencio gather regularly in the small northern Mexican desert town of Espinazo, Nuevo León, for curing rituals. Although this famous healer died in 1938, they believe that his spirit continues to manifest itself there through trance mediums. The *fidencista* movement is based on the appropriation and manipulation of sacred places within the town and the surrounding area whose sacrality is defined by past events in El Niño Fidencio's life. The survival of the movement depends on the preservation of these places, yet it also requires a continuing redefinition of their physical appearance that will fulfill the expectations of pilgrims. In this chapter, I cover some changes that have taken place in these definitions during the past 25 years, a time when the last living links to the historic person of Fidencio have disappeared from the scene and the movement has adapted to new conditions in Mexican society.

FIDENCISMO AND SAINTHOOD

The Mexican healer José Fidencio de Jesús Síntora Constantino (1898–1938), better known as El Niño Fidencio (Fidencio the Child), is probably closer to the traditional Christian saint than any other figure considered in this volume. There is little doubt that he believed he was "chosen by God" for his healing mission, and both his followers and detractors measure his personal traits and healing acts in terms of Christian sainthood. The Roman Catholic Church's emphatic rejection of that attribution places him in a special category.

This antagonism focuses attention precisely on the attributes of sainthood and the significance of official rejection. In anthropological terms, Macklin (1974b, 1988) identifies Fidencio as a "folk" saint, although from the Church's view, perhaps "anti-saint" is a more appropriate term. Looking at the official Christian saints, she identifies some (the "pious") who are recognized for their contributions to the Church itself, while others (the "popular") achieve sainthood through the fame of their acts and their acclaim among the faithful. Folk saints, like El Niño Fidencio and others (Macklin and Crumrine 1973), often share the attributes and charisma of popular Christian saints such as San Martín de Porres, but their appearance beyond the pale of the Church resists orthodox classification and official incorporation.

Even during his lifetime, Fidencio manifested many saintly attributes. His image in a famous historic photograph makes this identification quite explicit. The tunic he wears recalls the vestments of the itinerant friars who first evangelized the northern desert frontier of New Spain in the 17th and 18th centuries. The photo shows him barefooted and kneeling with a heavy wooden cross on his shoulder in a replication of the Christian Passion. *Fidencista* oral tradition (Heliodoro y Fabiola 1997:59) recounts that in these Holy Week representations, Fidencio took the role of Christ, and this scene may be a photographic testimonial of one such event.

Other saintly attributes are suggested indirectly. The male chastity implied by his popular name "El Niño" (the Child) replicates the religious vow of celibacy. In Fidencio's case, it was clearly fulfilled (although not necessarily for the same reasons as those of an ordained priest). *Fidencista* oral tradition also identifies specific consecrating events in which El Niño was visited by Christ and received his spiritual mission as a healer (cf. Berlanga et al. 1999:14ff; Garza Quirós 1980:41; Heliodoro y Fabiola 1997:14). Photographs show that in life, Fidencio received the personal veneration accorded a "saint" from his followers (Terán Lira 1980). Even the desert landscape around Espinazo, Nuevo León, where Fidencio lived and worked as a healer seems to recreate the world of Jesus of Nazareth.

For one part of the *fidencista* movement today, the "Iglesia Fidencista Cristiana" (Fidencista Christian Church), Fidencio is simply a modern saint unrecognized by the Church. Its adherents plainly identify themselves as Catholics and freely incorporate popular Mexican Catholic religious symbols into *fidencista* practices. Yet in 1993 when federal legislation required official registration of religious groups, the Iglesia Fidencista Cristiana was incorporated as a separate and distinct "religious association." *Fidencismo* thus became northeast Mexico's only officially sanctioned "native" religion, reaffirming its "otherness" from both the Roman Catholic Church and any other identifiably Christian denomination. One can only assume that this was done with the approval of the Church authorities and fully reflects their view of the situation.

For the Church, El Niño's canonization is not so much improbable as unthinkable. The Church's opposition to *fidencismo,* like that of the medical profession, has been consistent and categorical. It began during Fidencio's lifetime

(Garza Quirós 1980:61ff) and continues today in pulpits and through the mass media. *Fidencista* images or banners are officially banned inside any Roman Catholic church (although individual parish priests may have some leeway in applying this prohibition). In those areas where *fidencista* groups are known to exist, catechists are given special instructions for recognizing and refuting *fidencista* claims and beliefs.

The Church's counteroffensive touches on a variety of themes. As Macklin (1974b) points out, *fidencismo* was from the beginning a syncretic fusion of traditional Mexican Catholicism and 19th-century spiritism. For orthodox Catholics, the spirit possession practiced by the *fidencista* healers is charlatanry, and Fidencio's representation (analyzed in Macklin 1988:85) as "El Niño Guadalupano," replacing the Virgin of Guadalupe, Mexico's official patron saint, is a sacrilege (Figure 1.1). Official rejection rests, however, on more than just the heterodox elements of *fidencismo* incorporated from its spiritist origins. It also stems from a historic memory that provides the content of *fidencista* oral tradition.

El Niño Fidencio's career spanned a critical phase of the Mexican Revolution during which the Church was openly persecuted. In Nuevo León, Pancho Villa's forces burned and desecrated churches and forced the clergy to flee. The anticlerical frenzy reached its height in the 1920s during the Cristero War, which produced martyrs now officially beatified for defending the Church against the emerging revolutionary leadership. For the *fidencistas,* the Mexican Revolution is sacralized as the time when Fidencio lived, but for the Roman Catholic Church, this revolutionary past is a permanent reminder of its darkest hour, a time when Mexican Catholics died for their religion. Although rarely enunciated in these terms, this disjuncture in historic memories probably informs the Church's position far more than any point of doctrine or peculiar practice.

No clear evidence exists that present-day *fidencistas* inherited their faith from anticlerical revolutionary grandparents, but the movement's leadership, ideology, and oral tradition continue to emphasize this historic continuity (Heliodoro y Fabiola 1997:5). Fidencio's principal patrons and protectors were all closely connected to the Revolution, and Macklin (1967,1974b) documents his popularity among the revolutionary elite of Saltillo and Monterrey, many of whom were spiritists. Villa's spirit still possesses *fidencista* healers on occasion.

In this light, *fidencismo* can be understood as a kind of sacralization of the Revolution's own ideological pretensions. President Plutarco Calles's famous visit to El Niño in 1928 (and subsequent published testimonials) is Fidencio's consecration as a "saint," not of the Church, but of the Revolution itself. It marks the high point of his career and receives special emphasis in *fidencista* oral tradition (Terán Lira 1980:48ff). His honey-based treatment of President Calles's skin disorder was apparently successful, if not exactly miraculous, since the medicinal properties of honey were known even in ancient Egypt (Maino 1975:115ff) and its efficacy as a wound dressing has been rediscovered by armies in battle all over the world.

This episode also marks quite precisely Fidencio's irreconcilable separation from the official Church. Among devout Mexican Catholics, President Calles is known as the "Anti-Christ," and Fidencio simply became one of his admiring servants and willing political tools. This disjuncture in historic memories persists today, still charged with powerful emotions for many faithful on both sides of the split.

THE MAKING OF A SACRED PLACE

The historical context focuses attention on what is perhaps the modern *fidencista* movement's most unique element: its sacred landscape. This 20th-century "holy land" is located in and around Espinazo, Nuevo León, the isolated desert ranch on the Nuevo León–Coahuila border where El Niño Fidencio lived and cured in life, roughly between 1923 and 1938. It is the "other world," where *fidencismo* defines the salient features of the landscape, a Mexican town without a priest and a church on its plaza, a place unincorporated into the official Church even today.

Espinazo's landscape combines the most typical and the most improbable features of northern Mexico. It lies in the hot, dry rain shadow of the Eastern Sierra Madre, a land forming the southeastern fringe of the Chihuahuan desert. In pre-Hispanic times, it was inhabited by nomadic hunter-gatherer bands, but the Spanish colonial conquest rapidly erased or assimilated these groups and replaced their lifestyle with a ranching and horticultural economy based on large isolated haciendas. Espinazo was one of many such haciendas throughout the north, although it went practically unnoticed on the economic and social periphery until well into the 19th century.

The construction of the main rail line from Mexico City to the U.S.–Mexico border at Piedras Negras, Coahuila, in the 1880s changed all this. It created a new landscape that dramatically juxtaposed the isolation of a desert hacienda and the most modern communication network then available. It placed Espinazo within a new spatial dimension, Estación Espinazo, a train stop on the growing continental rail system, and the hacienda lost its isolation forever. This rail network was the pride of the Porfirian regime and the trigger for the new economy it fostered. It was also a major focus of military operations during the Mexican Revolution, and an important battle between Villistas and Carrancistas was fought not far from Espinazo at the rail junction of Paredon, Coahuila.

The railroad is thus both an original feature and an integral part of the *fidencista* sacred space. This linkage is made explicit in *fidencista* tradition by the *pirul* (pepper; *Schinus molle*) tree located right beside the railroad tracks, where El Niño was supposedly visited by Christ. In 1923, the railroad brought the young man of 24 who would become El Niño Fidencio to work as a cook at the hacienda. Later it would bring the thousands of patients who sought his healing ministrations. In fact, critics at the time even suggested that Fidencio's entire ministry was simply a railroad promotion (Garza Quirós 1980:155ff).

Although Fidencio's activities at the height of his career were widely reported in the media, his early life is known almost exclusively through *fidencista* oral tradition. The incidents it records are not necessarily fabrications, but the tradition is selective and hagiographic, emphasizing those attributes and events that anticipate his later image. Thus, despite many photographs and newspaper articles, Fidencio's personal history is hard to separate from this image and remains elusive on key points.

Information on his life before his arrival in Espinazo, for example, is limited to his birth certificate and baptismal records that confirm he was born in Irámuco, Guanajuato (Garza Quirós 1980:38ff). According to tradition, he traveled widely in Mexico during the troubled times of the Mexican Revolution and manifested his healing gifts on several occasions before he arrived in Espinazo. Evidently, he also developed the distinctive personal characteristics that set him apart: the falsetto voice, boyish demeanor, and lack of secondary male sexual attributes—traits that earned him the nickname "El Niño."

Although it chose particular strands, Fidencio's healing career follows a classic pattern shared with other Mexican healers (Romano 1965). When Fidencio arrived in Espinazo, the hacienda's owner was Teodoro von Wernich, a wealthy German with close connections to the revolutionary elite and an ardent follower of the spiritist teachings of Alain Kardec. He was the first to recognize Fidencio's healing gifts and spread his fame. Although his exact relation with and influence over Fidencio are hard to measure (see Macklin 1974b for further details), he is an identifiable source of many spiritist elements present in *fidencismo* today.

At the hacienda, Fidencio gained access to the German's remarkably extensive library and may have learned more about medical practice. His empirical skills were undoubtedly self-taught and were thoroughly adapted to the limited resources available at the hacienda, but from these books, he may have acquired some knowledge of human anatomy and learned to recognize and use the medicinal plants that grow in the Espinazo region.

In *fidencista* oral tradition (most recently recounted in Heliodoro y Fabiola 1997:20–23), his first important healing act was successfully curing his own master's gangrenous leg through the application of fresh tomato paste. In gratitude, von Wernich promptly spread his fame outward from the immediate household to the local community, then to the surrounding region through his personal contacts in Saltillo and Monterrey. The presidential visit (mentioned above) extended his fame to the national and even international level.

Fidencio's cures may have appeared miraculous to von Wernich and many of his patients, but what kind of medicine did Niño Fidencio actually practice? Here one comes face to face with another kind of separation in time and a key question about healing saints: the definition of miracles. Although both the Church and the medical profession denounced Fidencio from the beginning, they did so for different reasons, and these differences also point to elements relevant to his saintly status.

For scientifically trained doctors, there are no miracles, only more or less probable outcomes, and a doctor's personal charisma or religious convictions are irrelevant to that outcome. This automatically places "faith" healing in opposition to scientific medicine. My students in the university's medical program nearly always attributed *fidencista* healing to psychological factors, condemning it to an obscure "gray zone" in which science claims only limited expertise.

This characterization may indeed be apt for the patients who come to Espinazo today, but in his own time and place, Fidencio's healing acts showed a more complex combination. Fidencio was not a "trance healer"; instead, he created a unique role somewhere between "the saint" and "the doctor" by uniting the power and authority of religious inspiration with the empirical resources of the traditional Mexican *curandero.* Although he invoked a powerful personal charisma, from a medical point of view, Fidencio's cures are not miraculous. They rely on an assortment of traditional remedies combined with practical skill and close attention to the outcome of specific cases. During his lifetime, Fidencio was an accomplished *curandero,* especially famous as a male midwife, and an empirical surgeon who used broken pieces of glass to extirpate tumors.

Admittedly, Mexican *curanderismo* is alien to modern medicine, perhaps being more akin to the modern "natural health" movement, but its cures are fully comprehensible in scientific terms. For scientifically trained doctors, Fidencio's cures are miraculous only in the sense that they were achieved with limited resources by a person without any formal training. For the *fidencistas,* however, testimonials of these surgeries are preserved in jars and photographs at his tomb shrine today, a physical link of talismanic power bridging one time with another. They are symbols of Fidencio's spiritual presence, rather than medical evidence of his curing methods.

At its height after the presidential visit in 1928, Espinazo became literally a tent city of thousands seeking Fidencio's attention. Although his healing continued to rely on the charismatic power of his ecstatic visions, Fidencio received financial support and notoriety from President Calles's visit. Political support came from the President's allies when Fidencio was formally denounced by the

Church and the medical profession. These funds were applied to convert and equip part of the hacienda as a hospital. In later photos, Fidencio frequently appears in the vestments of a doctor and is accompanied by nurses similarly garbed.

Later, however, the affluence of patients declined. Perhaps it was the changing times or the growing opposition of the medical profession, but by the 1930s, the tent city disappeared, leaving behind only the phantom cemeteries of those who had died there. Fidencio also began to show signs of the physical deterioration that led to his premature death at age 40, but he continued his healing mission unabated to the very end. The specific circumstances of his death are much debated, and no medical autopsy records exist to resolve the issue, but his later photos fit the clinical picture of Klinefelter's syndrome, an endocrinal disorder often associated with increasing obesity and premature death.

With Fidencio's death, the *fidencista* movement was born. Exactly how its peculiar fusion of spiritism and popular piety took place remains mysterious and a blank chapter in *fidencista* history, but it evidently occurred among some of those who had worked most closely with Fidencio. They became the first trance mediums (*cajitas* or *materia,* if female, and *cajones,* if male) to receive his spirit after death and continue his healing ministry. As they dispersed to the nearby towns and cities, they developed their own followings and established local *fidencista* shrines.

Pilgrimage to Espinazo, either individually or in groups called *columnas* (columns), became the principal link between these otherwise isolated *fidencista* groups, and participation in these pilgrimages still defines *fidencista* identity. It also transforms their setting into a sacred landscape where Fidencio's miraculous healings continue to take place. *Fidencistas* believe that El Niño's spirit still inhabits this place and continues to communicate his counsels to the living through the mediums who are possessed by his spirit. Thus, the features of the holy land acquire meaning and consecrating power, combining time and place by fusing historic memory and spiritual presence into a single identity.

Pilgrimage to Espinazo is undertaken for both healing and fulfillment of promises (*promesas*). It follows a pattern deeply rooted in Mexican popular tradition (cf. Hudson 1951; Romano 1965) but with a peculiarly early 20th-century twist. Since the railroad was the vital link that created the *fidencista* movement, after Fidencio's death it continued for a time to be the usual access to the sacred landscape for his followers. *Fidencista columnas* came by train from Monterrey and Saltillo nearly every Sunday, while the "*fiestas grandes*" in March and October brought special trains from more distant locations, recreating the heyday of Fidencio's mission. My initial fieldwork in the early 1970s confirmed that *fidencista* pilgrimages actually began when the train left its originating station and headed for Espinazo. *Fidencista* songs were sung and stories told en route. The transfer at Paredon, Coahuila, brought together groups coming from different directions, and all anticipated the arrival in Espinazo with heightening fervor and expectation.

For these visitors, Espinazo was a place where time seemed to have stopped (Macklin 1967:555–556). Its rustic adobe constructions and horse-drawn carts preserved much the same aspect as when Fidencio lived and provided a polar contrast to the increasingly urban Mexico in the second half of the 20th century. For the rural migrants who made up the new urban working class, it recalled their origins—the way of life "back on the ranch" where they grew up. Even the train cars appeared to date to the Mexican Revolution and reinforced the picture.

A visit to the *fidencista* shrines in Espinazo (Figure 7.1) recreated a consultation with El Niño in life and fit comfortably into the half-day provided by the train schedules. The pilgrims always began at the sacred *pirul* tree. Here, the mediums were first possessed by El Niño's spirit and began to heal their *columna* of followers. The sacred *pirul* was also the starting point for penitentiary processions, whose route proceeded up the stony main street to the old hacienda building ("*la Iglesia*") where Fidencio once had his hospital and is now entombed. Penitents normally covered this route on their knees in a procession led by the *cajita* and accompanied by other members of their *columna* who sang *fidencista* hymns in the trajectory.

These processions led to Fidencio's tomb, where the *cajita*'s possession by Fidencio's spirit was often manifested in consultation and healing acts (*limpias*). Flowers and a large glass urn filled with water on Fidencio's tomb allowed the pilgrims to partake of El Niño's spirit sacramentally. The walls were covered with photographs and testimonials. Historic relics associated with El Niño, such as his deathbed, were preserved in adjoining rooms and often venerated by the *fidencista* pilgrims.

Pilgrimages always ended in the pond (*charco* or *charquito*), whose murky waters are thought to be especially charged with El Niño's spirit. As the final stage of their consultation, patients were ritually immersed three times by the *cajita* and covered with the pond's healing mud. This mud was left on the skin and served to identify the *fidencista* pilgrims as they returned to the city on the evening train. This ritual can also be seen as their baptismal introduction into *fidencismo*.

CHANGES IN THE HOLY LAND

The three core features of the sacred landscape—the *pirul*, the hacienda, and the *charco*—are still visited in much the same way today as in the past, but the gradual demise of rail passenger service in the 1980s and 1990s redefined the pilgrimage's spatial context and permanently changed the *fidencista* landscape.

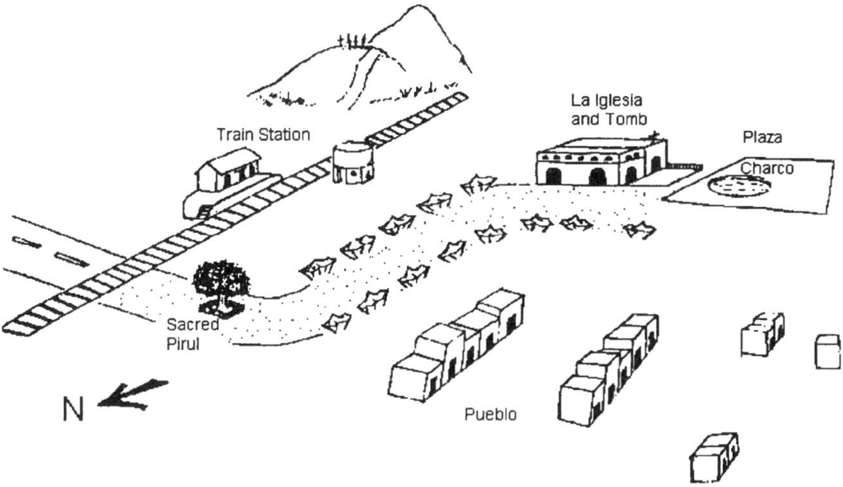

Figure 7.1. Espinazo's sacred core. (Adapted from Berlanga et al. 1999:anexo 3)

A part of Fidencio's world disappeared forever as a result of forces well beyond *fidencista* control. This forced change of access did not directly affect the sacred places; it stimulated modifications in the pilgrimage that reaffirmed the landscape's sacredness by expanding its dimensions and incorporating additional features.

Even before the end of railroad service, some *fidencista* groups, especially those from nearby south Texas, came to Espinazo in buses or auto caravans. For them (and local permanent residents), the 26-kilometer dirt road to the nearest paved highway was always an unpredictable obstacle, often made impassable by flash floods, and a true test of any vehicle's suspension. When passenger rail service finally ended, pressure rapidly mounted for paving the road. This was accomplished late in the Salinas administration (1988–1994) and reoriented the sacred landscape along a new axis. A large cement memorial next to a new Pemex gas station now greets visitors at the highway junction and defines a new boundary of the *fidencista* holy land.

Further, the new access was sanctified by converting the mundane paved highway into a sacred avenue. Especially during and after the celebration of the 50th anniversary of El Niño's death in 1998, *fidencista columnas* constructed shrines at regular intervals along the highway. These are now visited on arrival and departure, and on these occasions the highway shoulder itself becomes a ritual setting. Although some of these shrines are rustic and temporary, others are permanent monuments, destined to perplex any archaeologist in the future. The highway's sacrality is further reinforced by twin shrines on each side at the point where the visitors first view Espinazo, followed by two elaborately constructed "welcome" arches, one about three kilometers before reaching the town and the other at the entrance to the town itself.

Sanctification of this wider landscape is also achieved by attributing sacrality to its natural features. Many of these are analogues to the sacred core itself, and each is linked in some way to El Niño in *fidencista* oral tradition. For example, a new healing site adjoining the paved highway exploits a natural hot spring where El Niño is said to have cured. Here, one *fidencista* leader built a chapel and a series of open-air tanks for bathing in the sulphurous water. Its properties are analogous to those of the holy waters of the *charco,* and a *fidencista* shrine beside the largest pool permits modern pilgrims to be cured in the same way.

Plants are another link between *fidencista* spirit possession and the natural landscape. The significance of the sacred *pirul* in Espinazo is extended to any *pirul* growing in the surrounding area. *Fidencista columnas* often try to camp near one or incorporate them into their roadside shrines. Moreover, although modern *fidencista* healers do not attempt to replicate El Niño's empirical skills, they do use the standardized repertory of herbal remedies attributed to him, many of which remain common in the Espinazo region. *Fidencista* pilgrims often collect herbs during their stays because those harvested in the holy land are considered especially powerful and efficacious.

Within the town of Espinazo, motor vehicle access generated new demands for parking space and changes in the pilgrimage ritual. Bus access created a new kind of urban traffic congestion that grew steadily worse, especially during the *fiestas grandes,* when vehicle movement in the sacred core had to be severely restricted. Even the sacred *pirul,* which once symbolized the movement's link to the railroad, had been affected by the motorized traffic. When the pilgrims came by train to Espinazo, they first circled the *pirul* tree three times counterclockwise on foot. This tradition was preserved when access changed—except the same ritual is now performed in a motor vehicle. This quickly converted the surrounding plaza into a dusty thoroughfare and the *pirul* into an isolated relic in the middle of traffic. For a time, the *pirul* appeared to be succumbing to the effects of its new surroundings, but recently it has recovered its original verdure, protected for the moment from further damage by a reinforced iron fence and spiritual warnings not to remove its leaves or branches.

The town of Espinazo also changed in response to the new circumstances. Many *columnas* set up temporary accommodations by camping on the town perimeter, but others eventually bought land and constructed permanent quarters. These buildings are usually occupied only during the *fiestas grandes* and at other times become a phantasmal perimeter extending well beyond the original town core. Dirt access roads are now transformed into streets with appropriately religious names, including "San Niño Fidencio" street (the penitentiary route from the *pirul* to Fidencio's tomb), the only place in Mexico where El Niño's canonization has already been confirmed. Although this road is still unpaved, the recent appearance of curbing suggests that even this aspect of the pilgrimage may soon change, perhaps better to accommodate the affluence of vendors' stalls that line the route from end to end during the *fiestas grandes*.

Meanwhile, a generational crisis in leadership within the *fidencista* movement created new uses of the sacred core. As Macklin has documented, the initial *fidencista* movement developed around mediums (often *cajitas*) who had known and worked with El Niño in life, and institutionally it was unstructured. As these individuals died, a new form of legitimation was required to identify those with the "gift" of receiving El Niño's spirit. This usually centered on a collectively recognized possession by his spirit at the sacred places. The use of the sacred places to consecrate new *materias* obviously intensified their power, but it also heightened the competition for access and control and polarized the movement into competing factions (cf. Berlanga et al. 1999; Macklin 1974b). In some of these consecrating events, older *cajitas* evidently attempted to pass their spiritual powers to younger proteges, but not all those selected ultimately succeeded in the healing role. Success depends too much on personal charisma and the ability to manage the trance experience to make patronage or pedigree the primary criterion. The role remains open-ended and new *fidencista columnas* continue to form around any *materia* who fulfills their expectations.

The landscape's consecrating power was more precisely articulated by the appearance of many "new Niños." After Fidencio's death, the spiritist beliefs incorporated into *fidencismo* opened the door to other healers who claimed to be reincarnations of El Niño (cf. Garza Quirós 1980:120ff). None of these claimants were ever accepted by the older *cajitas,* but their threat to make the sacred landscape of Espinazo obsolete by establishing a new and distinct spiritual center raised the question of legitimacy and continuity almost immediately.

The search for new *materias* also initiated a slow and still incomplete process of gender change in the movement's leadership. In the years immediately after Fidencio's death, mediumship was exercised almost entirely by women. This gender transformation is facilitated by the androgynous characteristics attributed to El Niño, but it does give women a male identity when they are possessed by El Niño's spirit. In fact, the empowerment bestowed by *fidencista* trance possession is still one of the few sacerdotal roles open to women in Mexican society and points out another key difference with the official Catholic Church. This identity does not involve transsexuality because the mediumship role is neither permanent nor sexually charged. Rather than replacing men with women in the preexisting social order, the transformation defines a distinct (but temporary) intermediate gender role, different from but fully as unique as Fidencio's combination of doctor and saint.

The chastity implied in El Niño's name is not that of a "third sex," but the purity and innocence of the presexual child. Nevertheless, the search for new Niños inevitably centers on young men, many of whom would be considered effeminate by usual Mexican standards. Although the movement's leadership is still predominantly matriarchal women, the number of male *materias* has clearly increased in recent years. Their effective power is limited to their mediumship, but their potential transformative power is much greater. If a new Niño were found, it would make the present leadership obsolete by replacing the historic Fidencio with a new apostolic tradition based on the spiritist idea of reincarnation. It would also emphasize precisely those ideological elements of *fidencismo* most alien to orthodox Mexican Catholicism.

Motor vehicle use also permitted longer stays in Espinazo, especially by the more distant *columnas* during *fiestas grandes*, and provided greater mobility to reach points outside the town itself. This has led to the creation of a more elaborate network of sacred places for visitations. Although regular pilgrimages to most of them appear to be very recent, all are sanctified by their presumed historical association with El Niño, and some of them are now as elaborately marked as the original sacred core.

Probably the most frequently visited is Cerro La Campana, a low hill about 4 kilometers north of Espinazo where El Niño is known to have conducted some of his mass healings. One side of the hill is a semiactive mine, but its rocky summit is now covered with *fidencista* crosses, the earliest of which appear to date to the mid-1980s. Most of the crosses are dedicated to *materias* who healed there, and all are positioned to "look out" on the surrounding "holy land." The hill is crowned by an elaborately decorated shrine with an impressive panoramic view.

My documentation of the contemporary sacred landscape is still incomplete, but all of its features form part of a creative ongoing redefinition. It negotiates the immediate needs of the permanent residents and the unchanging vision and expectations of the *fidencista* pilgrims on whom they depend. Although key changes were imposed by conditions external to the movement and its setting, their implementation has been managed and controlled to maintain the landscape's sacredness. New boundaries are drawn, but for the *fidencistas,* the holy land is still a "separate place" charged with the presence of El Niño's spirit. Thus, Fidencio's sainthood merges personal identity with place and time, creating a "magical" land.

FIDENCIO: SAINT OR SHAMAN?

In recent years anthropological studies have provided another perspective on the *fidencista* movement that relates it to "shamanism" (Atkinson 1992). Both *fiden-*

cista mediumship and shamanism involve "possession states" achieved through the ritualized use of one or more physical stimuli to produce an altered state of consciousness. Neurological studies show that these stimuli alter the brain waves to the theta rhythm, manifested by physical signs (a vacant gaze) and behavioral changes (personality dissociation). Some cultural evolutionary schemes identify shamanism as the Ur-religion of all humankind and the trance experience as the original source of all spirit worlds. Yet each culture has its own means of achieving trances and explains the behavioral changes associated with them according to its own tradition.

In her earlier studies, Macklin (1967, 1974b) noted the similarities between classical shamanism and *fidencista* trance possession and readily characterized El Niño Fidencio as a kind of modern-day shaman. *Fidencistas* use penitential devices (a crown of thorns or a cactus pad tied to the chest), repetitive song in a distinctive keening tone, and the sensory deprivation involved in crawling on one's knees in the hot sun to achieve this altered state. *Fidencista* spirit possession is manifested dramatically in the healer's behavior, usually by physical tremors and a change in voice to the high-pitched tone attributed to El Niño.

Even so, El Niño Fidencio's identification as a shaman is misleading in several ways and glosses over the differences in time and culture that separate shamanism and the spirit mediumship incorporated into *fidencismo.* More specifically, *fidencista* practices lack any historical basis in indigenous culture and incorporate only those native traditions that are part of Mexican popular culture. *Fidencista* trance possession derives not from the native Mexican tradition of the Huichol *mara'akáme* or the Mazatec healer María Sabina. Its roots are found in the 19th-century spiritist tradition (Mexican version) and the ecstatic religiosity of "popular" Mexican Catholicism. In fact, folk sainthood and shamanic possession belong to distinctive cultural worlds, and *fidencismo* illustrates these critical differences in specific ways.

Again, the most dramatic example is found in the *fidencista* landscape. At least two of the places now visited by the *fidencista* pilgrims preserve archaeological remains left by Archaic hunter-gatherers: prehistoric petroglyphs associated with fire pits and lithic material. The most elaborate of these petroglyph/hill shrines is about one kilometer south of Espinazo along the rail line. It faces the town cemetery used since the late 19th century and was known to El Niño. Its ascent has been extensively reworked into a natural amphitheater with a well-constructed permanent shrine along its back wall and a stunning panoramic view all around. At the hill's base is a giant atlatl and other nonrepresentational petroglyphs like those at many other sites in the region (Murray 2001). Two other locations just to the east of Espinazo show similar associations with prehistoric petroglyphs, although their *fidencista* ritual shrines are more modest.

The two time horizons are easy to separate, both spatially and artifactually. The *fidencista* visitors leave very different traces and usually exploit other aspects of these places than did the Archaic inhabitants who made the petroglyphs. Their carvings include many ambiguous geometrical shapes, but also atlatls, projectile points, and the antlers of the white-tailed deer. The *fidencistas,* on the other hand, mark the highest points on each hill by placing on them crosses and altars festooned with colored paper streamers, flowers, candles, and other offerings, all of which are renewed on each visit.

Despite the physical proximity, the *fidencista* shrines usually do not interfere with the rock art nearby and do not use the earlier petroglyphs. Only two modern petroglyphs can be firmly identified as being of *fidencista* inspiration and their motifs and execution are easily distinguishable from the earlier ones. They contrast as well with other modern petroglyphs (graffiti) nearby, some of which must date to Fidencio's lifetime. The modernity of the *fidencista* movement is thus reaffirmed by the spatial and artifactual separation manifested at its sacred places. *Fidencismo* draws neither inspiration nor ideological support from the Native American religious traditions reflected in the petroglyphs.

This separation is further illustrated in relation to the use of peyote (*Lophophora williamsii* and its variants), the hallucinogenic cactus whose consumption is still central to several existing Native Mexican and Native American religious traditions. Peyote is abundant in the Espinazo region, and modern Huichol pilgrims harvest it in the canyons of the nearby Sierra Madre. Ethnohistoric evidence from the early colonial period clearly documents peyote use among the Amerindian cultures of northeast Mexico and describes its ritual use in considerable detail. In nearby Texas, the Archaic Pecos River–style paintings may be linked to prehistoric peyote use (Boyd 1998).

It is significant, then, that the *fidencista* healers do not use peyote, either to achieve an altered state of consciousness experience or even (to the best of my knowledge) as a home remedy, although it is widely used among local ranchers for many purposes quite unrelated to its hallucinogenic properties. Instead, *fidencista* trance possession is produced by the same kinds of collective singing and penitential acts as are performed at other Mexican religious shrines, such as the famous Franciscan church at Real de Catorce. *Fidencista* trance possession is not, after all, the shamanic journey of indigenous healing traditions, and Espinazo serves to warn us that the ethnographic analogies sometimes used to identify shamanism in archaeological contexts must be drawn with extreme caution (cf. Kehoe 2000).

This difference also serves to distinguish *fidencismo* from the many new neoshamanic cults that have appeared in the past two decades, spawned in part by anthropology itself. In Mexico, these sects often aim to recover and reinterpret pre-Hispanic religious beliefs and practices, frequently by reenacting modern versions of rituals at archaeological sites. Macklin (1997) describes one of these neo-shamans or spiritual guides, Francisco Jiménez, in greater detail, but he is only one of many who have become familiar figures at Mexican archaeological sites. Neo-shamanism converts the demonstrable antiquity of these places into a magical attribute. Archaeological sites become "power centers" where ancient spirits continue to reside, whether they are the temples and altars at major Mesoamerican sites or the petroglyphs carved on the native rock at places like Espinazo (cf. Vargas Somoza 2001). In this way, *fidencismo* and Neo-shamanism share an important general trait: both create new sacralized landscapes by juxtaposing time dimensions. The *fidencista* landscape is defined by oral historical tradition, whereas the neo-shamanic landscape is invoked by reconstructions and a selective treatment of scholarly knowledge about its prehistoric features.

For the Neo-shamanists, the structures and artifacts at prehistoric sites often encode knowledge left by their ancient inhabitants and only glimpsed in conventional archaeological analysis. This knowledge is manifested in calendrically determined building alignments, light-and-shadow effects, and hidden metrological proportions, all waiting to be shown to those with insight enough to see them. Neo-shamanism fills the time gap by relating them to daily life in their present-day surroundings, although this transformation may cause problems for the archaeologists in charge of preserving their original context. Macklin (1997) concludes these beliefs decisively separate *fidencismo* from most Mexican versions of Neo-shamanism. The *fidencistas* claim no special knowledge of the petroglyphs' meanings and do not use the prehistoric features within their sacred landscape. Apparently, the prehistoric past plays no part in *fidencista* imagery or the definition of its sacred places.

Unlike Neo-shamanism, the eclectic mix of *fidencismo* is radically different and emphatically Mexican (with a bit of European spiritism). It is defined by the multiple symbols of popular Mexican religiosity and national identity that it incorporates. Today, it reflects the increasing globalization of both the local region and the country as a whole. Thus, although the vendors who come for the *fiestas grandes* may sell fat Buddhas or Indian incense, for them, Espinazo is just another stop on a "religious articles" circuit that covers most of the major shrines and pilgrimage centers all over Mexico.

CONCLUSIONS

The fusion of place and time is characteristic of many kinds of settings: historical monuments, archaeological sites, battlefields, neighborhoods that preserve the architecture of a given period, and even mythic settings like Mount Ararat, where Biblically inspired explorers still search for the vestiges of Noah's ark. Each place transforms the present into the past by spatial association. Their sanctity is defined by the nature of the events recalled and the kind of magic required to realize the transformation.

In the *fidencista* tradition, elements of traditional Christian sainthood define the historic identity of El Niño Fidencio and reveal its cultural links with popular Mexican Catholicism. On the other hand, the transformation represented by *fidencista* spirit possession depends on 19th-century spiritist beliefs imported from Europe and popular at the time of the Mexican Revolution. This spiritist element dissociates the historic Fidencio from the Christian apostolic tradition of healer-saints and defines the present-day movement's antagonism with the official Church. *Fidencismo*'s magic is also antagonistic to science, particularly scientific medicine as practiced today. Many educated Mexicans consider *fidencista* beliefs pseudoscientific, a manifestation of popular ignorance and even a national disgrace. The medical profession often rejects *fidencista* practices for these reasons and is perhaps its most direct threat. The medical establishment views the sacred *charco* as a public health menace and the *fidencista* healers as frauds whose herbal remedies can cause dangerous intoxications.

Such charges, of course, merely heighten the polarity between material and spiritual explanations of the same phenomena and intensify the magic involved in *fidencista* spirit possession. They mark off the distance between scientific medicine and the faith healing still carried out within the orthodox Christian tradition (both Catholic and Protestant). *Fidencismo*'s reliance on faith explains why scientific critics often describe it as "medieval" despite its recent origins. It uses precisely the charismatic healing resources that scientific medicine largely eschews. *Fidencismo* is not a protest movement, but it clearly represents the theoretical and practical antithesis of scientific medicine and appeals to many people left uncured by the Mexican medical system.

On the other hand, definitive separation from the official Church has served to define a new orthodoxy and structure from what began as simply a popular tradition. By creating a legally constituted religious sect, the Iglesia Fidencista Cristiana now proclaims its legitimate representation for the entire *fidencista* movement. It has an officially sanctioned liturgy and hymnal and a church hierarchy of its own, and even organizes an annual convention. Its authority is sanctioned both by a kind of *fidencista* apostolic tradition (its leaders are direct descendants of the family who later owned the hacienda) and the legitimacy accorded by recognition from the state. Even so, Fidencio's saintly status is still in doubt and will depend on future developments in the movement's ideological and institutional definition.

NOTE

I have drawn from my own research and fieldwork in preparing this chapter, some of which began many years ago (Murray 1980). Persons who have been of particular assistance include colleagues Olympia Farfán (INAH-Nuevo León) and Jon Olson (California State–Long Beach) for oral information on historical aspects of the *fidencista* movement; archaeologists Moisés Valadez and Evaristo Reyes Gómez (INAH-Nuevo León) for information on recent archaeological reconnaissance in the Espinazo area; and Michael Van Wagenen of Brownsville, Texas, for additional details on recent developments.

8
Saints and Stars
Sainthood for the 21st Century

James F. Hopgood

A man who could not seduce men cannot save them either.
Søren Kierkegaard

What could a folk saint and a movie star possibly have in common? In the present case, what could two people so clearly different in background and culture as the Mexican curer and folk saint José Fidencio de Jesús Síntora Constantino (1898–1938) and the American actor James Byron Dean (1931–1955) have in common? Despite apparent differences I believe there is much to be learned from a comparison of these two figures and their followers. I seek homologues and see Fidencio and Dean in analogous structural positions, as "saints" or "icons," with regard to their respective sociocultural systems. I view them as foci for emotive expressions of devotion and questing, although what is sought may differ. The answers offered here, though tentative, include recognition of the role of the sacred and of sacralization in any explanation of the process of making saints of whatever variety (Demerath 2000).

A comparison of these two figures provides a basis for exploring processes of deification of secular personages—creating icons and making of them a "new" type of saint. Even with very strong pressures of secularization, or in spite of them, this process continues today and is expressed in many extant forms. But what is required to transform admiration into adoration? The comparison itself is problematic and will involve examination of general "commonalities." This exploration, however, cannot be undertaken as a classic cross-cultural comparison because the conditions for such a comparison cannot be met (Ember 1996). Nevertheless, the basic task appears simple enough in identifying factors involved in the selection and perseverance of certain persons as "saints" or "icons." "Factors" include any relevant psychological or sociocultural data and "selection" refers to the sociocultural, historical, and environmental processes in operation at the time and subsequently. After considering a series of these comparative points, such as the role of *place* in grounding, situating, and localizing the folk saint and icon, I turn to the role of the image and certain aspects of visual appeal. Specifically considering still photography, I seek points of similarity and difference, such as the contribution of still photography and particular image forms in the genesis of folk saint, Fidencio, and icon, James Dean. Particular attention is given to those that will illuminate their attraction and genesis, to saint and icon formation, as a kind of "modeling."

Each case will help to clarify apparent similarities and differences. And, despite some significant differences, this comparison will suggest several points regarding (1) how apparently disparate manifestations and forms of adoration exhibit "merging"—a process of "borrowing" and expanding similarities—and (2) the sharing of many key features, including similar sources in their genesis—that is, how the making of folk saints and modern icons has many common impulses and sources. This comparison reveals how these two phenomena derive from and function in their respective social and cultural contexts, each indicating possible equivalencies in the other and suggesting commonalities.

Despite the presumed religiosity of one and the presumed secularity of the other, within their respective sociocultural "frames" they stand in very similar positions, and, despite obvious differences, each fulfills a selection of personal needs for their devotees within those cultural matrices. Being clear about the analytical distinction of religion and the sacred is important for the sake of the present argument. The sacred exists typically within religions, but the sacred does not require the frame of religion. The *sacred*, and the process of sacralization, is a central concept in understanding what two such seemingly disparate phenomena as these have in common. Consequently, the role of "icons," "stars," "celebrities," and many "saints" today becomes intelligible only when placed within a framework devoid of the strictures of religion.

Throughout this chapter, some events in the life histories of James Dean and Fidencio will be used for comparison. For those unfamiliar with one or either, a very brief synopsis of the lives and careers of each is in order.

JAMES DEAN AND EL NIÑO FIDENCIO

James Dean is remembered by most people as a movie star of the 1950s and may be recalled by a postage stamp, poster, or cardboard standup.[1] Some may remember one or more of his three major film roles. Only the first of the films, *East of Eden*, was in release at the time of his death at age 24 on September 30, 1955. For most people, Dean may only be a link with other American "icons" representative or symbolic of a near-mythical 1950s. "Deaners"—his most devoted followers—however, find in James Dean an array of meanings and significance well beyond the simple facts of his life and accomplishments (Hopgood 1998b, 2000).

Signs of adoration of Dean followed immediately upon his death. Fairmount,

Indiana, Dean's hometown, became a pilgrimage site beginning with Dean's funeral on October 8, 1955, when some 3,000 people attended and the first Deaners were born (Hopgood 1998b:106). Dean's second film, *Rebel Without a Cause,* opened across the country a few days later, but *Giant,* his final film, was not seen until November 1956. Despite only *East of Eden* being in release before Dean's death, his death sparked an outpouring of grief, remorse, and shock not seen since the death of Rudolph Valentino. Legions of fans appeared, fan clubs were founded, pieces of his wrecked Porsche were offered as mementos, suicides were reported, tributes were made in song and film, monuments were built, two posthumous Academy Award nominations were made, co-actors described him in charismatic terms, books about him appeared, magazine articles were everywhere, film documentaries were scripted, Dean merchandise was offered via magazine ads, and so on.

What is remarkable is that the adoration has continued for over 50 years and today Deaners come in all ages, genders, ethnicities, and nationalities.[2] Fairmount continues as the pilgrimage site for Deaners, fans, and the curious. He is honored several times during the year, but every September the city holds the "Jimmy Dean Days" weekend festival and on the 30th, a special memorial service is held at the small Quaker church Dean attended as a boy.

José Fidencio de Jesús Síntora Constantino was born in a small village in Guanajuato in 1898.[3] Little is known of his parents and much of Fidencio's life is shrouded in mystery until the time he became widely known for his curing abilities in the 1920s. Around 1923, Fidencio traveled to the hacienda of Teodoro von Wernich at Espinazo, Nuevo León, where he would remain for the rest of his life.

The narratives concerning Fidencio's gifts of healing are many. Apparently his early successes with curing farm animals and assisting with animal birthing led to attempts with local people, including midwifing. He was very successful and his fame soon spread to other communities in northern Mexico. During this period it is said that Fidencio had many visions, some of Jesus, and through some of these he received the power of healing and knowledge of medicinal plants. Fidencio's fame continued to grow and by 1928 he was getting some attention in the national press, in part because of a visit by the Mexican President, Plutarco Calles. In the following months, even more people took trains to Espinazo, with as many as 30,000 people reported living in the little desert pueblo at one time.

His followers began calling him "El Niño" as a term of endearment but also because of his childlike qualities and the growing view of him as a "Child of God." From 1928 until his death at age 40 in 1938, Fidencio continued to cure the sick of any and all ailments, sometimes while in a trance.

Fidencio continues to cure today through dozens of mediums in Mexico and the United States. His body is entombed in the old hacienda house, now called "*la Iglesia*" (the Church). On the days marking his birth and death (both in October) and in March (his saint's day), thousands of pilgrims make the journey to participate in healing rituals. The pilgrims come as individuals or in organized groups called *columnas*, sometimes led by traditional dancers called *matachines*. Still, for those in need, any day is a good day to visit Espinazo.

COMPARISONS AND THE PROBLEM OF COMPARISON

The potential breadth of coverage in making a comparison of this sort is such that some limits are needed. To consider all relevant factors that contribute to the making of a saint or an icon would be a daunting task and beyond the scope of a single paper or chapter. For example, some issues involved in a study of the genesis of saints and icons concern the nature of charisma (Eisenstadt 1968:xxxiv–xxxviii; Lindholm 1990; Weber 1963:2) and of religious movements.[4] Here the focus will be specifically on a few comparative questions regarding Fidencio and Dean and what ingredients are involved in constructing these two deified, semideified, or sanctified, sacralized figures. Even that is an issue, of course. After all, to the Catholic Church, Fidencio is not a saint and despite recent increases in canonizations of popular folk by Pope John Paul II, Fidencio remains outside the fold, perhaps forever an aberration.

However, there is also a fundamental question: Are these equivalent "cultural units" (Munck 2000:285, 2002)? My assumption for the purposes of this chapter is that they are equivalent units and the categories I use serve as etic concepts, although they are simply heuristic in this context. Whether these do adequately encompass phenomena like the Deaner movement and *fidencismo* is an issue for the future. Why make such a comparison in the first place? For example, the differences between Mexico in the 1920s and 1930s and the United States of the 1950s, when these two phenomena developed, are obviously quite substantial. Yet, each country experienced considerable sociocultural change and stress during those periods. The 1950s in the United States may have been the heyday for the Boy Scouts, Davy Crockett, the Marlboro Man, Norman Rockwell, McCarthyism, Eisenhower Republicans, and the Cold War, but it was also a time of considerable social and cultural ferment with strong counterculture undercurrents: Jackson Pollock and abstract expressionism, existential angst, humanist Marxism, ban-the-bomb and civil rights, bebop and Miles Davis, rock 'n' roll and Elvis Presley, Jack Kerouac and the Beats, *Mad Magazine* and *Playboy*, the Actor's Studio and "Method Acting," new conceptions of American masculinity (or, better, masculinities [Early 2002]). It was an era of "the individual" and of individual expression and imagination (cf. Bellah et al. 1985: 144–147) and of television and the ascension of image over word. It was also a time when contradictions within American society, culture, and politics came to the foreground and American youth was "discovered" and, in time, empowered as an economic force.

For Mexico the 1920s and 1930s were times of great change (Benjamin 2000; Womack 1986). The Mexican Revolution may have concluded, but violence continued to erupt from time to time, maintaining conditions of uncertainty, instability, and further economic hardship and threatening to push the country into civil war. Religion was officially repressed; the Cristeros revolted while many Catholics and Protestants practiced secretly, if at all. Coupled with these were the pressures of modernity's challenge to traditional folk cultures. New ideas of modernity, predating the Revolution, the consolidation of political power by the National Revolutionary Party and the Party of the Mexican Revolution (both precursors to the PRI, Mexico's long dominant party), and a pronounced anticlerical and socialist bent confronted traditions as never before. Though relatively unscathed when compared with many other regions of Mexico, remote, rural places like those in the desert of northern Nuevo León experienced losses in population and major disruptions in agricultural activities and all services (what there was of them). The normalcy of daily routines in family and ritual life was disrupted. Fidencio, at first employed as a cook at the *hacienda* of Espinazo, met the needs of a largely rural people recovering from many years of war and hardship in a difficult desert environment. The owner of the hacienda, a German named Teodoro von Wernich, was bankrupted during the Revolution but is often cited as being very influential in Fidencio's genesis as a healer. He is also thought by many to have supplied Fidencio with many spiritist ideas then current in Mexico that were to be incorporated into what is now *fidencismo.* Perhaps analogous to an agent and given his situation, he may have seen certain advantages to promoting Fidencio. Some narratives also have him being cured of gangrene by Fidencio.

Clearly, the cultures and personal "styles" of Fidencio's Mexico and Dean's America differed in profound ways. Yet, Fidencio and Dean, after all, were products of those cultures and of certain regional, ethnic, and class sectors, and what they did in life, even if innovative, was within certain given cultural parameters. Nevertheless, each possessed a culturally produced "style" that not only "fit" but appealed to certain sectors of people in each setting and both touched, and continue to touch, those sectors. Fidencio's and Dean's charisma or, specifically, the particular style or expression of charisma of each, attracted, stirred, and influenced many followers. Dean's appeal was and remains (to some extent) to that broad societal construction called "middle America" and ranges from the broad level of American popular culture to serious Deaners. Dean is not for everyone and neither is Fidencio. Fidencio's appeal, in contrast, at the level of Mexican (national) popular culture was brief; it was local to regional for the most part and initially fit a more or less traditional religious mold of the *curandero* (though later altered and made syncretic). His appeal is wider today than in the 1920s and 1930s, but the core still comes from the least economically well-off among *mexicanos* and Mexican Americans. Although he has followers outside the core area, even in the American Midwest, the core continues to come from northern Mexico and Texas, and nearly all his followers are of Mexican origin.

What, then, is there to compare? Can this be a "comparison" in any of the usual sociocultural senses? Is this so much "apples and oranges" that no actual comparison is possible, or is this Fujis and Big Reds? Is the point to find common underlying causes? I see Fidencio and Dean as parallel forms—two different charismatic types arising in two stratified societies under conditions of significant culture change, with each addressing "needs" among certain sectors of the populace at large. Still another issue is this: Can these two cases provide an understanding of commonalities about issues that distinguish or fail to distinguish folk saints, secular saints, and their movements? Given the differing specific historical and cultural contexts, are folk saints like Fidencio and icons or secular saints like Dean equivalents or simply spurious, happenstance cases? I obviously see similarities that include both social and psychological factors, though they are expressed differently by their respective followers.

At first glance these two phenomena may appear quite distinct, sharing very little. Closer examination, however, reveals a series of commonalities and similarities. The "Meccas" of Espinazo and Fairmount are both small towns, which may suggest only a superficial similarity. Yet, today small towns like Fairmount and *pueblitos* like Espinazo have a nostalgic ambiance, a quality more in demand as both countries approach total urbanization and urbanized populations seek a nostalgic past. This does not explain the attraction of Fidencio or Dean; it only supplies a common field for each of these charismatics and, importantly, grounding in an actual place.

Both Fidencio and Dean had difficult and disrupted childhoods. Fidencio was born in a small village in Guanajuato in 1898. At age six he was "lent" to another family in nearby Irámuco who became his "adoptive" family. He had, perhaps, three years of formal schooling. He worked in Michoacán and Yucatán on *henequén* (sisal) farms from age 10 to 16. From age 16 to 25 or so, he worked as a cook on a ship. In 1923 or 1924, he traveled to Espinazo where his adoptive family then lived. Dean was born in Marion, Indiana, in 1931 to Winton and Mildred Dean. He was an only child. His father, Winton, was a dental technician. When the future Hollywood star was five years old, his father was transferred to Santa Monica, California, but four years later his mother died. Her body was sent by train back to Indiana for burial. Along with his grandmother Dean, nine-year-old Jimmy accompanied his mother on that long trip from

California. There he was given over to Marcus and Ortense Winslow (Winton's sister and brother-in-law) to be raised on the family farm just outside the small Indiana farm town of Fairmount.

Fidencio's beginnings were in poverty and Dean's would be called "modest." Both experienced what can only be regarded as major psychological trauma because of separation from their natal families. Both factors, origins and separation, have figured significantly in their appeal: Fidencio rose from a poor and obscure origin to be selected by God to cure the poor, "*la gente humilde*" (humble people), and Dean rose from modest and difficult beginnings by his own initiative to become a great, talented actor. Both these narratives have wide appeal in their respective social and cultural contexts.

Several important differences need brief attention. The major one is Fidencio's claim to divine selection by Jesus of Nazareth and the obvious relationship of *fidencismo* to Mexican folk Catholicism. Fidencio began curing before this divine selection, as one narrative has it, with farm animals or local workers. Just how he came to that vocation is not clear, and how it led to his encounter with Jesus at the now sacred *pirul* tree (pepper; *Schinus molle*) in Espinazo is the "stuff of myth." Nothing along similar lines can be claimed by or for Dean. His movement into the sacred is by a different, initially secular route. Deaners do commonly speak and act within religious metaphors and while the deification and spiritualization of Dean may be regarded as un-Christian, it is nonetheless sacralization. In the same way that *fidencismo* does not form a complete theology or system of belief independent of that larger complex of folk Catholicism and spiritism, the beliefs of the Deaners too are part of that larger thing often called American "civil religion" (Bellah 1980).

Closely related to these points of difference is the emic question of how individual *fidencistas* and Deaners consider themselves vis-à-vis their respective devotions. Few Deaners, in my experience, would openly call their devotion to Dean a religion. Many Deaners belong to established churches and many others consider themselves "religious," having "faith" or a "belief" in God or some supernatural power although they do not practice a particular religion. Some, given the nature of American categories of thought and attached values, have difficulty conceiving of their Deaner devotion as religion. A woman of 25 explained to me about coming from an Italian Catholic background and having her mother, who is very religious, become concerned about her obvious devotion to Dean. Consequently, for her mother's benefit, she began referring to her "thing" for Dean as her "fetish." This, she said, "seems to satisfy mother." Other Deaners refer to their, and others', devotion to Dean as "idolatry," an expression clearly within the parameters of Christian negative judgment. Yet, some do admit their devotion to Dean is of a "religious" nature, and a few refer to "conversion" experiences (another religious metaphor).

Fidencistas, in contrast, present a different problem. They regard their devotion to Fidencio as nothing but faith and religion with a set of beliefs and practices in keeping with the wishes of God, even if the Church of Rome does not agree. *Fidencistas* believe Fidencio is a saint. They are marginalized by the established Church, whose hierarchy is officially highly suspicious and critical of their practices and of Fidencio for many reasons, including the elements of spiritism and Fidencio's appearance in the guise of the Virgin of Guadalupe.

Another point of contrast concerns the nature of Dean's and Fidencio's respective organizations. Until quite recently the *fidencistas* could not be characterized as having a centralized organization. Today, there is at least one formalized organization and maybe two competing *fidencista* organizations. There were always efforts at organization and control ("routinization of charisma" in Weber's terms) following Fidencio's death, but the move to establish legally a church in his name is very recent. The Deaners, as an organization, are best referred to as acephalous or "liminal." Although there have been, and continue to be, various clubs, these do little to formalize the social processes engaged in by the Deaners. There are web pages, of course, and these, along with the fanzines and newsletters, provide news and many other features for Deaners. Many Deaners maintain regular contacts and often make pilgrimages together to other Dean sites. There are several "centers" of Deaner sociality, in fact, but not a dominant, "official" one.

One of the more intriguing issues of similarity concerns the "sexual ambiguity" of Dean and Fidencio. For example, neither married or had children. But for each, "sexual ambiguity" has very different origins and expressions. For Fidencio, not to marry simply replicates the accepted case of Jesus. Yet, he often appeared as the "Guadalupano," that is, in the guise of the Virgin of Guadalupe (Figure 1.1). His appearance as the Guadalupano is a great sacrilege to some and especially to the Church, but to Fidencio's followers it is a clear sign of his closeness to, as the child of, the Virgin of Guadalupe. However, his physical appearance and characteristics, especially in the early years of his career, can be described as androgynous.[5] He never developed secondary masculine characteristics and always spoke in a high-pitched voice, as do mediums (*materia*, *cajitas*, or *cajones*) when possessed by his spirit. Today the notion that Fidencio may have been homosexual is sometimes overheard among followers. Others note obvious feminine characteristics of some of his male followers.

With Dean the sexuality issue is more open today than in the 1950s, though even then there were "stories." Today the debate continues with respect to his sexuality: was he heterosexual, homosexual, or bisexual? There are narratives and supporters for each interpretation. The debate is perhaps most pronounced in his hometown of Fairmount, where many citizens emphatically deny that he was homosexual. Whether he was is not an issue here, of course, but his androgynous appeal cannot be denied. The issue, as with Fidencio, is simply that contrary beliefs help explain some of Dean's wide appeal.

The observation that each is of "rural social origin" is, perhaps, most significant in reference to the public festivals held in Espinazo and Fairmount today, not in the fact of each having been raised in rural settings. The Fidencio connection to Espinazo and Dean's to Fairmount are played out several times each year on the occasions of Fidencio's saint's day and death anniversary and Dean's birthday and death anniversary. It is the close association of each with these particular places, along with a certain nostalgic aura, that is important to their followers, not their rural origins, per se. Espinazo has taken on a "quaint" quality for today's visitors, like small towns such as Fairmount in the Midwest.

It is important to note that neither Espinazo nor Fairmount is an "outdoor museum," a historic site, restoration, or park. Neither is operated by a government or a public or private agency. The "messages" presented by these places, whatever those may be, are not controlled by a hegemonic entity. In fact, the "presentation," or public face, of towns like Espinazo and Fairmount are often contested, but that is another part of the story and one that will not be detailed here.

Interesting general similarities in the arrangement of things in Espinazo and Fairmount can be seen. During my first visit to Fairmount, in 1989, I picked up an expressly prepared map of Fairmount while visiting the James Dean Gallery. The map showed the major places associated with Dean when he lived in Fairmount: his uncle and aunt's farm where he grew up following his mother's death, the high school he attended, the motorcycle shop he frequented, the church he attended, his grave, a memorial built for him in the cemetery (its bust of Dean stolen long ago), the local historical museum with the "James Dean Room," and the new gallery dedicated to him. It was a mapping of special (or *sacred*) places and sites for all to visit.

The similar case Fairmount suggested to me was not another small town somewhere in the Midwest, although Fairmount is much like other small Midwestern towns. I was reminded of Espinazo, Nuevo León, Mexico, the Mecca of the *fidencistas.* This small desert *pueblo* has many places considered sacred by the *fidencistas: el Pirulito* (the little *pirul* or pepper tree), *el charco* or *charquito* (the pool), many nearby hills where Fidencio cured or sought retreat, and of course *la Iglesia,* Fidencio's final resting place as well as the site of his deathbed, other important rooms, and thousands of sacred objects. More differences between Fairmount and Espinazo exist than similarities. Eventually, though, the differences become insignificant to what has emerged as a series of interesting similarities in the events and movements associated with these two small towns.

Most people who go to Fidencio and to Espinazo are seeking a cure for a physical ailment or, sometimes, a well-being problem. Many people go to Dean and Fairmount seeking help with problems of well-being, usually of a social or psychological nature. While their devotees may seek different things or results, in both cases there is no question why it is that they have come to seek them in those particular places. Those places are sacred and by being there it is possible to contact or touch the divine.

On the issue of memorabilia, relics, and sacred objects, both Espinazo and Fairmount overflow with them. Sacred items are displayed in the old hacienda building in Espinazo and items are for sale both inside and outside in the streets. Sacred Dean items may be viewed at the museum and the gallery in Fairmount. Gift shops at both places and a few stores in Fairmount sell memorabilia. Pilgrims visit the sacred sites and purchase mementos for home altars. It is more common to see an image of Fidencio on a home altar in Mexico than Dean in one, but many Deaners do maintain special rooms or altar-like places for their displays of Dean objects and memorabilia.

The selling of Dean and Fidencio, and their memorabilia, is making money for many people, sometimes a good deal of money.[6] But, the capitalist enterprise is not the issue here, nor the consumption of commodities, nor the interests they may serve. The image industry, in fact, constantly attempts to create the next big star (dead or alive). However, to focus on the issue of who stands to profit from these activities only begs the question since the issue "why him or her?" remains unaddressed. My concern is with the people who view and interact with the objects and the issues of what brings them to that particular saint or icon.

Returning to those efforts, I attempt to provide a partial answer by focusing on the role of the image and, specifically, the role of the photographic image in placing the saint or icon in concrete reality. As indicated above, I think the importance of *place* in the origin and genesis of saint and icon may be critical, first, to the essence of the saint's and icon's appeal and, second, for the continuation of that appeal. I also see the merging or blending of forms of expression and devotion that perhaps point to the emergence of a new variety of saint. Although I had given thought to the role of photography and mass media in the genesis of the iconic James Dean, and I interviewed Magnum photographer Dennis Stock in 1991 concerning his self-perceived role in the Dean saga, the specific "inspiration" for the direction now taken is Kay Turner's chapter "'Because of This Photography': The Making of a Mexican Folk Saint" in Dore Gardner's book *Niño Fidencio: A Heart Thrown Open* (1992).

While it may be true that the "evolution of media has decreased the significance of physical presence in the experience of people and events," as Joshua Meyrowitz (1985:vii) suggests, my observations in Fairmount and Espinazo suggest many people are not satisfied with anything less than the "real thing." They want to be close to where the subject of their devotion walked, worked, and lived. They want "hands-on" experience of those sacred places. Perhaps it is the increased feeling of "no sense of place," of which Meyrowitz (1985:307–308, 315–317) also writes, that motivates people to seek out concrete experiences in actual places. Consequently, images that tie the saint or icon to actual places and link him to other important sites are critical to this experience.

EL NIÑO FIDENCIO—MEXICAN FOLK SAINT

The importance of photography in the spread of celebrities generally is outlined by Braudy (1997:491–499) and more recently by Rojek (2001:125–129). Kay Turner (1992:122), however, points out that with the development of photography, images of "living saints" could be made that documented their work and could be easily replicated. This is significant because before the use of the camera, living saints (like anyone else) had to be represented by drawings, prints, engravings, paintings, sculpture, and so on. While prints and engravings may have been portable and relatively cheap, they could not equal photography on either score. Photography has the added advantage of depicting the actions of a living saint *in situ* and, presumably, correctly in regard to actual actions. As Turner also points out, photographs of living saints "became a part of their holy posterity, just as paintings and prints had been for saints of earlier periods" (1992:122).

Turner argues for a special role for photography in Fidencio's "rise to sacred status" by "documenting, preserving, and enhancing the powers of this holy man" (1992:122). She continues by insisting that Fidencio's "cult largely thrives due to the widespread duplication and distribution of photographs of him taken during his lifetime—photos that record the life of a healer and charismatic figure who might otherwise have remained unknown beyond his lifetime" (1992:122). This position may be overstated, but I would agree that the photos played a significant role in spreading the word about Fidencio and have continued to provide proof, reinforcement, and demonstration of his acts. Given the paucity of contemporary written commentary, the photographs provide invaluable documentation of Fidencio's activities.

Existing images of Fidencio show surprising range, given the circumstances and conditions of the time and place.[7] The devoted can see Fidencio in a riding outfit, in the stylish wear of the day, wearing a pith helmet, in the dress of a contemporary medical doctor; with a wide range of wild and domestic animals; carrying a cross, posed with a cross; doing surgery with broken glass, attending patients in his "hospital" in the company of his "nurses"; taking the role of Jesus Christ in plays and skits during Holy Week; and dressed as "El Niño Guadalupano."

Taken together these photographs provide a complex ideological view of Fidencio. He is a man of the people, yet he is extraordinary: he is seen riding a horse and with his pet mountain lion. The theatrical aspects of Fidencio's activities emerge in photographs of him in his guise as Jesus donned for performances during Holy Week and in the photos of him in a stylish riding outfit, à la Valentino. There are a few photos of Fidencio taken with Mexican President Plutarco Calles during a visit to Espinazo in 1928, cementing that connection. Nevertheless, the image that typically emerges of Fidencio is that of an ordinary man, though sometimes "stylish."

In the images of Fidencio, Espinazo's streets, buildings, and backgrounds are clearly seen. Better still, the devoted today can see Fidencio's image in the same *charquito,* in the same rooms of the old hacienda house, and in the nearby *sierras* and *cerros*. Perhaps most important of all is that the *fidencista* can see Fidencio with the people in those photos. Viewing Espinazo today the pilgrim can observe the same sacred *pirul* tree where Fidencio received his powers to heal, the locations where he cured the sick, and where he prayed. Despite many outward changes much in Espinazo still looks as it did when Fidencio lived, and the overall ambiance of a remote, rural desert village remains.

In her discussion of photography's role in the rise and promotion of Fidencio, Turner (1992:128) considers two images in particular that are most frequently seen and used. One is a formal-looking portrait of Fidencio, taken at about age 20, as a well-dressed young man in a dark suit, white shirt, and tie (Figure 8.1). He is posed sitting with hands on a walking cane. This may be the most frequently copied and duplicated image of Fidencio. And, as she points out, Fidencio in this image can be seen as urban with Anglo conventions, yet his "facial features are markedly indigenous" (Turner 1992:128). Although Fidencio was not an indigene, I suggest that this coupling of attributes is an excellent expression of a transitional personage and, seen in the context of early 20th-century northeastern Mexico, a figure bridging the traditional past and the future, an expression still viable today.

Another image, and one seen nearly as frequently as that of the well-dressed young man, is Fidencio as "El Niño Guadalupano" or "child of Guadalupe" (Figure 1.1). In this image Fidencio is seen in the dress and aura of Our Lady of Guadalupe. It is significant to note that no other Mexican folk saint is depicted "assuming the mantle of the patron saint of Mexico and one of the singularly most powerful manifestations of the Virgin Mary in the world" (Turner 1992:128). Another attribute of this image is Fidencio's Christlike pose with His Sacred Heart. Acceptance of this image by the viewer indicates an acknowledgment, if not ratification, of blending in three dimensions: (1) a powerful traditional religious and national symbol with Fidencio, (2) male with female, and (3) Fidencio with Jesus Christ. The richness of such images is part of the footing and substance of the sacred.

Figure 8.1. A young, fashionable Fidencio. (James F. Hopgood Collection)

Taking these two key images together, along with the additional images of Fidencio at work and play, creates and portrays a saint of broad appeal, a sort of saint for everyone.

JAMES DEAN—ICON (AMERICAN FOLK SAINT)

Among the hundreds and hundreds of images of James Dean, some are reproduced so frequently they are commonplace and clearly a part of that monster machine known as American popular culture. Interestingly, some images of Dean have acquired names, such as the "torn sweater" series (Schatt 1982:7–23), "the crucifixion," "the last supper," and "the outsider." As with Fidencio, certain images of Dean carry more weight with the devoted, because of what is attributed or attached to them (Hopgood 2000:354–356). It is granted, of course, that every Deaner has his or her favorites. Still, some are emblematic. One such image is the "rebel" (Figure 8.2). This has been duplicated in dozens of ways and by dozens of artists (including Andy Warhol).[8] Another is Dennis Stock's photo of a "beat" Dean in New York's Times Square and, again, this is an image reproduced hundreds of times with many variations. Both are favorites of Deaners in their own ex-voto–like creations in drawings, paintings, sculptures, and tattoos.

Among the dozens of photographers who made images of Dean, there are three professional photographers in particular whose photos of Dean, taken together, provide a chronicle of his life and work from February 1954 until his death on September 30, 1955. Each has published at least one book of his photos of Dean, adding measurably to the accessibility of Dean's image (Roth and Roth 1983; Roth and Ohnishi 1987; Schatt 1982; Stock 1978, 1987). Because of the work of these three photographers, a concrete, "real life" image of Dean is solidly established. With these photos the devoted can see Dean in many extant places: in the streets, television and theater sets, dressing rooms, cafes and other haunts of New York; playing his congas at the photographer's apartment and hanging out at the Museum of Modern Art (Schatt and Stock). Likewise, in Los Angeles we see Dean in his apartment, washing his Porsche, playing his congas, backstage on the sets of his movies, at the race track, hanging out, chatting at a party, goofing around, going for walks, playing with his cat, sculpting, and driving to the races at Salinas on September 30, 1955, and we see his crashed car (Stock and Roth). In all these images, what stands out is an absence of the posed studio image. Instead we see the young actor going about his daily and nightly life; his interaction with friends and colleagues; and him at work and play—all of which show him as "very human" and often quite ordinary. No doubt Dean played and worked photographers to his own ends (Dennis Stock, interview, September 29, 1991), but with rare exception this is not apparent in the images.

Figure 8.2. James Dean's "rebel." (David Loehr Collection)

THE IMPORTANCE OF PLACE, CONTINUED

The case of James Dean and Fairmount, Indiana, presents a similar situation to that of Fidencio and Espinazo. Like Espinazo, Fairmount draws thousands of people yearly on special marked days and for special sites and events because of one person. Deaners in particular come to Fairmount seeking to make an intimate connection with Dean's spirit (Hopgood 1998b, 2000), just as *fidencistas* do in seeking Fidencio in Espinazo.

What is of specific interest, however, are those images that create a special sense of place and, like those of Fidencio, establish a reality for the icon. "He *really* did live here!" fans often say. The most significant collection of photos of Fairmount was taken by Magnum photographer Dennis Stock and published in many books and magazines in the United States, Europe, and Japan. What makes Stock's photographs so significant is that they are the only ones that show the 24-year-old rising star in Fairmount. Fortunately for the devoted, most of these images can be found in the several editions of Stock's own book, *James Dean Revisited* (1978, 1987), and in many other books and documentaries. They are ubiquitous.

Stock's photos show Dean in the streets of Fairmount, in the family home, on the farm, in the local cemetery, in the motorcycle shop, attending the high school's Sweethearts Ball, and visiting other haunts in Fairmount. These images place Dean firmly in an actual place, and, importantly, the images capture the future icon with ordinary people. He is shown with people in the street, with his aunts, uncles, and a nephew, old friends and acquaintances, and with farm animals. In those images he is shown as one of them and his dress is "like everyone else," including his work clothes. Private moments are also captured by Stock with Dean reading his favorite poet, browsing through old phonograph records, posing in a coffin, visiting the Fairmount cemetery, and so on.

As with Fidencio and Espinazo, these images of Dean place him in locations that can be visited today. Stock's Fairmount can still be seen today along with the Winslow family farm. They have scarcely changed. The devoted can walk the same streets in Fairmount and visit the same cemetery and high school (now closed). If the family is at home, you may be treated to a tour of the farm and, if lucky, visit "Jimmy's" bedroom. The small Quaker church that Dean attended is the same one used for his memorial service every September 30.

CONCLUSIONS

One way to view Fidencio is as manifesting a syncretic mix of Mexican folk Catholicism, traditional curing practices, and spiritism, and as being the product of a particular place (northeastern Mexico) and time (early postrevolutionary Mexico). He can also be profitably viewed as a transitional figure bridging the Mexican "traditional" and "modern." James Dean can be viewed similarly using the same dimensions: as manifesting a genre of American civil or secular religion, as the product of a particular place (middle America and Hollywood) and time (post–World War II America), and as transitional (bridging the postwar years and the culturally "revolutionary" years that followed). Still, why certain persons are selected, and not others, for devotion and sainthood is an issue attached to the questing by devotees. The sentiments for making deities of our "living saints" and "personalities" are similar to those involved in recognizing certain living and dead persons as *kami* in Shintō tradition, only for our icons, no formal, institutionalized process of selection exists. Of course, "it is not what a saint *is,* but what he *signifies* in the eyes of the non-saints, that gives him his world-historic value" (Nietzsche 1996:78).

The merging or blending of styles and forms of images seen in the expression of devotion (T-shirts and buttons with photos of Fidencio as well as Dean; Fidencio shown in ways reminiscent of Elvis) is of interest. This only represents the continuing process of image "updating" and the next move, no doubt, will be the digitalization of their images in new ways. Yet, in both cases, these products continue to express the deeply felt emotions of followers and devotees, just as images, ex-votos, *retablos,* and other forms did in the past.

Regarding the idea of emerging forms of "new" sainthood, something should be noted for the "blurring" of forms in a broader sense; that is, the fact of icons serving as saints in different cultural contexts and saints taking on characteristics of icons and "celebrities" or "personalities" to meet new expectations. Social and religious institutions may attempt to maintain the secular/sacred line of separation, yet ultimately saints come from the people they served and represented and will continue to reflect the sentiments of their followers. Creating saints and icons out of certain celebrities in today's postindustrial, globalizing societies appears to be an ongoing process and enterprise, together with making modifications to previous ones. Given the great potential of current communications technology in the hands of greater numbers of people everywhere, and the sorts of "communities," virtual, imagined, and otherwise, that are emerging because of this technology, the possibilities for creating "saints" for any and all purposes appear great indeed.

NOTES

This chapter has benefited from the reading of a paper by N.J. Demerath III (2000) that neatly summarizes and focuses much that was "floating around out there" concerning issues of the sacred. I first "met" El Niño Fidencio on October 31, 1971, on a field trip to Espinazo. Later that year when I was conducting research in Monterrey (Hopgood 1979), I was "cured" of a back problem by a *cajita* (female medium) possessed by Fidencio. However, for my research on Fidencio I am indebted to June Macklin for her many years of assistance in understanding "El Niño" and the *fidencista* movement. I also want to acknowledge her comments on an earlier version of this chapter. Likewise, I appreciate Walter Adams's comments on that earlier version. To Breen Murray I offer my thanks for his willingness over many years to share up-to-date information with me on *fidencistas*. Dorothy Willner also commented on earlier versions of this chapter and shared her knowledge in clarifying several concepts and methodologies. The Deaner research would not have been possible without David Loehr's generous assistance with his time and his willingness to share information. He is a recognized James Dean archivist and displays the world's largest collection of Dean memorabilia at the James Dean Gallery in Gas City, Indiana (formerly in Fairmount). My research on the Deaners began in 1989. Initially it was to be a "weekend" project.

1. There are many biographies and hagiographies of James Dean that I have consulted. One of the best is David Dalton's *James Dean: The Mutant King* (1974). Reprinted often, it has the distinction of being the most frequently read and reread biography of Dean. The first biography written on Dean by his friend Bill Bast (1956) is a standard reference, and it and Dalton's book constitute the Deaner "bibles." Riese (1991) may also be consulted for seemingly endless details of Dean's life and legacy. (For specific information on the Deaners and events in Fairmount see Hopgood [1998a, 1998b, 2000].)

2. Among Americans, most Deaners are white and about equally divided between males and females, with ages ranging from early adolescent up. Most have Protestant or Catholic backgrounds; a few are Jewish. Very few African Americans or Mexican Americans are currently among his followers. Outside the United States, the largest numbers of fans are found in Japan, Germany, Canada, England, France, Australia, Spain, and Switzerland, roughly in that order.

3. In writing about Fidencio's life and work I have consulted Macklin's writings (esp. 1967, 1974b, 1988), Macklin and Crumrine (1973), Garza Quirós (1980), Heliodoro y Fabiola (1997), Berlanga et al. (1999), Zavaleta (1998), and my own limited fieldwork on the subject. In the sketch I avoid engaging the various debates on the details of his life.

4. Elsewhere I have explored some dimensions of what I call an "iconic movement" and the adoration surrounding Dean (Hopgood 1998a, 1998b, 2000).

5. It is interesting to note in this context that the reinterpretation of Jesus as androgynous, or even feminine, may be a late 20th-century phenomenon, although this is hardly a simple issue (see Steinberg 1996:239ff, 364ff).

6. In the case of James Dean, it was reported that he ranked 13th of the 13 "richest deceased celebrities," by earning $3 million in 2000 for "James Dean, Inc." (Fong and Lau 2001:14). For some perspective, Elvis Presley was number one with $35 million.

7. For photographs of Fidencio I have consulted those reproduced in Gardner

(1992), Garza Quirós (1980), Heliodoro y Fabiola (1997), Terán Lira (1980), and several miscellaneous sources.

8. Dean's rebel pose has become a (visual) trope. It is probably the most commonly reproduced and imitated image of Dean, of which there are several versions or variations. It is also reenacted every September in Fairmount, if not elsewhere, by nearly every contestant in the James Dean lookalike contest.

9
I Quit My Job for a Funeral

The Mourning and Empowering of a Japanese Rock Star

Carolyn S. Stevens

> The death[s of celebrities] . . . ha[ve] oftentimes been viewed through converging psychologies of denial and rationalization. The first dictates that death, and specifically the horror of death, be repressed in social practice and cultural remembering. The second transforms death into spectacle, entertainment, banality. Relayed through new communication technologies, death is constructed and circulated as an object of consumption, knowledge, and desire. . . . Such decontextualisation is part and parcel of the standardized, repetitious presentation of death in the mass media, the most important consequences of which are a fading of its emotional significance and its reconstruction as something trivial.
>
> Elliott 1999:148

Death changes the way we view life. Science has increased our potential to live longer and increasingly pain free; in the modern and postmodern era, the "key notion is fulfilment" (Huntington and Metcalf 1979:205). Many argue that because of this, our ability to deal with death is diminished. Anthony Elliott (1999), in his book on John Lennon, hypothesizes that the cultural field seeks to avoid direct confrontation with death through trivialization, while Little (1999:86) notes the trend toward manipulation of these events as means to a political end. Meanings that arise from a public death are fluid.

Public figures who die in their prime years are frozen in time. Their permanent association with earlier life stages allows them to retain an ideal physical memory; furthermore, their early deaths mean they gain knowledge of the afterlife unnaturally soon, enhancing their spiritual status and power. Taken too soon, these celebrities are idealized and romanticized.

WHAT MAKES A JAPANESE ROCK STAR A CANDIDATE FOR SAINTHOOD?

Matsumoto Hideto, also known as "HIDE" or "hide," former lead guitarist of X Japan and promising solo artist, died in unusual circumstances in 1998.[1] The ensuing expression of public mourning and the media frenzy surrounding it sparked interest not only in fan circles but in the general population as well. Why did this promising young musician die? Why did his fans have such a difficult time coming to terms with his death? Why the adoration? Why did he die and for what purpose? Some said it was due to depression over his band's breakup while others blamed alcohol. Or he was merely a highly strung individual who met with an accident. Either way, he had crossed boundaries that few at his age had. He gained power through death and unleashed a powerful public reaction. Today, fans gather to commemorate hide's death at the hide Museum in his hometown of Yokosuka. The museum was opened in 2000 and built with the cooperation of Japanese Prime Minister Junichiro Koizumi.

The Japanese mass media contributed to the empowering of hide. The nonstop coverage of fan grief encouraged public emotion (either sympathy or disbelief), which then, in turn, encouraged further expression of sadness or cynicism. The banalization of a Japanese rock star's death served to critique the outburst. Why would such a senseless death be considered holy? Saintliness appears to be enhanced by a combination of humanity and holiness. For saints, their faults are often as endearing as their virtues. Take, for example, the appeal of St. Augustine (as the sinner in *The Confessions*), St. Teresa of Avila (with her "unconventional" sense of humor [Peers 1960:16, 20, 39]), and the nature-loving St. Francis of Assisi (who was the first saint to show human attributes of Christ in the form of stigmata). Yet hide's act of self-denial was harshly criticized by many who said he had a greater responsibility to the public to face his problems. Some said he was a failure as a role model, but fans created their own mythology: hide was too sensitive, too kind, and too gentle to exist in this world.

WHO WAS HIDE?

Matsumoto Hideto was born December 13, 1964, in Yokosuka. His hometown is described as a place where "lead-colored ships float in the sea and the dried-out sound of U.S. military radio networks fills the air" (*Shukan Josei* 1998b:56).[2] Yokosuka is known for its U.S. naval base with all its cultural baggage: greasy spoons that accept both yen and American dollars, raucous nightclubs, and tacky Japanese souvenir shops. In this uneasy mix of imitative and resistant culture, Matsumoto heard a KISS album and decided he wanted to learn to play guitar. Meanwhile, he studied to become a hairstylist and was interested in fashion design. His love of fashion was also expressed in his music; early photos of HIDE and X Japan in their amateur days reveal a taste for outrageous costumes, full theatrical makeup, and long, spiky dyed hair.

In 1987 Matsumoto joined "X"—the members couldn't agree on a better name—and they soon achieved success on a minor, alternative music recording label.[3] In the late eighties, the Japanese pop music scene was undergoing change: young Japanese listeners had tired of the sometimes saccharine and always manufactured sounds of pop idols and yearned for a rougher, more authentic musical expression that resonated with their real-life experiences. "Live houses" or smaller nightclubs that hosted amateur and semiprofessional acts gained in popularity, offering a more genuine musical experience than the mammoth stadium concert.

X Japan started as an independent, alternative band that gained a large following in the live house music scene. Their music and live performances have frequently been described by Japanese music critics as unusual and at times violent ("*atarashii kosei*" [a new individuality] with "*kageki na raibu*" [extreme performances]) (Takahashi 1993:170–171). Hard rock numbers were occasionally balanced with ballads: the general tone of X Japan's music was "large scale" heavy metal with classical influences, a hard guitar sound, and a driving beat (Take and Maeda 1995:77).

Their music was striking and their appearances were equally extraordinary. The band members' dyed spiky hair was teased ever higher and their makeup created dramatic masks on stage. HIDE himself authored the copy to the concert pamphlet distributed during their first major concert tour that succinctly describes X Japan's aesthetic sense: "PSYCHEDELIC VIOLENCE CRIME OF VISUAL SHOCK" (Take 1999:267). It is thought that the term "visual" (*bijarukei*) type rock was first used to describe X Japan (Take 1999:267). This genre of pop/rock (including other bands such as Seikimatsu and BUCK-TICK from the eighties and Sharan Q, Luna Sea, Glay, Penicillin, and Malice Mizer from the nineties) was established by a generation of Japanese influenced by the seventies glam rock movement in the United States and the United Kingdom; X Japan was no exception.[4] Their visual impact was promoted through the proliferation of newly established music magazines such as *Pachi Pachi* and *B-Pass*, which carried glossy photographs of the bands in full costume (Takahashi 1993:170). X Japan and their hard rock and "visual" colleagues presented a further choice in music consumption to Japanese youth interested in "independent" music.

In 1988, X Japan was signed by a major label, Sony. In 1990, they won one of the Japanese record industry's highest awards (best new artist); in 1991, they won best video of the year and appeared on NHK Television's prestigious New Year's Eve program. In 1993, HIDE became "hide" when he signed a solo contract with MCA Victor records. He and the other X Japan members marketed themselves wisely, putting their names to perfume, underwear, clothing and accessories, condoms, animated cartoons, and computer game software. Their concerts regularly filled the Tokyo Dome.[5] However, rumors abounded that the band's leader, YOSHIKI, had total creative and financial command of the group;

the other members were so squeezed out of profits, X Japan's vocalist TOSHI had to put out a solo album and a nationwide tour just to pay his bills.

In September 1997, the members announced the band's demise. Reasons given were few, but hide appeared to rebound with great energy. He formed a new band (entitled, unfortunately, "hide with Spread Beaver") and his 1998 single "Rocket Dive" was well received. Three singles followed in early 1998, with plans for two albums and a nationwide tour: hide was a busy man, and the public was eating it up. He was riding on two waves of consumer desire: nostalgia for the fame that was X and excitement for the new hide to come.

Hide's new band had a misogynist name, yet he cannot be so easily categorized as a stereotypical sexist metal rocker. In 1997, before the breakup, he became involved with charity work after participating in a "Make a Wish Japan" program. Fourteen-year-old contest winner Kishi Mayuko asked to meet HIDE just before her bone marrow transplant operation.[6] An employee of the Make a Wish office noted, "We were surprised at the speed with which hide responded to our request. We were also touched at his earnestness at the actual interview" (*Josei Jishin* 1998:45). Not only did HIDE appear gracious and caring, but X Japan fans also rallied around Mayuko, illustrating the tight fan community. Months later HIDE saw her in the hospital and his purported two-hour visit was widely publicized. He then registered as a donor for the bone marrow bank and encouraged fans to do the same. These actions were denounced as "self-advertisement" (*Josei Jishin* 1998:47), but after his death, Mayuko's mother claimed the rock star had maintained the relationship through e-mail. "Thanks to him, Mayuko really recovered," she insisted. After his death, hide was presented as a contradiction in terms: a wild musician versus a kind man who gave honestly of himself to a sick girl. This image certainly contributed to the construction of secular sainthood after his death.

Death, violence, and even suicide were constant motifs in X Japan songs.[7] Whether this contributed to hide's death is a matter of speculation, but it is important to note that the band cultivated an aesthetic appreciated by a select group. Beauty to some is ugliness to others; rather than analyzing the content, my aim here is to show that this aesthetic also served to demonstrate in-group knowledge and taste. This knowledge represented a clear boundary between those who understood hide and those who did not. This cleavage was further deepened following the media reaction to his suicide.

MASS MEDIA FRENZY

"Searching for information . . . may not only help survivors make sense of the death, it can also lessen their sense of isolation," as Wertheimer (1991:69) says. Fans—not immediate family or friends—had nothing but indirect access to news surrounding hide's death. It was the mass media that filled the informational vacuum. Because fandom is an increasingly common way for postwar Japanese consumers to construct their identity (cf. Kelly 2004; Stevens 2002), answers to their questions were of the utmost importance.

The desire for knowledge feeds human agency; it can both fuel and amplify the motivations and outcomes of individual actions. Fans wanted to know why hide died; others wanted to know why they should care. The facts were spare: on May 1, 1998, after appearing on a late-night television show called "Rocket Punch," hide went out for drinks with colleagues and was driven to his home in the fashionable Azabu section of Tokyo about 3:00 A.M., May 2, by his brother. Later that morning, the woman with whom he lived found him hanging from the bathroom doorknob by a towel. It appeared as if he had tied the towel around his neck, fastened it to the doorknob, and then sat heavily against the door, legs perpendicular. It would have been simple for him to stand up and stop the strangulation process, but this was not to be. He was rushed to the hospital but was pronounced dead just before 9:00 A.M. Police reports immediately after the incident confirmed that he had been drinking heavily. Suicide was suspected, and depression over the breakup of X Japan was thought to be the cause. The other possibility was an autoerotic experiment gone awry, as the circumstances of his death resembled those of Michael Hutchence, the lead singer of the Australian band INXS, who died in late 1997.

Another theory was alcohol-induced short-term amnesia (*Shukan Josei* 1998a: 37). Blaming hide's death on this syndrome (called "*nemuri shokogun*" in Japanese) meant that, in other words, hide did not know what he was doing when he hung himself (supporting the theory that it had been an accident). Later, it was revealed that he had suffered from stiff muscles in his neck and shoulders (*katakori*) and he had used the towel to help relieve the discomfort. Police investigations eventually ruled hide's death to be an accident as he had numerous engagements planned to promote his new album and this meant a premeditated suicide was unlikely.

Whether a suicide or an accident, hide's death affected his public deeply and immediately. Soon after his death was announced, a junior high school student hung herself; several teenaged girls tried to commit suicide by jumping off a bridge in Chiba on May 4. On May 6, at the Honganji funeral, a 19-year-old woman tried to cut her wrists with a paper cutter (*Shukan Josei* 1998a:36).[8] That evening, YOSHIKI, the former leader of X Japan, called a press conference and stated his strong belief that hide's death was an accident, cancelling the need for copycat suicides.[9] He said he understood the fans' feeling that they had lost their "reason for living" (*ikigai wo nakushita*) but he thought it was more important for fans to stick together and "be strong" (*Shukan Josei* 1998b:14–15).

The leader's plea to fans for strength was clipped to a three-second sound bite and televised repeatedly while the press-conference transcript was printed in all major newspapers and magazines. The media's treatment of this important speech focused on simplified warnings to fans: do not try this at home! There was no mention of hide's complicated emotional life, though the audience was more interested here in YOSHIKI's pain. He was scrutinized for any admission of guilt; could *he* have known what was to be?

Concern for the moral health of the populace also served to mock the fans by objectifying their subjective feelings, contributing to the trivialization of death in public mourning that Elliott (1999) described. It is precisely this process of denying feelings that the fans rejected so strongly. If they didn't, hide's death (and therefore life) would become meaningless.

ANALYSIS

Modern social life insists on drawing a line between private and public within the individual. Fans refute this divide and personalize the public face of a celebrity. Although "professional celebrities" should keep their "private" selves segregated from their "public" ones, hide broke down the barrier by allowing his private act of self-denial to become a public matter, producing on the one hand deep emotion through his vulnerability and accessibility and, on the other, criticism through his irresponsibility.

As a foreign observer, I was most struck by comparisons to the public mourning of Princess Diana. In the case of Diana, there were many who felt her death struck a deep chord. Diana was symbolic of "the contemporary struggle of the self . . . emblematic of the therapeutic self, of the subjectivity at the heart of our modern therapeutic culture" (Little 1999:11). Little noted that Diana's death brought out unexpected reactions in a variety of people, who identified strongly with the mourners as "griefs tend to run together, the death of one person . . . reviving our sorrow for another" (1999:11). But Little points out there were different kinds of mourners. "True" mourners were contrasted with those who experienced "recreational grief" (1999:21), which was "enjoyable . . . [in that it] promoted the griever from the audience to an on-stage part in the final act of an opera . . . the dead heroine had provided the most marvelous story and the grief of her spectators may have been genuine in the sense of unfaked. But it was grief with the pain removed, grief-lite" (Ian Jack, cited in Little 1999:21–22). Hide's death, also an "accident," similarly reminded many of the fragility of life and the meaninglessness of fate. He, like Diana, burst on the scene suddenly, broke convention, made a lot of money and mistakes, but was considered sensitive and caring. Those who did not count themselves as hide fans were also fascinated as they reevaluated their own identification with the trappings of youth culture.

Some realized they had grown up and were saddened. Others admitted they had not: they were closer to the fans than they liked to think. While the media's manipulation of Diana's death attempted to unite the nation (and perhaps the world) in a kind of emotional solidarity (Myers 2000:183), hide's death and the reaction to it, objectified and displayed to others, was consumed for enjoyment but also for moral edification. While hide's fans wept before the cameras, non-fans also mourned, but in a more diffuse manner: "look what Japanese society has become!"

Wertheimer says, "Suicide is also a violent, often ugly act and a funeral which is made beautiful—whether by flowers, music, the support of friends, words that are spoken, or all of these—can help to counteract the survivor's more disturbing memories" (1991:97). At the time of hide's funeral, suicide had not been ruled out and the need to sanitize his death was great. His funeral was one of the largest public funerals in Japanese modern history with approximately 50,000 fans paying respects, and this massive demonstrated outpouring of emotion contrasted with the stereotypical image of modern Japanese society as logical and efficient. The young people pictured by the media were more concerned with emotions and interpersonal relationships—real ones between fans and perceived ones between fan and star—than with rational behavior exemplified in traditional Japanese social organizations (e.g., family, school, workplace, and community). A fan told me that she had quit her job the moment she heard of hide's death and rushed to Honganji, saying, "Why work when the only reason I toiled is gone? I earn money so that I can see hide [attend his concerts]. If I can't see hide anymore, there is no reason to work." A youngish mother of a 14-year-old told me, "Personally, I disapprove of all this. But I fear that if my daughter represses her feelings it will be unhealthy. So I am accompanying her to these places because I want her to get over it (*sukkuri suru*)." People touched by hide were willing to forgo social expectations, like the unemployed fan, because the stakes were no longer so high. Others, like the mother, were willing to bend rules precisely because the stakes were so high.

A weekly tabloid magazine printed a collection of messages from letters and cards left at the funeral that illustrate the fan construction of hide's saintly attributes: he is an angel watching over his fans (*mimamoru*); he appears to have sacrificed himself to the image, the music, and the success; and so on. These fan letters were so numerous that volumes of them were published soon after hide's death (e.g., Hattori 1998; Shirai 1998). This sampling of fan sentiments is instructive:

> Thank you [for your music]. I'll work hard so please watch out for me.
> I don't know what else to say but you were great. You worked too hard . . .

> Hide *chan*[10] will live forever in my heart. Please look after me from your spot in heaven . . .
> Naughty hide *chan* . . . Lonely hide *chan* . . . [*Shukan Josei* 1998b:30–33]

Rather than blossoming in material success, hide burned out psychologically, rejecting fame. This only served to heighten his spiritual presence (*Shukan Josei* 1998b:30–33).

Harvey Cox writes that despite the increasing secularization of society, the belief persists that "true holiness" can only be achieved through "extended periods of isolation and loneliness" (1984:79). To categorize it in this way, we need to understand the reasons for hide's death and place the person and his art in a cultural and historical context. However, fans could not objectify the incident, as hide was a large part of their subjective identity. How could they reconcile the gap between the image they loved and his unthinkable deed? His funeral represented the real "death of author." Who knows what hide wanted? Did he deserve this adulation? Was it all a media stunt? All that is certain is that hide's "dark night of the soul" was insurmountable and this transformed his life into a manipulated narrative for both youthful and middle-aged angst in this postmodern society.

NOTES

Although I spent two days at the funeral and interviewed several fans (and their parents), the bulk of useful information for this chapter came from television and popular magazine articles, not from my own ethnographic enquiries. At first I was disappointed in the fieldwork but gradually realized that the cameras were in more than one place at a time and what they saw was edited down to easily digested, action-packed visual bites. Furthermore, major network cameramen had access to press conferences that I could not hope to obtain. Learning more from TV than from actually being there made me realize how much reality is constructed by the mass media. My interviews were conducted at Honganji, Tokyo, on May 4 and 7, 1998.

1. All personal names are presented in Japanese customary order: family name first, personal name second. In Japanese, all vowels are pronounced as in Italian, so that the first part of Hideto, or "hide," is pronounced "hee-day." Also note that I have endeavored, where possible, to preserve the native romanization of musicians' names: as a member of X Japan, HIDE's name is written in capitals, as are those of all his bandmates; as a solo artist and after his death, he is referred to as "hide."

2. All translations are mine.

3. The band changed their name to X Japan in 1992 after signing with Atlantic Records in the United States.

4. Elsewhere a colleague and I make the argument against orientalist explanations

that the kabuki tradition contributed to the aesthetics of X Japan and other visual bands (Stevens and Hosokawa 2001:245).

5. The Tokyo Dome, the largest arena in the city, seats more than 56,000.

6. GM_1 gangliosidosis is an extremely rare condition. One course of treatment is bone marrow transplant.

7. Perhaps because of its samurai-influenced history, Japan has been termed a "suicide nation" (Pinguet 1993:14) by many industrialized nations that hold suicide to be a sin in a moral or religious sense. According to statistics, Japan's suicide rate is higher per capita than that of the United States but on par, approximately, with that of many European countries: "people are no more inclined to kill themselves in Japan than they are in the West: rather more than in France, maybe, but less than in Germany" (Pinguet 1993:14). The majority of suicides in Japan are committed by the elderly and middle aged with 75.9 percent of suicides in 2002 committed by people 40 years old or older (Keisatsucho 2003:2).

8. Over a year later, a radio announcer committed suicide in a similar fashion (using a necktie rather than a towel to string himself from the bathroom doorknob) and the Japanese tabloids called this a copycat hide suicide.

9. Studies in the United Kingdom show that heavy media coverage does appear to affect the number of copycat suicides, but "there is little evidence that such effects occur in isolation of other vulnerability factors" such as prior history of mental illness (M. Williams 1997:136–137); thus the media's direct role in imitation suicide is still unclear.

10. "*Chan*" is the diminutive form of the address "*san*" and implies a sense of intimacy.

10
Popular Culture Canonization

Elvis Presley as Saint and Savior

Erika Doss

August 16, 2002, marked the 25th anniversary of Elvis Presley's death. Despite pouring rain, some 40,000 Elvis fans gathered at Graceland, Presley's home and grave site in Memphis, Tennessee, and paid their respects in an all-night ceremony called the "Candlelight Vigil." Presley's tomb in Graceland's Meditation Gardens, a small plot of land where Elvis, his parents, and his paternal grandmother are buried and where his stillborn twin (Jesse Garon Presley) is memorialized with a bronze plaque, was piled high with gifts and tributes from fans, including bouquets of flowers, stuffed teddy bears, votive candles, photographs, records, trinkets, handwritten letters, and poems reading "From Graceland to the Promised Land/We followed you here/We will follow you there." During the vigil, fans held candles and listened to Elvis songs such as "If I Can Dream" and "How Great Thou Art" broadcast over loudspeakers; they also listened to the reading of Psalm 23 and joined in singing "Can't Help Falling in Love." Some fans queued for nearly 24 hours to pass through Graceland's gates and visit Elvis's grave; among the last to appear were Lisa Marie Presley, Elvis's daughter and inheritor of his estate, and her new husband, the actor Nicolas Cage. As one fan from Chicago put it, "This isn't a fascination. This is a love. A love forever" (Blank 2002).

Another fan who deeply loves Elvis is a former language and psychology teacher from Athens who in 1985 married a Greek-American and emigrated to Memphis to "be closer" to Elvis. "The day he passed away, it hit me like lightning," she recalls. "That very day I started making my arrangements, using the gold foil from cigarette packages, and decorating Elvis pictures. I feel so blessed that I can live in Memphis and do this. Elvis, his image, is so alive inside me."[1] This fan, whose Memphis apartment is covered with pictures and photographs of Elvis, spends every spare moment she can at Elvis's grave, honoring him with small portable shrines and handmade angels featuring images of Elvis.

Her image-making and grave-site rituals symbolize her deeply spiritual relationship with Elvis. A devout Catholic (raised Greek Orthodox), this fan does not worship Elvis but sees him as a man sent by God "to wake us up, to shake us, to ask us, what are we doing, where are we going?" She views Elvis as a mediator, an intercessor, between herself, and between other fans, and God. As she says, "There is a distance between human beings and God. That is why we are close to Elvis. He is like a bridge between us and God." If, along with other fans, she imagines Elvis as a saint, she also sees him as a redemptive figure. "I believe in Jesus Christ and I believe in God," she remarks, "but Elvis was special. Elvis was in our times, he was given to us to remind us to be good." A servant of God and Christlike savior, Elvis brings this fan joy, intensity, pleasure, and purpose. "I don't go to church much now. I don't ask for anything else from God, my prayers have been answered," she says, acknowledging that her personal relationship with Elvis and the artworks she makes and the rituals she performs express that relationship and are the most meaningful cultural and social practices in her life (Harrison 1992:53, 68).

WHY ELVIS?

Why has Elvis Presley become sanctified as the central figure in what some call a quasireligion? Despite dying in 1977, Elvis remains everywhere: his image is seen on the surface of every conceivable mass-produced consumer item, his music is honored in multiple tribute concerts and greatest-hits re-releases, his life is dissected in endless biographies, art exhibitions, and documentaries. Contemporary folklore has it that the three most recognized words in the world are *Jesus, Coca-Cola,* and *Elvis.* Elvis fans are everywhere, too. Some belong to the 500 or so official Elvis Presley fan clubs that currently exist around the globe. Others habitually visit Graceland, making it the second most popular house tour in America (after the White House). Each year during the anniversary of his death, during Elvis International Tribute Week, Memphis swells as thousands of fans gather in grief and celebration around Elvis's grave, displaying a kind of emotional intensity and reverence that clearly intimates Elvis's popular culture canonization.

Indeed, comments like "it's a religious thing" dominate the discourse surrounding Elvis Presley's abiding presence in contemporary America and around the world. Eager to explain, and often to debunk, the emotional and collective behavior of Elvis's fans, many journalists and critics relate how Elvis "culture" has become a "cult." Some point out that Elvis's rags-to-riches life story and his tragic death neatly parallel the secular/sacred narrative of Jesus Christ, and they hint at the contemporary possibility of Elvis's own eponymous cult foundation.

Others cite a long list of quasireligious factors that seem to confirm Elvis's contemporary deification: how in the years since his death, a seeming Elvis religion has emerged, replete with prophets (Elvis impersonators), sacred texts (Elvis records), disciples (Elvis fans), relics (the scarves, Cadillacs, and diamond rings that Elvis lavished on friends and fans), pilgrimages (to Tupelo, Elvis's birthplace, and to Graceland), churches (including the 24-Hour Church of Elvis in Portland, Oregon, and many website shrines), and all the appearances of resurrection (with reported Elvis sightings at, among other places, a Kalamazoo, Michigan, Burger King). Ritualized fan activities that occur each August in Memphis during Elvis International Tribute Week further suggest how Elvis is increasingly perceived, desired, and constructed in religious terms.

Multiple scholars have probed the Elvis cult's Celtic, Gnostic, Hindi, and vodun derivations; contemplated Graceland's status as "sacred space"; and considered how and why some insist that Elvis, like Jesus, defeated death.[2] Less charitable writers cynically attribute the entire phenomenon to the highly successful mass-marketing techniques of his estate (Elvis Presley Enterprises, Incorporated) and to the susceptibility of an apparently passive public bent on real-world escapism through, especially, the "transformative" ideology of consumerism. "Explicit manifestations of 'Elvis Christ' did not exactly evolve," carps British journalist John Windsor (1992:33): "They were cunningly contrived for a mass market" (Stromberg 1990).

Easy explanations that Elvis's omnipresence and the devotion of his fans embody a cult or religion bring up all sorts of questions, including the issue of religious essentialism. What is it about the revered images, ritual practices, and devotional behaviors within Elvis culture that is essentially religious? Do these images and practices constitute the making of a discrete and legitimate religion? Why is it that *images* of Elvis, unlike those of most other popular contemporary figures, seem to have taken on the dimensions of faith and devotion, viewed by many Elvis fans as links between themselves and God, as ex-votos for expressing and giving thanks, as empowered objects that can fulfill wishes and desires?

These questions are complicated by the fact that most fans quickly dismiss intimations that Elvis is a religious figure or that Elvis images and Elvis-centered practices form any sort of Elvis religion. Such protestations may confuse Elvis's cult status: What does it mean when adherents deny the religiosity of something that looks so much like a religion? Yet their resistance warrants consideration. Some fans object in order to avoid charges of heresy or iconoclasm, because their religion forbids sacred status for secular figures, because seeing Elvis as a saint violates, for example, Protestant dogma. Still, most do so to avoid being ridiculed as religious fanatics. Fringe religions, moreover, are usually held up against the standards and values of mainstream religions, which means that most media accounts of Elvis's "cult" status frame his fans as abnormal outsiders whose faith does not follow institutionalized spiritual practices. Canny to their media marginalization, it is not surprising that many fans deny fidelity to any sort of Elvis cult or religion, suspicious of facile analyses that attempt to equate them with the Branch Davidians or the Japanese followers of Aum Supreme Truth.

Without discounting their objections, however, recognizing the following is important: from its "city on the hill" creation myth to present-day proliferation of New Age spirituality and the growth of fundamentalism, religiosity—mainstream and fringe—remains central to American identity and experience. As a profoundly religious people, Americans tend to treat things on religious terms, apply religious categories, and generally make a religion out of much of what is touched and understood. According to a 1980 survey, Americans "value religion" and maintain "strong religious beliefs" to far greater degrees than the citizens of any other Western industrial nation (Hatch 1989:210). In 1999, the Gallup Poll found that 96 percent of Americans interviewed "believed in God."[3] Yet, Americans tend to be predominantly private and diverse in their religious beliefs and practices. In fact, historian Nathan Hatch (1989:212, 218) observes that much of America's "ongoing religious vitality" can be attributed to the long-standing democratic, or populist, orientation of American Christianity: as "custodians of their own beliefs," Americans have traditionally shaped their religious practices to mesh with individual, rather than strictly institutional, desires.[4] It may be that when Elvis fans protest that their devotion to Elvis is not "religious," they are really objecting to an institutional definition of the term. In fact, their privatizing veneration of Elvis is one strong historical form of American religiosity.

My references here to "religion" are not meant as metaphorical flourishes, nor do I want to mitigate the reverence that many fans have for Elvis as a "kind of" religion. Religion makes up those practices and attitudes that imbue a person's life with meaning by linking him or her to a transcendent reality: that which is beyond purely immanent, or secular, experience and understanding. Assertions of affinity between religion and the generally privatized spiritual beliefs and practices of Elvis fans stem from their similarly supernatural, and inexplicable, character and authority. Collecting Elvis stuff, creating Elvis shrines, and going to Graceland are not, in and of themselves, religious acts and practices. However, they can become religious if they affect a transcendent and all-powerful order that can influence human affairs and is not inherently apprehensible.

CONSTRUCTING RELIGION

The issue of Elvis's place in America's democratic, diverse, and individually synthesized religious realms may best be considered by asking why so many Americans have come to place their faith in an image of Elvis. Why is Elvis an icon, and what does this reveal about how contemporary Americans visualize faith?

Examining how and why his fans have made him a figure of popular culture canonization, as well as how his iconic dominance is actually embedded in and extended from their religious beliefs and practices, may provide some answers.

Elvis was, of course—and remains—a profoundly charismatic figure, which clearly contributes to his popular, and perhaps religious, status (Figure 10.1). Mainstream religions are fronted by charismatic types (Jesus, Confucius, the Buddha, Muhammad, Joseph Smith), as are their cult counterparts (most recently Jim Jones, David Koresh, Shoko Ashahara). The diversity of Elvis's extraordinarily magnetic image, whether sexually provocative teen idol or jumpsuited superstar, has generated his appeal on many different levels for many different fans. But being charismatic does not automatically translate into reverential status: plenty of contemporary rock stars and sports figures are objects of adoration, but few sustain religious veneration. Elvis's religious import hinges on his multifaceted image, which is for many fans imbued with a certain mystical greatness and looked upon for access to a transcendent reality. It is long-standing, too. As early as 1957, some fans were trying to start an "Elvis Presley Church"; as recently as 1995, a St. Louis group (Congregation for the Causes of Saints) sought his canonization (Morin 1960:71–108; Pierce 1994:136). Most fans, however, prefer to commune with Elvis privately, in their homes.

The domestic sphere can be a safe haven from an unfriendly outside world, a sanctuary where fans can be with Elvis without drawing attention. Many fans have special rooms or areas in their homes especially dedicated to Elvis, which they describe as "quiet places" where they can think about and "be really close to Elvis." Some spend hours each day in their Elvis Rooms, listening to Elvis's music, watching his movies, looking at pictures of him in books and magazines. "I like to go to my Elvis Room, down in the basement, after supper," remarks one Roanoke fan. "It's a quiet space and time for me." Filled with Elvis stuff that she has collected since the 1950s, the room "helps to keep memories of Elvis alive." As places where secular thoughts and tasks are suspended, Elvis Rooms allow personal and private moments of contemplation and solitude. As places where fans spotlight their collections of Elvis stuff, they also speak to the ways in which material culture plays a major role in sanctifying and legitimizing Elvis as a special, important entity.

This combination of religious and commercial sensibilities in the American home is nothing new: in the 19th century, Protestants and Catholics alike linked religiosity with domesticity, creating a more sanctified home front with parlor organs, Bibles, and religious pictures and sculptures.[5] Filling special rooms, and sometimes whole houses, with Elvis paintings, plates, trading cards, limited-edition lithographs, watches, dolls, and all sorts of other mass-produced and handmade items, Elvis fans sacralize their homes in similar sorts of ways, using images and objects to declare their deep-felt devotion to Elvis. The ways they

Figure 10.1. Elvis, *Jailhouse Rock* (1957). (Library of Congress, Prints and Photographs Division, LC-USZ6-2067)

organize their Elvis Rooms reveal how they freely appropriate the look and feel of domestic religiosity to cultivate a reverential atmosphere in a secular realm. Whatever their religious affiliation, or lack thereof, Elvis fans choose patterns of visual piety that closely correspond to the home shrines that have long been a "vital part of domestic Christianity" for Americans of African, Irish, Italian, Latino, Polish, Portuguese, and many other backgrounds (McDannell 1995:275). From modest groupings of a framed religious motto and a few family photographs on top of a living room piano or TV set, to more elaborate assemblages of holy cards, votive candles, and school photos, home shrines sacralize domestic interiors. Uniquely coded by their primarily female makers, home altars integrate personal and sentimental items with more purely devotional offerings, thus blurring distinctions between the domestic and the divine.

The circulation of these Judeo-Christian visual and material traditions within Elvis culture is evident in the homes of many fans. Stepping into the Florida home of one fan, for example, is like walking into a private Catholic chapel, but in place of crucifixes, religious pictures, and reliquaries there are dense rows of neatly displayed Elvis posters, decanters, pennants, spoons, and plates. This fan calls her home a "memorial to Elvis" and calls Elvis her "guardian angel." She is a practicing Catholic and has special allegiance to Our Lady of the Miraculous Medal, but few Catholic religious items are displayed in her home. Born in 1942, she describes her father as an "abuser" who beat his wife and three children and kicked her out of their South Miami home at the age of 15. "All I had was my record player and my Elvis records," she recalls, "and I listened to them over and over." Married in 1967, her only child died at birth in the early 1970s; her second marriage, in 1982, lasted only six months. "I was alone and Elvis was there for me," she remarks. "Elvis has brought so much to me, and when he died I wanted to make sure his image wasn't mutilated. He gives me the boost to overcome the hurdles. Through him I know that things can be done."

For such fans, Elvis Rooms are creative means to help them cope with the difficulties and needs in their lives, refuges where they experience their feelings for Elvis privately, on their own terms. Judeo-Christian home shrines are similarly powerful forms of domestic piety, especially for the women who have traditionally made them. Generally excluded from public forms of religious leadership and expression, Christian women often use the domestic sphere to express their personal spiritual needs and desires. Home altars are one of these manifestations, both private religious endeavors and visibly conscious expressions of family relationships, traditions, and memories. By making them, women strengthen those relationships and traditions, their religious beliefs, and their own identities (K. Turner 1986). By blending the domestic and the divine, home altars nurture female and family spirituality and transform the private sphere into a powerful locus of religiosity. The look and feel of many Elvis Rooms suggest that various

Judeo-Christian traditions of domestic religiosity that allow believers to decorate their homes and venerate their chosen deities or holy figures in highly personalized ways appear to have been absorbed by many Elvis fans.

Elvis Rooms are also places where fans rehearse public expressions of devotion. Shrines, as William Christian comments in his study of relationships to the divine between communities and individuals in a small Spanish village, "are energy transformation stations—the loci for the transformation of divine energy for human purposes and the transformation of human energy for divine purposes" (1989:101). Many images, effects, and rituals that fans use in their homes to articulate their devotion to Elvis are repeated in the public sphere, especially at Graceland each August, during Elvis Week.

THE ROLE OF PILGRIMAGE

Pilgrims make their way to shrines, the sites of saints, sacred relics, or miracles. Generally enclosed and set apart from the secular world, shrines are wherever the special qualities of a holy person, thing, or event are "believed to be more concentrated" than anywhere else. In their study of contemporary Christian pilgrimages in Europe, Mary Lee and Sidney Nolan argue that a place becomes a shrine "if people think of it in that way and behave accordingly" (1989:13). Pilgrims visit shrines "in order to commune more intimately" with whomever (or whatever) is thought to be sanctified there (Nolan and Nolan 1989:36). As the Nolans further determined, pilgrimage sites are commonly marked by two conflicting features: centrally located, to attract and benefit the largest number of devotees, they are also often found in uncomfortable and hard to get to places (Nolan and Nolan 1989:291–292). A shrine's special or sacred character is enhanced, in other words, by the difficulties of pilgrimage.

Religious terms like *pilgrimage* and *shrine* are generally not part of the average Graceland visitor's vocabulary, and many fans might be offended if they heard these words used. Still, Elvis's estate has become the object of veneration for thousands of fans who visit it every year and for thousands more who wish that they, too, could go to Graceland. The homes and graves of other American icons and celebrities cannot compete with the powerful, magisterial, and transcendent image that fans give to Graceland, an image that plays a central role in Elvis's contemporary iconic status.

Set back on a hill and surrounded by fieldstone walls and white picket fences, Graceland is conceptualized by thousands of Elvis fans as an especially hallowed place whose every surface is charged with the spirit of Elvis. Going there, much more so than visiting Elvis's humble childhood home in Tupelo or taking a peek at the cramped Lauderdale Courts Apartments in Memphis, where the Presley family moved in the late 1940s, is a deeply significant, and generally formidable, act for most of them. Graceland itself is easily accessible, just a few miles from Memphis International Airport and near the crossroads of several major interstates. But the blistering heat and paint-stripping humidity of August make Memphis a hellhole during Elvis International Tribute Week. Going to Graceland is expensive: the average fan spends hundreds of dollars on travel, car rental, motel costs, meals, admission to the mansion, and souvenirs. Rarely impulsive, fan pilgrimages to Graceland are carefully planned journeys that usually entail months, if not years, of scrimping and saving.

Despite pilgrimage hardships, going to Graceland is the deepest desire of most Elvis fans. "My dream was to see him in concert and see Graceland," writes a fan from Chisholm, Minnesota. "Well," she adds, "one dream came true when my husband took me to Graceland on our honeymoon." Many fans try to go as many times as they can, hoping to partake of Graceland's spirit as often as possible. Graceland's significance, in other words, depends on the meaning Elvis's fans give it. As the focus of their pilgrimage, Graceland is special because they make it special: their beliefs and behaviors transform it from historic home to shrine. To be sure, Elvis Inc. facilitates their faith, eager to profit from Graceland's spiritual significance, but the fans themselves ensure its home shrine glory.

Of course, not everyone who goes to Graceland is an Elvis fan. As with any shrine, Graceland's audience is a blend of pilgrims and casual tourists—families on vacation, RV retirees, on-the-road college students. Still, however diverse this crowd might be, it is safe to say that most are drawn to Graceland, and drawn together, to try to come to terms with Elvis's abiding popularity. Their presence feeds the phenomenon—even the most ambivalent tourist who goes to Graceland to see why everyone else goes adds to Elvis's popular culture canonization.

That is not to say they all share the same insights about Elvis. During Elvis Week, especially, Graceland draws a diverse population not only of fans but also of journalists and documentary filmmakers in search of a good story about "the Elvis thing." Most fans resent the intrusion of "the media" and other outsiders into Elvis culture and onto their turf. Some are even suspicious of recently declared fans making their first trip to Graceland, eyeing them as "fake fans," as inauthentic wannabes who have not loved Elvis long enough. While Graceland brings many different people together, it may also see conflict as fans, tourists, reporters, and lots of other people argue over who Elvis was, what his image represents, and what (and who) accounts for, and profits from, his contemporary popularity.

For most fans, the desire to see and experience Graceland is akin to the desire to see and feel Elvis. From 1957, when he bought the "big house on the hill," to 1977, when he died in it, Elvis withdrew from the outside world inside Graceland's fences, escaping from the pressures of performing (he gave few live concerts in the 1960s), from the repetitious B-movie sets of Hollywood, and from the rapacious appetites of his fans. Touted as the authentically preserved stomping grounds of the real-life Elvis (although most fans seem to know that Priscilla Presley had the main house "tastefully refurbished" before its public unveiling in 1982), Graceland lends authority to Elvis's real time, 1957–1977, existence (Marling 1993, 1996). "I was on cloud nine walking around there, seeing in person how Elvis lived and played," writes one fan. "It's so hard to describe the feelings when you're there," another says, "to know you're in his home, walking where he has walked."

Resonant with Elvis—his possessions, his body, his spirit—fans go to Graceland to walk in his mansion, gaze at his things, mourn at his grave site, and be that much closer to the man they adore. Some leave things for Elvis: a tour guide who worked at Graceland in the mid-1980s recalls finding slips of paper tucked under vases or hidden behind curtains with messages like "Elvis, we miss you. Love, Bob and Marge." Others cannot resist the temptation to take a little piece of Graceland home with them, pocketing leaves, pebbles, sticks, and pinches of dirt as tokens of their pilgrimage and their brush with Elvis. Again, it is the stuff of material culture—here, Graceland and its relics—that is pivotal to the devotional practices and beliefs of Elvis's fans.

The house itself is not that remarkable: a pseudo-Georgian structure of about 4,500 square feet and a teeny guitar-shaped pool. If it is ironic that this mundane mansion has now become the most public house shrine in America, drawing well over 750,000 visitors a year, the fact that Elvis died and is buried there has a lot to do with it. Elvis was originally interred at Memphis's Forest Hill Cemetery, but after many reports of tomb break-ins, Vernon Presley had his son reburied at Graceland. It was a smart move. Contemporary Americans are increasingly drawn to the sites of tragic death (Doss 2002).

Mostly insulated from death and disaster, and discouraged from public displays of grief, people go to these places to see and touch real-life tragedy, to weep and mourn and *feel* in socially acceptable situations. As shrines, these places not only memorialize the horrible events that occurred there but also the feelings of visitors. Ghoulish fascination with inexplicable death—the death of unfortunates, the death of innocents—is matched by feelings of guilt and gratitude, with worries about personal responsibility, with thanks that we were not inside that federal building or high school. Similarly, however morbid it might seem to make the pilgrimage to the grave of their favorite American icon, Elvis fans go to Graceland to emotionally indulge themselves, to become overwhelmed by their feelings of love, loss, and loneliness for Elvis. Elated inside his house, many openly weep beside his grave.

Graceland's shrinelike sensibility is particularly evident during Elvis International Tribute Week, when fans engage in specific rituals such as touring Graceland, attending fan festivals and memorial services, watching Elvis impersonator contests, visiting Sun Studios near downtown Memphis, eating at local restaurants, and tagging their names on the fieldstone walls in front of Graceland. They spend much of their time buying Elvis stuff at the gift shops that surround Graceland. Fans at area motels participate in elaborate window decorating competitions; others submit pictures and crafts to the annual Elvis Art Exhibit held at the Graceland Plaza Visitor Center. Ordinary spaces—motels and restaurants, for example—become sacred spaces during Elvis Week, because Elvis fans occupy them and fill them with images and objects that they deem to have special significance. Simultaneously a shrine and a shopping mall, Graceland's multiacre complex is no different from other pilgrimage sites: from Lourdes to the Basilica of the Virgin of Guadalupe in Mexico City, devotional practices, material culture, and commercialism are typically mixed.

Elvis Week culminates in the all-night Candlelight Vigil on the anniversary of Elvis's death, when fans gather at the gates of Graceland and walk up the mansion's steep pathway to the Meditation Gardens for a brief, private tribute. Each solemnly bears a glowing candle, lit from a torch at the start of the procession. Once back down the driveway and outside Graceland's gates, they snuff it out. The tone of this ritual is clearly borrowed from traditional religious practices, from the ceremonial ambience of midnight mass services at Christmas to the precisely timed vigils at the Shrine of Saint Jude in Chicago, where candlelighting marks the beginning and the end of each pilgrim's devotional encounter (Orsi 1991:222). It also resembles secular-realm rituals, from the Bic-flicking encore summons at rock concerts to the lighting of the Olympic torch. For those who are unfamiliar with sacred or secular ceremonial behavior, Elvis Inc. provides some "special guidelines": "Please avoid loud talking or laughter or any behavior that might be offensive to, or unappreciated by those who take this tribute seriously. The Candlelight Vigil is intended to be a solemn, respectful tribute."

For most Elvis fans, the Candlelight Vigil is a hushed and somber ceremony, the cathartic moment of a highly emotional week. If rituals have special meaning because of their tangible and sensual qualities, this one is a particularly sensational ceremony. The sounds of cicadas, low murmurs, hushed cries, and Elvis's music, broadcast over strategically placed loudspeakers all over the mansion grounds; the visual spectacle of Graceland lit up at night, of flickering candles and a seemingly endless line of fans slowly parading up, then down, Graceland's serpentine driveway; the smells of wax, perfume, flowering magnolias, mounds of roses, and sweat; and, of course, the damp and steamy heat, made even more oppressive from standing in line pressed against tens of thousands of other fans for hours on end, all combine to make the Candlelight Vigil an especially spectacular ritual.

OFFERINGS

The special character of the Candlelight Vigil is further enhanced by the offerings that fans leave at Elvis's tomb, including flowers, photographs, pictures, dolls, toys, teddy bears, and records. A fan from Missouri often leaves tableaus at Elvis's grave, usually incorporating letters or mementos from other fans who cannot make the trip to Graceland. One, sculpted out of tinfoil, gift wraps, and plastic flowers, included a pledge of devotion from Ralf, a disabled 15-year-old fan from Germany. Some of these gifts, especially those that feature images of Elvis, are like ex-votos or *milagros*, made of tin and shaped like body parts (hearts, hands, feet). Commonly left at the shrines of saints or holy figures, ex-votos act as petitions or thanks for cures and healing (King 1992:103; S. Wilson 1983:21). Offerings of Elvis dolls and pictures that simulate his body or face and are placed in close physical contact with the spot where he is buried seem to have similarly powerful connotations for the fans who leave them at the Meditation Gardens.

These grave site gifts are expressions of gratitude and heartfelt thanks to Elvis from his fans. In a culture in which mourning often takes material form, offerings left at Graceland, especially during Elvis Week, help fans express their grief about Elvis's death. The images and objects that they place on Elvis's grave are the physically expressive focal points of their tributes to both his greatness and his absence and help atone for the pleasure he gives them, for the pain of his death, and for the sorrow of their loss.

"CHURCHES"

Other quasireligious manifestations within Elvis culture, too, such as the Elvis "churches," have sprouted over the past few years, including the First Church of Elvis ("pastored" by Doug Isaacks of Austin, Texas, since 1991). In 1996, the First Presleyterian Church of Elvis the Divine staged a widely publicized two-day "Elvis Revival" bent on "E-vangelizing" students at Lehigh University, in Bethlehem, Pennsylvania (Girardot 1996). The First Presleyterian, like most of these manifestations of Elvis divine, is mostly realized online—a click-in church of the cyberspace that, says the founder of Lotus software, Mitch Kapor, is the "great new spiritual frontier" (E. Taylor 1994).

Primarily the products of Generation X fans who recognize Elvis's vast spiritual appeal, these Elvis churches are more cynical than the home shrines and Graceland rituals of "authentic" Elvis fans. Such a distinction is facile, however, especially since the tricksters who organize these campy parodies of an institutionalized Elvis faith say that they are Elvis fans, too. A lot of time and energy is invested in producing "sacred" cyberspace Elvis texts and shrines, such as the

First Presleyterian's online "sermons" with weekly topics like "How to be Spiritually Correct" and "The Contract with Elvis." "Although I see all this as satire," says Isaacks, "Elvis may actually evolve into a major religion some day. Let's face it, it's no sillier than any other religion." Or as religious studies professor Norman Girardot (1997) comments, "The Presleyterians remind us [that] the seriousness of religion can only be rediscovered in relation to all of its glorious absurdity." Humor, jokes, and derision, after all, are all forms of participation and ways of mocking and celebrating at the same time.[6] Embedded in all of the quasireligious revelations of Elvis along the electronic highway, there lurks a true contemporary yearning for spiritual intensity and belonging.

People build shrines and make pilgrimages for religious reasons and because of deeply felt needs for meaning and enlightenment, in hopes of salvation or with expectations of spiritual satisfaction, and as tributes to special, sacred figures, things, or places. The burgeoning of Elvis home shrines, Elvis Week rituals, and Elvis cyberspace temples and texts suggests that Elvis culture has taken on the dimensions of religious faith and belief. The central component in this quasireligious construction is, of course, Elvis himself and the ways he is increasingly imagined as a special, wondrous, virtuous, transcendent, and even a miraculous figure. "Elvis was no god," his fans say repeatedly, but the ways they revere him suggest that he is often perceived as a saint and a savior, an intercessor and a redeemer. Devotion to Elvis dovetails with this contemporary religious blending—New Age spirituality, therapy, mysticism, and a host of New Religious Movements—particularly among Americans who have long made a habit of spiritual synthesis and reconfiguration. As one fan remarked, "I've got Elvis sitting on my left shoulder and God on my right and with that combination, I cannot fail."

A RELIGIOUS ELVIS

Not surprisingly, fans' understandings of Elvis's religiosity generally correspond to their own particular religious persuasions. Fundamentalist Christians say Elvis was "very religious" and cite his Pentecostal upbringing, his religious faith ("All good things come from God," said Elvis in 1956) (Steif 1956:3), and his various gospel albums (including *How Great Thou Art* of 1967). Other fans see Elvis as a New Age spiritualist, recounting his interest in alternative religions, mysticism, and the occult and pointing out that the book he was reading when he died was *A Scientific Search for the Face of Jesus* (about the Shroud of Turin). Recently, many fans have imaged Elvis as an angel—not a teen angel but a radiant personality appointed for spiritual service. He was the cherub of the month for a 1995 issue of *Angel Times*, a glossy magazine with the publishing philosophy that

"God's angels appear to all peoples of the world regardless of religion, race, culture" (Shamayyim 1995). Southern fundamentalist, supernatural New Ager, or rock and roll angel—fans make Elvis the religious icon they want.[7]

Understanding the faith that fans have in Elvis does not lend itself easily to deterministic models of cultural or historical analysis. Fans talk about the "wonder" and "mystique" of Elvis and repeatedly describe him as a "miracle." As one writes, "Elvis is an emotion that entails everything we are capable of feeling. It cannot be captured. It cannot be bought. You cannot draw it. You cannot write it. You cannot take a photograph of it. You can't even explain it. YOU HAVE TO FEEL IT—IT MUST BE FELT BECAUSE IT COMES STRAIGHT FROM THE HEART!!" "Popular ways of knowing" include the emotive, irrational, superstitious, and revelatory, and these are the ways that fans feel about Elvis and how they see him as a special and transcendent figure in their lives (Fiske 1993:181). Their faith in him is made "real" through the tangible stuff of material culture, through Elvis's image.

Some argue that materialist forms of Elvis's "deification" are only a facet of the American obsession with transformative consumerism. Elvis is an intercessor in this scenario, but he only mediates between his fans and their faith in consumption; collecting Elvis stuff and making Elvis shrines, in other words, may help fans construct meaning in their everyday lives but it mainly keeps them addicted to an ideology of buying things to feel better. Obviously, Elvis culture is thoroughly drenched in the world of consumerism, and fans readily admit that they "need" Elvis stuff to "take care" of Elvis and participate in his fandom. But such a view fails to take into consideration the ways in which fans rely on Elvis's image as an all-powerful, nonreferential, and largely incomprehensible transcendence. As such, Elvis's image does not simply prop fundamental beliefs in consumerism but raises the issue, as art historian David Freedberg writes, of the "deep cognitive potential that arises from the relations between looking—looking hard—and figured material object[s]" (1989:432).

Looking plays a large role in the formation and practice of religious belief or in the "identification of the *seen* with what is to be *believed*," Michel de Certeau (1984:187) argues. There is a plurality of visual pieties, as well, and different fans see Elvis in different religious roles (cf. D. Morgan 1998). Some see him as an especially integrative spiritual figure. One remarks: "Although I am a Christian, I have never experienced such unity in any form of worship. Elvis bonds us between nations, religions, and across all age ranges" (Young 1994:123). He was a "gentle man," writes one fan, who "never hurt us, but instead, left so much for us to enjoy." Still others see Elvis as a healer. In an especially poignant memoir, a fan from Duluth writes that her mother's long and painful bout with cancer was eased by her vast collection of Elvis memorabilia throughout her house: "In the final stages of illness, when she was heavily medicated on morphine, she often commented that the various Elvis's [*sic*] . . . were talking to her, comforting her."

CONCLUSIONS: ELVIS A "SAINT"?

Most religions make distinctions between a higher god (or gods) and lesser divines. In the Christian world, saints are seen as advocates, mediators, and intercessors between believers and the divine. Only Christ is viewed as a figure of salvation. Based on their comments and behaviors and the way they look at Elvis, it appears that many Christian Elvis fans, and even those who are not Christian, see Elvis as both a saintly mediator and a redemptive, Christlike figure. Blending religious archetypes, or simply mixing them up, fans liken Elvis to a spiritual intercessor whom they produce and personalize—in art and in ritual practices—as an instrument of therapeutic relief.

Admittedly, some fans say Elvis "was no saint," but these are often Catholic fans for whom the term *saint* strictly connotes a canonized figure who performed miracles and was especially virtuous during his or her lifetime—which Elvis, most fans agree, did not and was not. Others point out differences between religious beings and contemporary celebrities, but they ignore the way secular figures (from Eva Perón to Che Guevara) can become saints by way of shrines, pilgrimages, and popular veneration. Saints, as historian Stephen Wilson remarks, "belong to and reflect the societies which produce and honor them, and no one would expect late 20th century believers or nonbelievers to have the same saints necessarily as the contemporaries of St. Simeon Stylites" (1983:6–7). The fact that so many fans look upon Elvis's image as a source of protection and relief, and think of him as a special man who was "beyond human" and "bigger than life," suggests that they have extended sanctity to include the King of Rock and Roll.

Whether viewed as Saint Elvis or "alter *Christus*," Elvis is venerated and admired by many—more so than any other popular culture figure in contemporary America. Fans' understandings of Elvis as saint and savior follow from their imaging of him as a legendary entertainer, a down-home Southern gentleman, a patriot, a philanthropist, and a sad man who died alone—each image an amalgamation of Elvis fact and Elvis apocrypha. Some suggest Elvis be especially seen as a "permissive savior" who encourages his followers to indulge and consume and enjoy themselves. As much as fans find pleasure in Elvis's image and his music, it is pain, and the sense that through their devotion to him they can somehow ease that pain, that is most evident in their ritualistic behaviors during Elvis Week. Besides assassinated political figures, Americans have historically embraced few secular-realm martyrs. Elvis's pain and suffering, his drug-addict's death in a gilded bathroom, his failure to find happiness *despite* achieving the American Dream, may be what attracts so many of his fans, similarly caught up in pursuing the myth of the American Dream. They identify Elvis as a fellow sufferer, which may explain why the image of Elvis most loved by contemporary American fans, and most frequently evoked by his impersonators, is that of the Vegas Elvis, the "Late, Fat, Pain-Racked, Self-Destructive Elvis" (Gottdiener 1997:189–200). That image of Elvis embodies the pleasure *and* the pain of his devotees.

Elvis Rooms and Elvis Week rituals testify to the profound manner in which Elvis is understood by many fans as a revered figure of enormous capacity who mediates between them and their particular theological constructs. Images of Elvis, by extension, are understood by fans as icons with the explicit power to intercede between themselves and a higher power (a god). This works because images of Elvis are multifaceted, mercurial, and mysterious and because American religiosity is essentially flexible and democratic. On one level, then, fans place their faith in images of Elvis because they correspond to the personal mores and ecclesiastical self-image they desire. On another level, fans place their faith in images of Elvis because he provides a kind of "secular spiritual succor," because he both shares and can minister to their pleasure and their pain (Rosenbaum 1995:52).

For many fans, the authority of Elvis's image lies in its iconic ability to satisfy spiritual needs and respond to *personal* notions of contemporary piety. Many critics lump these essentially private constellations of belief and practice together, eager to construct cultish apparitions of an Elvis religion. However, no totalizing institutional religious paradigm is at work in Elvis culture. Instead, Elvis fans independently construct a series of cultural and social practices that both foster a sense of belonging and allow room for individual beliefs. Faith in Elvis neatly corresponds to abiding American needs for spiritual community and spiritual solitude, which makes Elvis a profoundly democratic American icon.

NOTES

This is a shortened and revised version of my chapter "Saint Elvis" in my book *Elvis Culture: Fans, Faith, and Image* (Doss 1999:69–113, 266–270).

1. Quoted in an author interview, August 14, 1995. Unless otherwise noted, all quotations from fans in the chapter stem from my interviews conducted in Memphis and elsewhere from 1993 through 1996 or from surveys of Elvis fans collected during 1996.

2. On these points see, for example, Ebersole (1994), Vikan (1994), Alderman (2003), Beckham (1987), and Fiske (1993:181–205).

3. See Gallup Poll analysis from April 13, 2001, at http://www.gallup.com/poll/releases/pr010413.asp; see also "Barna Poll on U.S. Religious Belief—2001," at http://www.adherents.com/misc/BarnaPoll.html.

4. On these points see Bellah et al. (1985:220–221ff), Hatch (1989:212, 218), and Roof (1993). Ideas of personal religious pluralism in complex industrial societies were first advanced in the works of Berger (1967) and Luckmann (1967).

5. These issues are discussed in McDannell (1986, 1995) and David Morgan (1998). On religious iconography in contemporary American Catholic homes see Halle's (1993: 171–192) analysis.

6. On similar forms of derision see Heinich (1996:129–130), Olalquiaga (1992:45–46), and G. Marcus (1991:74–85).

7. See also Moody (1987), Mallay and Vaughn (1992), K. Turner (1986), and Albanese (1981:318–320).

11
Saints and Health
A Micro-Macro Interaction Perspective
Walter Randolph Adams

The primary purpose of a concluding chapter is to reduce the information provided in the preceding chapters to a coherent framework. From this vantage, it is important to state two perspectives I bring to the assignment. The first is derived from micro-macro interaction theory. While this approach is most often associated with the relationship of some locality to a larger system, I believe it equally useful with respect to an individual (as locality) and an institution. A benefit of this approach is the encompassing of interaction between the smaller and larger entities as dialectic—dynamic and interactive (cf. Dewalt and Pelto 1985:4–5). The micro-macro analysis approach also allows for the observation that no two cults or sects, although responding to similar pressures, respond in identical ways (Smith 1977). Differential responses may be due, in part, to differences in the extent to which they, as "movements of religious protest" (B. Wilson 1970:7), seek to participate fully in the larger system.[1]

Micro-macro interaction perspective allows for the consideration that some individuals may participate more fully and energetically than others. It can be used to explain why some cults and sects continue to grow and develop into more complex organizations, such as denominations and churches (Stark and Bainbridge 1985:22), while others do not. A corollary is best demonstrated in the introductory chapter of my earlier work (Adams 2000:3) on the nexus of anthropology and theology, which states that it is critical that religions be meaningful to believers. This notion is important here because membership in a cult or sect provides believers an efficient means by which religion becomes meaningful. How believers do so, however, can take many different forms because the locus of religion is an "individual experience," as William James reminds us (in Macklin's chapter).

The second perspective comes from medical anthropology and the treatment of dis-ease. Such an approach is appropriate because nearly all of the chapters mention that the hero, icon, or saint is associated with healing in some way. Whether an individual was *actually* healed by participating in events or activities associated with a particular hero, icon, or saint is not important; the important issue is that the *follower* believes the dis-ease ebbed or disappeared by virtue of the hero, icon, or saint's intercession. This idea is analogous to that epitomized by the work of medical folklorists and anthropologists (Baer et al. 1998; Hufford 1988; O'Connor 1998) who stress that patients are more likely to continue the treatment recommended by the caregiver if it is consistent with their worldview.

THE BELIEVER

Passariello provides us a common vantage point with her definitions of hero, icon, and saint from her chapter on Che:

> Whereas a *hero,* and sometimes an antihero, is remembered as someone endowed with special traits of courage and strength and is respected for his or her noble pursuits, an *icon* is a person whose being becomes an enduring symbol of cultural specialness, often with a tinge of religion-like awe. To complete the related trio, a *saint* is an officially recognized, often institutionalized person who is entitled to public veneration beyond simple respect and admiration and who also may be someone who is capable of interceding with the cosmos—someone with not only special status but perhaps even special power.

Obviously a gradation exists between these classes of individuals.[2] However, what seems to make a difference is not necessarily what the individual did in his or her lifetime, but what their followers have done to elevate him or her to particular statuses. Adding to the complexity, as Macklin tells us, in the early history of the Church there were at least two types of saints—"red" and "white." However, they all have in common at least one element, as Macklin observes: all serve as *role models.* The primary difference among these categories is how much sanctity is ascribed to them by believers and, for official saints, who does the sanctifying. Still, as Hopgood states, "The sacred exists typically within religions, but the sacred does not require the frame of religion. The *sacred* . . . is a central concept in understanding what two such seemingly disparate phenomena as these [Fidencio and James Dean] have in common."

All of the personages described in these pages have been sanctified by their followers and at one level they may be regarded as sanctified role models. But it needs to be noted that the matter of degree of sanctification may be important etically but not emically, a point that Doss makes in her chapter. That is, a follower may consider the adored individual a "saint," while others may not hold that person in high esteem. In complex societies, cherished individuals, as role models, may come from a wide array of social venues and may be movie stars, rock singers, and other celebrities. The cases described in this volume attest that those who possess sufficient charisma are candidates for elevation by their followers and may attain superhuman qualities that place them close to the level of deities.

The Compact Oxford English Dictionary (*Compact OED*) provides an appropriate definition of a role model: "Someone who, in the performance of a role, *is taken as a model by others*" (1991:1606). The last part of the definition is italicized because it emphasizes that role models cannot be self-selected; they *must be* chosen by others. Importantly, they must be chosen by believers, not by institutions that may want people to believe in a particular person, a point to which I will return later.

Once a person has been chosen as a role model, that individual can easily achieve higher status (as exemplified by the cases in this volume) by virtue of social and political machinations by others. It does not take a great leap of faith to see how a "miraculous" cure of a follower from a condition that had defied treatment helps this transformation. In October 2002, such events helped the beatification of Mother Teresa and the elevation of Hermano Pedro Betancourt of Guatemala to sainthood.

It also seems that the ability to identify the demigod as someone with very human qualities, as is described in the chapters dealing with James Dean, Elvis Presley, HIDE, Che (epitomized by his asthma inhaler), Fidencio, and Evita, is important. This enables the adorers to better identify with the role model, providing ground for the belief that attainment of specific qualities or characteristics of the adored one is possible. The logic for this behavior may be that if an adorer recognizes in advance that the object of adoration is a saint or a god, the adorer may not strive for the culturally accepted patterns of excellence because such goals are seen as unattainable.[3]

As suggested by the volume's contributors, another transformation occurs: it appears that the adored one's frailties ebb in importance after death or in the view of later generations of believers. It is still the case, however, that although the individual is portrayed as a human, the individual's specific qualities are presented and re-presented in fables, legends, myths, and other narratives. All these describe qualities deemed important by that culture, and the purpose of them is to instruct the listener to emulate those qualities. The stories told about the hero, icon, or saint inform the listener about these qualities and the qualities deemed important by the storyteller. Passariello makes an important point: "it is in the particulars of the narrative and how it builds that a hero grows and, perhaps, how the saint is made. And we can find cross-culturally repetition and constancy to the patterns of the structure and of the morphology of the stories, even if the details expressed, the culturally specific values, change with time, place, and culture." One result of the repetition and constancy of patterns manifested in the narratives is their transformation into a form of a liturgy, meaning "a form of public worship . . . a collection of formalities for the conduct of Divine worship" (*Compact OED* 1991:355). I will return to this below, because in many regards the development of a liturgy is a function of institutions, not of believers.

I want briefly to note a trait mentioned by Lord Raglan (1934) found in the biography of everyone considered in this volume: that little is known about the individual's early life (sometimes including who the parents were). This quality has the same function as having the founding clan ancestors in many Native American cultures be mythological nonhumans (Bears, Wolfs, Storks, etc.). It imbues the individual with an aura of unknown, perhaps mysterious, origins. Such ambiguity aids the addition of supernatural qualities and thus elevates her or him to the level of a deity. *How* the transformation occurs varies by culture; what does not vary is the fact of the transformation.

THE BELIEVERS

It is at the group level that the religious energy emanating from each person creates a force much greater than would be expected otherwise. Macklin observes this occurred with St. Margaret: "once the collective memory of her having been embalmed was lost, secular knowledge was transformed into sacred incorruptibility." The central issue now is how individual followers become part of a collective group in spite of the wide range of variation the objects of adoration may manifest, especially when, as Macklin observes, the "multivocality of the star/icon image" derives from their ambiguity. How does this ambiguity enable their acceptance by a wider audience? The volume's authors identify three important elements underpinning this transformation that deserve consideration: the child-parent relationship, the patient-healer relationship, and the impact exerted upon the individual by major change in the cultural system.

The Child-Parent Relationship

Stengs mentions that King Chulalongkorn's devotees place themselves in a childlike position in the child-parent dyad with the king. Bosca also states that Evita's role "was that of mediation between her husband . . . and the masses: she took the typically feminine and maternal role of protecting her 'children' from the harshness of the father and of obtaining benefits for them." The other authors do not make this point; it is, however, logical that it may occur in other cases as well.

Should the institution have a "clergy" (however defined or understood), those individuals function very clearly as parents and manifest this role when they provide what can be considered "religious instruction" to followers.[4] Where there is no group formally identified as clergy, the object of devotion may become like a "parent" because there is no intermediary. Then, information obtained from other sources—whether it is other followers, published literature, or something else—becomes especially important.

The implication of this is obvious. By placing themselves in the position of a child with respect to the adored individual, believers are more willing to accept instruction or example in how to better themselves by following the directives of their role model. Each devotee becomes a "brother" or "sister" to all other devotees in the same sense that Christians are "brothers" or "sisters" in Christ. Fictive kinship always assists in the development of relationships between otherwise unrelated individuals. It also reduces the friction that behavioral particularities may cause.

The Patient-Healer Relationship

A pattern that does not appear in Lord Raglan's list of 22 qualities of venerated persons is the individual's ability as a healer. Sometimes, such as with El Niño Fidencio and Teresa Urrea, it has led believers to believe them to be saints; in others, the adored person is equated with a saint (as with Evita) or a god (for King Chulalongkorn). I mention this cautiously, however, because there are two cases in which the healing connection is extremely weak (Che and HIDE) and it is nearly nonexistent in another (James Dean). When I asked Passariello to comment on Che as a healer, she responded:

> Che was actually trained as a medical doctor for many years, [and] was in his fourth year of medical school when he got a male nurse certificate and signed on as a "ship doctor" for several months. . . . [He] received an Argentine medical certificate in 1953 . . . and he interned for a while at a Mexican hospital.
>
> He did work on allergens because of his horrible asthma—he wanted to find a cure—[it was a] very serious affliction throughout life [and] it was part of his identity. Devotees know this, and appreciate his triumph over this physical adversity—his inhaler is on full display in the Che museum in Cuba . . . [and in the museum] he is called a dentist and his dental tools are shown. [e-mail communication, October 8, 2002]

Passariello also notes that he practiced as a "dentist" among the guerrillas during the early days of the revolution. This suggests that Che was a healer. The extent to which this quality is integral to his allure, especially since his death, is yet an unanswered question.

HIDE was asked to visit a fan suffering from GM1 gangliosidosis. Stevens states that the patient's mother attributed her daughter's recovery to HIDE's intervention, which is possible because he signed up to participate in the marrow donor program and encouraged his fans to do similarly. Whether *his* marrow was used to cure the girl is unknown and not particularly relevant. What is important, though, is the extent to which other fans share the mother's belief that HIDE cured her daughter, because the recognition of his intercession by a group of followers may be the catalyst necessary to transform his fan club into a sect. This transformation could occur if his call to participate in bone marrow donation programs took on a philosophical tenor, thereby providing "religious instruction."

As for James Dean, Hopgood does not discuss the issue of Dean as a healer in his chapter. Elsewhere, however, the notion of therapy is apparent (Hopgood 1998b:107). Also, when I asked him to comment on this, he responded:

> Many Deaners have told me of being "helped" with their personal problems and dilemmas by Dean. I hear things like "he [Dean] would understand what I feel." It seems that "getting close" or "closer" to Dean is helpful in the process, at least based on what they say on visiting Fairmount. They can get closer to him in Fairmount. . . . Much of this is therapeutic and not always in the "healing" sense; rather it is a renewal of the spirit. The healing and the self-therapy seem to go hand in hand, but I suppose renewal can be a form of healing. I have heard of a case or two of physical healing, but I have not been able to confirm these. [e-mail communication, September 25, 2002]

Renewal, or any other form of "therapeutic relief," is a form of healing, as anyone who has stayed at home to rest under a doctor's orders knows. As a result, the patient-healer connection may not be as much of a stretch as it might otherwise appear, even for James Dean.

The stretch is reduced even further when one considers the role that desperation (which can be seen as a form of mental distress and, therefore, dis-ease) has in the contributions. Many chapters mention that desperation is a factor that compels a person to seek relief from the adored personages. Such is the case, for example, when Bilu refers to Rabbi Yaakov Ifargan's weekly performances as "deftly concocted and professionally marketed performances, palatable to the New Age sensibilities of young, spiritually deprived Israelis." Stengs quotes one of the king's followers as saying "those who worship King Chulalongkorn feel desperate." Such comments point to the conclusion that the object of devotion is a healer of some sort, whether somatically or psychologically.

The central focus must be the adorer: if that person is afflicted by any condition, whether psychological (which often has somatic manifestations) or somatic, that no other source of treatment—whether the established medical or the established religious system—has been able to cure, that individual will seek another way to get rid of the dis-ease. Today, perhaps more than ever, it is likely that alternative sources of health care—whether chiropractic, acupuncture, aromatherapy, or something else—will be sought. Turning to a hero, icon, or saint is to be expected. Faith healing is an option used by many people.

One could argue that the perspective presented here requires a leap of faith. However, the central issue is not whether outsiders believe an adored individual effected a cure but whether the *adorer* believes so. From this perspective, whether Che, James Dean, and HIDE are perceived as healers, etically, and *actually* did cure patients by virtue of their intervention is not the issue. After all, it is established that most conditions that afflict human beings will go away without professional medical intercession. As mentioned above, the only reason the issue of whether the adored individual *actually* healed people may be important is that it might help better distinguish cults from sects. This is because the attribution of healing often entails a philosophy (for example, acupuncture, aromatherapy, and others), as is eloquently stated in the following passage:

> Conceptions of disease, disease causality, and treatment are embedded in complex and coherent systems of thought and action that are articulated . . . with larger cultural world-views. Healing systems include bodies of knowledge production, evaluative processes, definitions and categories of health and illness, explanatory models of disease etiology and human function, theories relating cause and nature to preventive and therapeutic choices, specific repertoires of diagnostic and therapeutic actions and *materia medica*, generalist and specialist practitioners and the means to their training and legitimation, self care modalities, and generative principles for formulating system-consistent responses to new input. [O'Connor 1998: 146–147]

Even this, however, may occur only when many followers attribute the alleviation of their complaints to the intercession of the adored individual and they agree on a specific philosophy. Whether the transformation occurs or not may have little impact on the behavior of individual followers. It might, however, be another impetus for others to become followers of the adored individual.

The Role of Cultural Upheavals

A third element that contributes to bringing individual devotees together in search of some relief for their desperation is difficult times. Periods of substantial social and economic change appear to be critical for the elevation of a role model to higher stature. This interpretation is brought out clearly in many chapters. For example, both Teresa Urrea and El Niño Fidencio emerged during the period surrounding the Mexican Revolution; Evita also emerged in the context of economic change in Argentina; King Chulalongkorn, when Thailand was responding to the threats of colonialism; Che Guevara, when all of Latin America was trying to break away from the colonial domination of the United States. Similarly, James Dean, HIDE, and the rabbis Baba Sali and Ifargan became venerated figures when the United States, Japan, and Israel, respectively, underwent periods of major economic growth and the younger generations sought empowerment. Thus, if people were not seeking relief for a psychological or somatic ill, they did seek relief from social uncertainties regarding which there were few to turn for guidance.

INSTITUTIONS: FAN CLUBS, CULTS, AND SECTS

To this point, the focus has been on the individual or groups of individuals who have joined together to venerate a particular person. The chapters in this collection suggest that the longevity of belief in the adored individual depends, at least in part, on the extent to which formal institutions are constructed to perpetuate their memories. As demonstrated in this volume, some attempts have been successful and others have not.

Once adorers become aware of others like themselves, however, they may develop loose-knit organizations, such as fan clubs. Elvis fan clubs are legion, of course, and James Dean fan clubs exist as well. Stevens's chapter on HIDE does not directly refer to a fan club, but it is implicit in her discussion of his fans that such clubs, organized around popular entertainment celebrities, are common today in Japan.

Cults and sects are the next steps in organizational complexity and each is characterized by more structure than fan clubs. Stark and Bainbridge differentiate cults and sects in the following terms:

> Both cults and sects are deviant religious bodies—that is, they are in a state of relatively high tension with their surrounding sociocultural environment.[5] . . . To be a sect, a religious movement must have been founded by persons who left another religious body for the purpose of founding the sect. . . . Cults . . . do not have a prior tie with another established reli-

> gious body in the society in question. The cult may represent an alien (external) religion, or it may have originated in the host society, but through innovation, not fission. [1985:25]

Later Stark and Bainbridge state, "Many . . . cult movements function much like conventional sects" (1985:29); thus the separation of cults and sects may be difficult to establish. As Macklin notes, "The processes of modernization and democratization and the decline of organized religion along with postindustrial consumer capitalism have created a plethora of bereft, self-absorbed individuals, hungering for meaningful symbols and self-transcendence." This situation provides perfect conditions for the emergence of alternative forms of religious expression. Nowhere is this more clearly evident than among white women in Western culture, who have been clearly alienated from the Catholic Church (Douglas 2000) and other established denominations, which has been a primary stimulus for the feminist spirituality movement (Hariot 2000). Doss makes this point when she writes, "Generally excluded from public forms of religious leadership and expression, Christian women often use the domestic sphere to express their personal spiritual needs and desires." Similarly, Macklin implies the reason Pope John Paul II has canonized 63 percent of the women of the roster of saints may be that this is an attempt to entice women back to the Church by recognizing role models that could serve as a beacon for women.

The Compact OED defines cult to be "devotion or homage to a particular person or thing, now *especially* as paid by a professed body of adherents or admirers" (1991:374), while a sect is "the system or body of adherents of a particular school of philosophy" (1991:1695). Perhaps more poignant to the issue here, the same source also defines a sect as "a school of opinion in politics, science, or the like." Under strict definition, therefore, cults may be more generalized in that they pay homage to individuals for whatever reason—whether they are rock or movie stars, political figures, or something else—whereas sects focus attention on a particular philosophy or theology.

This difference may be important when one considers the consequence that healing has in the elevation of individuals. As mentioned above, healing is a philosophical construct. In fact, the proliferation and widespread acceptance of non-Western healing traditions such as acupuncture, aromatherapy, and chiropractic have been attributed to the rejection of Western biomedicine. Much has been written espousing the idea that patient acceptance of the treatment provided hinges tremendously on the extent to which the caregiver and the patient share the conceptions of what the disease is, what causes it, and how it is to be treated (viz. Baer et al. 1998; Hufford 1988; O'Connor 1998).

Some may believe a wide chasm exists between fan clubs associated with celebrities or other stars and cult and sect organizations. I believe the chasm can be spanned easily. In fact, I see very little difference between a fan club and a cult. The latter may be associated more with religious fervor as opposed to something initially more secular. In this regard, it is critical to recall the very close relationship between health (secular) and religion. If some followers believe that they were healed by participating in a particular activity or going to some museum, shrine, or other institution associated with their role model, hero, or icon, the chasm between a fan club and cult has been bridged. Again, whether they were healed etically is not important.

While this is the case for somatic diseases, the case can be made that the same holds for psychological conditions. It is possible to see why a person, suffering from psychological distress resulting from rapid or stressful culture change, might regard a particular hero, icon, or saint as the means to salvation that cannot be provided by any other caregiver. This is the rationale given by many patients who turn away from Western biomedicine and toward alternative health therapeutic traditions, including faith healing.

REFLECTION

What emerges, then, from considering the difference between a cult and a sect appears to be simply a matter of the complexity of organization. While some previous chapters (especially Hopgood's treatment of the Deaners) may be clear examples of cults because they are less formally organized, the other cases described in this volume are not so easy to place. What about the case of Fidencio described by Macklin, Murray, and Hopgood and that of the two rabbis presented in Bilu's chapter? What is to be made of cases where there are particular centers of worship (such as mausoleums and burial sites) and pilgrimages? Perhaps the only reason these manifestations have not been recognized as religious sects by the outside world is that the adored are generally not seen as deities. This does not seem to have deterred the *fidencistas,* who call Fidencio a saint. Perhaps the followers of Baba Sali and Rabbi Ifargan have done something similar, as have the followers of Che, Evita, and James Dean, even if they do so only secretly. These questions point to the possibility that cults and sects are endpoints of a single continuum, as Bryan Wilson (1970:35) suggested many years ago.

Would an observer group the cases of Evita, Che, King Chulalongkorn, and Baba Sali and Rabbi Ifargan separately or together? While it is undoubtedly the case that Evita, Che, and King Chulalongkorn were political figures, it is also the case that their admirers have placed them on the level of deities. While Baba Sali and Rabbi Ifargan are indisputably men of religious background, and thus their organizations are more clearly examples of religious sects, it is equally clear their elevations to this status are also products of political machinations.

Although etically the terms *cult* and *sect* may be used to define a religious group "in jest" (as indicated in the *Compact OED* [1991] definition of a sect), ask a Sunni and a Shiite or a Protestant and a Catholic whether the difference between their religious perspectives is a jesting matter and a battle royal may follow. Untold numbers of deaths have resulted from such differences. As a result, to avoid getting into a quagmire, I prefer the concept "institution" to relate to each organization described in the preceding chapters.

THE NEXUS OF INDIVIDUALS AND ORGANIZATIONS

Passariello refers to two concepts that now become important: *liminality* and *communitas* (V. Turner 1967). Both are also integral to van Gennep's (1960) classic description of the ritual process. Liminality is a period of reflection during which the participant in a ritual juxtaposes "the categories of event, experience, knowledge with pedagogic intention" (V. Turner 1967:106). During this process, the member becomes "as one with" the image being adored. As mentioned previously, because the member, by virtue of worshiping the image, places himself or herself in a childlike position relative to that image, it follows that any other individuals doing the same thing place themselves as brothers or sisters to any other adorer. In so doing, communitas comes into operation.

Because of this condition, the extent to which an organization is constructed around an image and can manipulate this social fact seems critical to whether the image is worshiped for a long period or merely is a flash in the pan. The level of organization also relates to the catchment area (whether the image is relatively local, as in the cases of Teresa Urrea and Fidencio, or national and international, as with King Chulalongkorn, Evita, and Che) and the range of individuals attracted to it—whether they are members of a particular class or sector (as with Evita and James Dean), a particular ethnic and socioeconomic group (for Teresa Urrea and Rabbi Ifargan), a particular loosely defined group, such as "disillusioned youth" (as with Rabbi Ifargan and Che), or individuals suffering from a particular psychological or somatic malady (for Fidencio).

It is in this context that pilgrimages, rituals, memorabilia, relics, museums, and mausoleums come into play. These events, things, and places must be maintained by some sort of organization. As Doss observes (citing Nolan and Nolan), "a place becomes a shrine 'if people think of it in that way and behave accordingly.'"

Many of the authors agree that purchasing memorabilia, going on pilgrimages, and visiting shrines and other places associated with the icon or saint serve to bring the individual to the conception of "being there" with the hero/icon/saint and then to the re-creation and/or re-presentation of history by the participant. As Doss observes, "Collecting Elvis stuff, creating Elvis shrines, and going to Graceland are not, in and of themselves, religious acts and practices. However, they can become religious if they affect a transcendent and all-powerful order that can influence human affairs and is not inherently apprehensible."

As Macklin observes, the relating of one's experiences to, during, and from their visit to the "*sacred space* in which the saintly one lived and worked" and the purchase of icons, memorabilia, and relics have the impact of uniting the member with his or her role model and imbuing the member with authority and prestige, if not a little sense of immortality or another desired or important quality. By virtue of "being there" with others who think, believe, and act like oneself, the pilgrim becomes a member of a larger community (via communitas) made up of others sharing similar values, beliefs, and sentiments. This is a healing process in the same way that membership in Alcoholics Anonymous is a healing process; indeed, the whole ritual of saying, "Hi, my name is ——. I am an alcoholic," then getting the response "Hello, ——," begins the process of healing for those for whom it works (Steffen 1997).

The Alcoholics Anonymous ritual is important to the ideas provided here for another reason, too. How and why a person becomes an alcohol abuser is as varied and complicated as how and why a person becomes a follower of an icon or saint. A consequence of the repetition of the Alcoholics Anonymous ritual is that, over time, the individual's story becomes more similar to those of the others (Steffen 1997). If the goal of the ritual is to integrate the person into the group, it becomes incumbent that the uniqueness of the individual's transformation becomes similar to that of others; otherwise, the emphasis will be on the uniqueness of the situation, which will keep the individual apart from the others. In short, communitas cannot occur if the focus is only on individual differences.

ORGANIZATIONAL TEMPORAL CONTINUITY

Communitas is critically important if an institution is to survive more than one generation. While memorabilia and visiting shrines and other places are important at the individual level, they take on added importance in the continuation of the organization from one generation to the next. Obviously, one function that institutions fill is to make these items available and otherwise see that other needs believers have are satisfied. As Bilu and Newell show, however, a fine line exists between achieving this goal and "manufacturing charisma," which, as Bilu mentions, is strained and fragile. Newell's chapter on Teresa Urrea provides an especially clear example of just how fragile "manufactured charisma" can be:

> Analysis of the remaking of Teresa Urrea as a Chicana counterpart to Guadalupe confirms that saints are the products of ongoing processes of

> selective traditions and illustrates how the construction of social memory and of a saint reflects present interpretations, needs, and political practices. . . . How Teresa failed to function as Chicana saint demonstrates the complex and multifaceted mechanics of selecting and constructing traditions and mnemonic figures. . . . La Santa de Cabora, reconstructed cognitively in academia to serve the Chicano community as Chicana saint, had no audience to receive, appreciate, or celebrate her. . . . [S]he could not be connected to a popular, public domain . . . [and] fell on deaf ears, unmade.

"Manufactured charisma" seems to be particularly fragile and strained if the institution's leaders emphasize values that prove to lack meaning to potential followers. Newell shows how the demise can occur quickly. Bosca (in a letter cited below) reveals that Evita's cult began to die in the 1970s and it continued to fade into the 1990s, yet it still survives after a fashion.

The administrative organization seems to be an important element. Unfortunately, very few of the preceding chapters focused attention on this feature, contributing greatly to the issue of whether they should be considered cults, sects, or denominations. An important difference is that the hierarchies described by Bilu, Passariello, and Bosca seem to be closed and rigid, while that described by Murray is not.

What accounts for this difference? Can it be that the society in which the veneration of the rabbis occurs, for example, is much more highly centralized and hierarchical than is the local society of northern Mexico, or is there another factor or set of factors that contribute to this difference?

The failure of an institution to deal with this issue may contribute in great measure to its ability to last more than one generation. The irony is that Bilu suggests the succession of leadership was an important feature to the perpetuation of the veneration of the two rabbis, while Murray suggests that it was not for the *fidencistas*. Indeed, if it were, mechanisms would have been in place to deal with factional schisms and other problems. Yet, it seems that the *fidencistas* (and the Deaners) have survived more than one generation, whereas others have not. Murray also deals with an issue not mentioned in the other cases, which bears on the institution's ability to continue for at least another generation:

> The search for new *materias* also initiated a slow and still incomplete process of gender change in the movement's leadership. In the years immediately after Fidencio's death, mediumship was exercised almost entirely by women. This gender transformation is facilitated by the androgynous characteristics attributed to El Niño, but it does give women a male identity when they are possessed by El Niño's spirit. In fact, the empowerment be-

> stowed by *fidencista* trance possession is still one of the few sacerdotal roles open to women in Mexican society and points out another key difference with the official Catholic Church. . . .
>
> . . . [T]he search for new Niños . . . centers on young men, many of whom would be considered effeminate by usual Mexican standards. . . . If a new Niño were found, it would make the present leadership obsolete by replacing the historic Fidencio with a new apostolic tradition based on the spiritist idea of reincarnation. It would also emphasize precisely those ideological elements of *fidencismo* most alien to orthodox Mexican Catholicism.[6]

How have the other institutions considered in this volume dealt with this stressor?

LEVEL OF RECOGNITION

One undercurrent evident in this volume concerns the level of recognition of the institution dedicated to the memory of a particular individual. The previous chapters, however, provide two alternative perspectives on this issue: the first is that, as Macklin writes, "the ambiguity of sanctified stars' images offers alternative, sometimes rebellious, models of behavior to their audiences." The absence of state recognition and support may be precisely what followers seek. On the other hand, some chapters clearly show that the state is (or was) involved in maintaining the memory or adoration of the individual. This is clearly the case for King Chulalongkorn, Che Guevara, and Evita. These chapters suggest that if the state is involved in the perpetuation of the memory of a particular individual, there may be greater likelihood that the catchment area will extend to the nation (as with King Chulalongkorn and Evita) or worldwide (like Che Guevara).

Just as the involvement of the state can have an influence in the elevation of an adored individual from role model to hero to icon or saint, it can have an influence on the individual's demotion, too. This idea came out clearly in a letter Bosca wrote in response to a question regarding the current state of the institution honoring Evita, which I have translated and provide here:

> There is no visible cult to Evita today. There is no sanctuary to her, although the day of her death is recognized with various activities and visits to her tomb. . . . Yet today, in the homes of the poor, one can still find her portrait, although less frequently than in the past. Her figure is so strong in Argentine history that she continues to be a myth.
>
> I believe that the cult to Evita has declined in recent years until it has

> almost disappeared. However, I also believe that so many people still worship her that she has acquired the level of a myth. The decade of the 1970s saw a renaissance of Peronismo, and consequently the resurgence of the Evita myth. . . . The Montoneros, a guerrilla group inspired by Peronismo, revived her memory with a new version of the myth, which disappeared along with the disappearance of that organization. [e-mail communication, October 8, 2002]

Sponsorships by less wide-ranging institutions seem to result in a more limited catchment area. This is clearly the case in the examples of the two rabbis, Teresa Urrea, HIDE, and Fidencio. HIDE poses an interesting case that does not appear to conform to this general pattern. He is recognized by many in Japan, where his appeal seems to be largely found among youth who are attracted to certain elements of Western-inspired culture and music.

Another element that provides an undercurrent, and related to the general issue of level of recognition, is the opposition of the Church to many of the individuals. Bosca (on Evita), Macklin and Murray (on Fidencio), and Newell (on Teresa) make it clear that these personages will not be considered candidates for sainthood by the Church because they either failed to do magnificent works for the Church or held definite anticlerical positions.

A question of some significance involves the extent to which a lack of official sainthood status for Fidencio and Evita is important. If it were greatly important, people would not participate in the institution's activities and rituals, and purchase memorabilia, or make pilgrimages. To be sure, while official recognition might serve as a deterrent for others to become followers, lack of it may have just the opposite effect: people might become members precisely because the individual is "a rebel." The "rebel" image of Dean and the revolutionary or anticlerical positions of Teresa Urrea, Fidencio, Evita, and Che are cases in point. One can make the same argument for Jesus Christ, who advocated a philosophy counter to that espoused by the state and was crucified for sedition.

CONCLUSIONS

Considered from a perspective of micro-macro interaction, we see the worshiping of adored individuals—whether heroes, icons, or saints—is a dynamic and stimulating interaction involving particular adorers, groups of adorers, and the institutions of which the individuals are a part. Whether the object of attention is a role model, a charismatic leader, a hero, an icon, or a saint seems to depend primarily on the extent to which the follower believes, or a group of followers believe, the adored person satisfies his or her needs (the micro level). The extent to which institutions evolve to facilitate that satisfaction (the macro level) becomes important primarily regarding the follower's continued belief in the adored or sacralized person. From the perspective of an individual believer, it seems to make very little difference whether that institution is a fan club, a cult, a sect, or a denomination.

The irony, however, is that as institutions become more rigid in their positions, increasing numbers of individuals may dissociate themselves from those institutions. This idea is perhaps best observed in the inability, reluctance, or lack of interest by the Roman Catholic Church in modifying its tenets concerning women as priests (Douglas 2000), homosexuality, and clergy who sexually molest minors. The inability to find a place within the context of established churches and denominations is a primary reason for the rise of the feminist spirituality movement (Hariot 2000). Such individuals, then, may find relief in organizations that, by virtue of being smaller and more loosely organized, are more open to their needs. Whether the relief they seek is from somatic or psychological dis-ease or is due to major societal changes makes little difference.

Pressures exerted by society can have an impact on the extent to which the institution may grow. This occurs no matter the type of institution. If the institution espouses behavior contrary to that accepted by the society—as with satanic cults—it is conceivable that the institution may disappear completely or go underground. To the extent that the institution can survive these pressures—perhaps precisely because the adored individual is perceived as a rebel—the institution may continue. Believers may continue to practice the rituals, go to common shrines, and otherwise engage in what Victor Turner might regard as liminal practices that contribute to communitas and thereby unite them to other followers. As long as the organization meets the needs of followers and attracts others as earlier cohorts die out, the institution will continue to exist, even if, by virtue of the change in cohorts (or other societal pressures), changes are required in the institution's tenets, structures, or activities. The dynamic quality of these institutions is clearly manifest in the fan clubs, cults, and sects.

Academia may not place high esteem on edited volumes for consideration in such issues as promotion and tenure, but such works are critical venues because they permit the voicing of novel and enigmatic questions that surface during any investigation. Such questions may be matters queried by other researchers independently investigating similar or parallel phenomena. These questions, then—far from being obscure or idiosyncratic—are part of our social and cultural world and deserve more serious attention. As such, the value of such volumes is found in bringing forward questions that need to be studied with greater care. I have presented many questions that emerged from reading and considering the preceding chapters; it is likely other readers will have identified other issues for future research on heros, icons, saints, and their institutions.

NOTES

1. The same concept applies to individuals (Adams 1988) and ethnic groups (Baureiss 1982; Gmelch 1986) and may be responsible for the schisms of sects and cults into other, often competing, groups.

2. The case can be made that most of the examples presented in this volume are representatives of cultures with direct ties to Europe, or, for both Mexico and Argentina, colonized by Spain, and may have been influenced by the imposition of European culture among the elite. Thus, the consistent patterns described by Lord Raglan and Landau in Passariello's chapter might be attributed, in part, to the impact Western culture had on narrative traditions. In any case, the preceding chapters show that Thailand (Stengs), Argentina (Bosca), Mexico and the United States (Hopgood and Doss), and Latin America in general (Passariello) all have long traditions of charismatic leaders. Although Stevens does not explore the role of charismatic leaders in Japanese culture, one merely has to consider the role that the Emperor had in World War II and the myriad of kamikaze pilots and others who engaged in forms of altruistic suicide in his name to know that charismatic leaders have been a part of Japanese culture.

3. Macklin observes "*humanness* . . . is one of the distinguishing characteristics of the sainted star performers, while that which traditionally has been demanded of religious candidates for sainthood is precisely their 'otherness.'"

4. I use the phrase "religious instruction" loosely. Religious instruction refers to any sort of information that the follower may take as "gospel" and uses as reason to change his or her behavior so that it more closely approximates the ideals epitomized by the object of adoration.

5. Bryan Wilson also considers sects as "movements of religious protest" (1970:7). As such, it is possible to consider virtually all of the movements described in these chapters as manifestations of individuals against secularism (another religious movement) (see Hopgood 2000:346–347 and Doss, this volume).

6. The extent to which homosexuals are ostracized by established denominations is the extent to which they—like women, who also feel excluded from these establishments—will seek refuge in alternative forms of religious expression.

References Cited

Abelardo Ramos, Jorge
1966 Revolución y contrarevolución en la Argentina. Buenos Aires: T. I.

Acuña, Rodolfo
1988 Occupied America: A History of Chicanos. 3rd edition. New York: Harper and Row.

Adams, Walter Randolph
1988 Fission, Maintenance and Interaction in an Anishinabe Community on Keweenaw Bay, Michigan, 1832–1881. Ph.D. dissertation, Department of Anthropology, Michigan State University.
2000 Introducing This Volume. *In* Anthropology and Theology: Gods, Icons, and God-talk. Walter Randolph Adams and Frank A. Salamone, eds. Pp. 1–30. Lanham, MD: University Press of America.

Akin Rabibhadana
1969 The Organization of Thai Society in the Early Bangkok Period, 1782–1873. Ithaca, NY: Southeast Asia Program, Cornell University.

Albanese, Catherine L.
1981 America: Religions and Religion. Belmont, CA: Wadsworth.

Alderman, Derek H.
2003 Writing on the Graceland Wall: On the Importance of Authorship in Pilgrimage Landscapes. Tourism Recreation Research 27(2):27–33.

Almada, Francisco R.
1938 La rebelión de Tomóchi. Mexico City: Privately printed.

Alonso, Ana M.
1988 The Effects of Truth: Re-Presentations of the Past and the Imagining of Community. Journal of Historical Sociology 1(1):33–57.
1994 The Politics of Space, Time and Substance: State Formation, Nationalism, and Ethnicity. Annual Review of Anthropology 23:379–405.

Anderson, Benedict
1991 [1983] Imagined Communities: Reflections on the Origin and Spread of Nationalism. Rev. edition. London: Verso.
Anderson, Jon Lee
1997 The Cult of the Guerrilla. The Geographical Magazine 69(Oct.):21–26.
Anzaldúa, Gloria
1987 Borderlands/La Frontera: The New Mestiza. San Francisco: Aunt Lute.
Aoyagi, Hiroshi
2000 Pop Idols and the Asian Identity. *In* Japan Pop: Inside the World of Japanese Popular Culture. Timothy J. Craig, ed. Pp. 309–326. New York: M. E. Sharpe.
Apinan Poshyananda
1992 Modern Art in Thailand: Nineteenth and Twentieth Centuries. Singapore: Oxford University Press.
Arce Gargollo, Rafael
1992 Los nuevos santos: beatos y santos elevados a los altares por Juan Pablo II. Mexico: Panorama Editorial.
Arias, Wil
1995 Teresa y Alfredo. Paper written for Dr. Rubio-Goldsmith in Mexican American Studies 485. Tucson, University of Arizona. Author's collection.
Armstrong, James A.
1976 Mobilized and Proletarian Diasporas. American Political Science Review 70:393–403.
Aronoff, Myron J.
1973 Development Towns in Israel. *In* Israel: Social Structure and Change. C. M. and M. S. Cherrtoff, eds. Pp. 24–46. New Brunswick, NJ: Transaction.
Arraras, Maria Celeste
1997 El secreto de Selena: la reveladora historia detras de su tragica muerte. New York: Simon and Schuster Libros en Español.
Atkinson, Jane M.
1992 Shamanisms Today. Annual Review of Anthropology 21:307–330.
Baer, R. D., L. Clark, and C. Peterson
1998 Folk Illnesses. *In* Handbook of Immigrant Health. S. Loue, ed. Pp. 183–202. New York: Plenum.
Barthes, Roland
1978 Image-Music-Text. Stephen Heath, trans. New York: Hill and Wang.
Barzun, Jacques
1959 God's Country and Mine: A Declaration of Love Spiced with a Few Harsh Words. New York: Vintage.
Bast, William
1956 James Dean. New York: Ballantine.
Bauman, Zygmunt
1982 Memories of Class: The Pre-history and After-life of Class. London: Routledge.
2000 Liquid Modernity. Malden, MA: Blackwell.
2001 The Individualized Society. Malden, MA: Polity.

Baureiss, G.
1982 Ethnic Resilience and Discrimination: Two Chinese Communities in Canada. Journal of Ethnic Studies 10(1):69–87.
Beckham, Sue Bridwell
1987 Death, Resurrection and Transfiguration: The Religious Folklore in Elvis Presley Shrines and Souvenirs. International Folklore Review 5:88–95.
Beit-Hallahmi, Benjamin
1992 Despair and Deliverance: Private Salvation in Contemporary Israel. Albany, NY: State University of New York Press.
Bellah, Robert N.
1980 Religion and the Legitimation of the American Republic. *In* Varieties of Civil Religion. Robert N. Bellah and Phillip E. Hammond, eds. New York: Harper and Row.
Bellah, Robert N., Richard Madsen, William M. Sullivan, Ann Swidler, and Steven M. Tipton
1985 Habits of the Heart: Individualism and Commitment in American Life. Berkeley: University of California Press.
Ben-Ami, Issachar
1981 The Folk-Veneration of Saints among Moroccan Jews: Tradition, Continuity and Change. *In* Studies in Judaism and Islam. S. Morag, I. Ben-Ami, and N. A. Stillman, eds. Pp. 283–345. Jerusalem: Magnes.
1984 Saint Veneration among the Jews in Morocco (in Hebrew). Jerusalem: Magnes.
Benjamin, Thomas
2000 Rebuilding the Nation. *In* The Oxford History of Mexico. Michael C. Meyer and William H. Beezley, eds. Pp. 467–502. New York: Oxford University Press.
Bennett, J. W., ed.
1975 The New Ethnicity: Perspectives from Ethnology. St. Paul: West.
Benton, Sarah
1998 The Princess, the People and Paranoia. *In* After Diana: Irreverent Elegies. Mandy Merck, ed. Pp. 87–102. New York: Verso.
Berger, Peter L.
1967 The Sacred Canopy. New York: Doubleday.
Berlanga, José Luis, Éric Lara, and César Ramírez
1999 Las fiestas del dolar: un estudio sobre las celebraciones del Niño Fidencio. Monterrey, México: Fondo Estatal para la Cultura y las Artes de Nuevo León.
Bilu, Yoram
1990 Jewish Moroccan "Saint Impresarios" in Israel: A Stage-Developmental Perspective. Psychoanalytic Study of Society 15:247–269.
1996 Encountering the Sacred: Saint Veneration and Visitational Dreams among Moroccan Jews in Israel. *In* The Sacred and Its Scholars. T. Idianopolus and E. Yonan, eds. Pp. 89–103. Leiden: E. J. Brill.
2000 Oneirobiography and Oneirocommunity in Saint Worship in Israel: A Two-Tier Model for Dream-Inspired Religious Revivals. Dreaming 10(2):85–101.
2001 Moroccan Jews and the Shaping of Israel's Sacred Geography. *In* Divergent Jewish

Cultures: Israel and America. G. Dash-Moore and I. Troen, eds. New Haven, CT: Yale University Press.

Bilu, Yoram, and Henry Abramovitch
1985 In Search of the Saddiq: Visitational Dreams among Moroccan Jews in Israel. Psychiatry 48(1):83–92.

Bilu, Yoram, and Eyal Ben-Ari
1992 The Making of Modern Saints: Manufactured Charisma and the Abu-Hatseiras of Israel. American Ethnologist 19(4):672–687.

Blank, Christopher
2002 Sense of Loss Same at Biggest Vigil of All, GoMemphis, August 16. http://www.gomemphis.com/mca/goelvis_king_weeks/article

Bloch, Marc
1924 Les rois thaumaturges. Strasbourg: Faculté des Lettres de l'Université de Strasbourg.

Boorstin, Daniel J.
1961 From Hero to Celebrity. *In* The Image: A Guide to Pseudo-Events in America, by Daniel J. Boorstin. Pp. 45–76. New York: Atheneum.

Bourdieu, Pierre
1977 Outline of a Theory of Practice. Cambridge: Cambridge University Press.

Boyd, Carolyn
1998 Pictographic Evidence of Peyotism in the Lower Pecos, Texas Archaic. *In* The Archaeology of Rock Art. Christopher Chippindale and Paul S. Tacon, eds. Pp. 229–246. Cambridge: Cambridge University Press

Braudy, Leo
1997 [1986] The Frenzy of Renown: Fame and Its History. New York: Vintage.

Brown, Kenneth, and Jean Mohr
1982 Journey through the Labyrinth. Studies in Visual Communication 8(2):2–81.

Brown, Peter
1981 The Cult of the Saints. Chicago: University of Chicago Press.

Brummelhuis, Han ten
1995 De Waterkoning: J. Homan van der Heide, staatsvorming en de oorsprong van moderne irrigatie in Siam, 1902–1909. Ph.D. thesis, University of Amsterdam.

Bynum, Caroline Walker
1987 Holy Feast and Holy Fast: The Religious Significance of Food to Medieval Women. Berkeley: University of California Press.

Caimari, Lila
1995 Perón y la Iglesia Católica, religión y sociedad en la Argentina (1943–1955). Buenos Aires: Ariel.

Cámara de Diputados de la Nación
1955 Diario de sesiones, May 19, p. 319.

Carvajal, D.
1999 Book Industry Study Shows Sales Increased 4% Last Year. New York Times, August 16:C1.

Certeau, Michel de
1984 The Practice of Everyday Life. Steven Randall, trans. Berkeley: University of California Press.

Chabrán, Richard, and Rafael Chabrán, eds.
1996 The Latino Encyclopedia, vol. 6. New York: Marshall Cavendish.

Chatelet, François, and E. Pisier Kouchner
1981 Les conceptions politiques du siècle XX, Historie de la pensée politique. Paris: Presses Universitaires de France.

Christian, William A., Jr.
1989 [1972] Person and God in a Spanish Valley. New rev. edition. Princeton, NJ: Princeton University Press.

Chula Chakrabongse, Prince
1960 Lords of Life. London: Alvin Redman.

Cisneros, Sandra
1991 Woman Hollering Creek. New York: Random House.

Cohen, Erik
1983 Ethnicity and Legitimation in Contemporary Israel. The Jerusalem Quarterly 28:111–124.

Comisión de Afirmación de la Revolución Libertadora
1987 Libro negro de la segunda tiranía. 2nd edition. Buenos Aires.

Compact Oxford English Dictionary
1991 Second edition. Glasgow: Oxford University Press.

Connerton, Paul
1989 How Societies Remember. London: Cambridge University Press.

Cornwell, John
2001 Breaking Faith: The Pope, The People, and the Fate of Catholicism. New York: Viking Compass.

Cox, Harvey
1984 Religion in the Secular City: Toward a Postmodern Theology. New York: Touchstone.

Crapanzano, Vincent
1973 The Hamadsha: A Study in Moroccan Ethnopsychiatry. Berkeley and Los Angeles: University of California Press.

Cunningham, Lawrence S.
1968 The Meaning of Saints. San Francisco: Harper and Row.

Dalton, David
1974 James Dean: The Mutant King. San Francisco: Straight Arrow.

Damrong Rajanubhab, Prince
1976 [1912] Sadet Praphat Ton, Phra Niphon Somdet Krom Phraya Damrong Ratchanuphap (Touring the Country-side, Writings of Prince Damrong). Bangkok: Sinlapabannakan.

Dare, Helen
1900 Santa Teresa, Celebrated Mexican Healer, Whose Powers Awe Warlike Yaquis in Sonora, Comes to Restore San Jose Boy to Health. San Francisco Weekly Examiner, July 26.

de Echevarría, Luís
1972 Canonización. *In* Gran Enciclopedia Rialp, vol. III. Madrid: Rialp.
Delbanco, Andrew
1999 The Real American Dream: A Meditation on Hope. Cambridge, MA: Harvard University Press.
Demerath, N. J., III
2000 The Varieties of Sacred Experience: Finding the Sacred in a Secular Grove. Journal for the Scientific Study of Religion 39(1):1–11.
Demitrópulos, Libertad
1984 Eva Perón. Buenos Aires: Centro Editor de América Latina.
Deshen, Shlomo, and Moshe Shokeid
1974 The Predicament of Homecoming: Cultural and Social Life of North African Immigrants in Israel. Ithaca, NY: Cornell University Press.
DeWalt, Billie R., and Pertti J. Pelto
1985 Microlevel/Macrolevel Linkages: An Introduction to the Issues and a Framework for Analysis. *In* Micro and Macro Levels of Analysis in Anthropology: Issues in Theory and Research. Billie R. DeWalt and Pertti J. Pelto, eds. Pp. 1–22. Boulder: Westview.
Dominguez, Virginia R.
1986 The Marketing of Heritage. American Ethnologist 13:546–555.
Doniger, Wendy
1998 The Implied Spider: Politics and Theology in Myth. New York: Columbia University Press.
Doss, Erika
1999 Elvis Culture: Fans, Faith and Image. Lawrence: University Press of Kansas.
2002 Death, Art, and Memory in the Public Sphere: The Visual and Material Culture of Grief in Contemporary America. Mortality 7(1):63–82.
Douglas, Mary
2000 Sacraments and Society: An Anthropologist Asks, "What Women Could Be Doing in the Church?" *In* Anthropology and Theology: Gods, Icons, and God-talk. Walter Randolph Adams and Frank A. Salamone, eds. Pp. 391–406. Lanham, MD: University Press of America.
Dreher, Rod
2002 What Juan Diego Saw: The Story of a New Saint. National Review, September 2: 26–27.
Durkheim, Émile
1915 The Elementary Forms of the Religious Life. Joseph Ward Swain, trans. London: George Allen and Unwin.
Dyer, Richard
1998 [1979] Stars. London: British Film Institute.
Eade, John, and Michael J. Sallnow, eds.
1991 Contesting the Sacred: The Anthropology of Christian Pilgrimage. London: Routledge.

Early, Gerald
2002 On Miles Davis, Vince Lombardi, and the Crisis of Masculinity in Mid-Century America. Daedalus 131(1):154–159.

Ebersole, Lucinda
1994 The God and Goddess of the Written Word. *In* Elvis + Marilyn 2 × Immortal. Geri DePaoli, ed. Pp. 136–145. New York: Rizzoli.

Ede, Yolanda van, ed.
1999 Personality Cults. Theme issue, Etnofoor 12(2).

Eguía, Carlos R.
1974 Sacro Imperio Romano Germánico. *In* Gran Enciclopedia Rialp, vol. XX. Madrid: Rialp.

Eickelman, Dale F.
1976 Moroccan Islam: Tradition and Society in a Pilgrimage Center. Austin: University of Texas Press.

Eisenstadt, S. N.
1968 Introduction—Max Weber on Charisma and Institution Building: Max Weber and Modern Sociology. *In* Max Weber on Charisma and Institution Building. S. N. Eisenstadt, ed. Pp. ix–lvi. Chicago: University of Chicago Press.

El Imparcial
1896 Reseña exacta del asalto dado a la Villa de Nogales la madrugada del 12 agosto de 1896 por indios en su mayor parte Yaquis, capitaneades por Arvizu. El Imparcial (Guaymas, México), August 26: 1.

Elliott, Anthony
1999 The Mourning of John Lennon. Melbourne: University of Melbourne Press.

Ember, Carol R.
1996 Cross-Cultural Comparison. *In* Encyclopedia of Cultural Anthropology, vol. 1. David Levinson and Melvin Ember, eds. Pp. 261–265. New York: Henry Holt.

Ewen, Stuart
1988 All Consuming Images: The Politics of Style in Contemporary Culture. New York: Basic.

Ferrazi, Cecilia
1996 Autobiography of an Aspiring Saint (The Other Voice in Early Modern Europe). Anne J. Schutte, trans. Chicago: University of Chicago Press.

Finke, Roger, and Rodney Stark
1992 The Churching of America, 1776–1990: Winners and Losers in Our Religious Economy. New Brunswick, NJ: Rutgers University Press.

Fiske, John
1992 The Cultural Economy of Fandom. *In* Adoring Audience: Fan Culture and Popular Media. Lisa A. Lewis, ed. Pp. 30–49. New York: Routledge.
1993 Power Plays Power Works. New York: Verso.

Floria, Carlos Alberto, and César A. García Belsunce
1992 Historia de los argentinos, vol. II. Buenos Aires: Larousse.

Folliet, Joseph
1963 Bourrage et débourrage de cranes. Lyon: Chronique Sociale de France.

Fong, Mei, and Debra Lau
2001 Earnings from the Crypt. http://www.forbes.com/2001/02/28/crypt.html.
Foster, George
1967 Tzintzuntzan: Mexican Peasants in a Changing World. Boston: Little, Brown and Company.
Freedberg, David
1989 The Power of Images: Studies in the History and Theory of Response. Chicago: University of Chicago Press.
Freze, Michael, S.F.O.
1989 They Bore the Wounds of Christ: The Mystery of the Sacred Stigmata. Huntington, IN: Our Sunday Visitor.
1991 The Making of a Saint. Huntington, IN: Our Sunday Visitor.
Frías, Heriberto
1911 Tomóchic. México, D.F.: Librería de la Viuda de Ch. Bouret.
Frías, Pedro J.
1989 Aproximaciones. Córdoba.
Frigerio, José Oscar
1984 Perón y la Iglesia, historia de un conflicto inútil. Todo es Historia, No. 210 (Oct.).
Gallardo, Juan Luis
1995 Crónica de cinco siglos: 1492–1992. Buenos Aires: Vórtice.
Gamson, Joshua
1994 Claims to Fame: Celebrity in Contemporary America. Berkeley: University of California Press.
Gans, H. J.
1979 Symbolic Ethnicity: The Future of Ethnic Groups and Cultures in America. Ethnic and Racial Studies 2(1):1–19.
Gaonkar, Dilip Parameshwar
2001 On Alternative Modernities. *In* Alternative Modernities. Dilip Parameshwar Gaonkar, ed. Pp. 1–23. Durham, NC: Duke University.
García de Loydi, Ludovico
1956 La Iglesia frente al peronismo. Buenos Aires: Cic.
García, Ignacio M.
1989 United We Win: The Rise and Fall of La Raza Unida Party. Tucson: University of Arizona.
1997 Chicanismo: The Forging of a Militant Ethos among Mexican Americans. Tucson: University of Arizona.
Gardner, Dore
1992 Niño Fidencio: A Heart Thrown Open. Santa Fe: Museum of New Mexico Press.
Garelick, Rhonda K.
1998 Rising Star: Dandyism, Gender, and Performance in the Fin de Siecle. Princeton, NJ: Princeton University Press.
Garibaldi, Giorgio Angelozzi
1988 Pío XII, Hitler y Mussolini. Barcelona.

Garza Quirós, Fernando
1980 El Niño Fidencio y el Fidencismo. 4th edition. Monterrey, México: Talleres de Impresora Monterrey.
Gaspar de Alba, Alicia, ed.
2003 Velvet Barrios: Popular Culture and Chicana/o Sexualities. New York: Palgrave Macmillian.
Geertz, Clifford
1968 Islam Observed: Religious Development in Morocco and Indonesia. Chicago: University of Chicago Press.
Gellner, Ernest
1969 Saints of the Atlas. Chicago: University of Chicago Press.
Gennep, Arnold van
1960 [1908] Rites of Passage. Monika B. Vizedom and Gabrielle L. Caffee, trans. Chicago: University of Chicago Press.
Giddens, Anthony
1991 Modernity and Self-Identity: Self and Society in the Late Modern Age. Stanford, CA: Stanford University Press.
Ginsburg, Faye, D. Lila Abu-Lughod, and Brian Larkin
2002 Introduction. *In* Media Worlds: Anthropology on New Terrain. Faye Ginsburg, D. Lila Abu-Lughod, and Brian Larkin, eds. Pp. 1–36. Berkeley: University of California Press.
Girardot, Norman J.
1996 But Seriously: Taking the Elvis Phenomenon Seriously. Religious Studies News 11(4):11–12.
1997 What Really Happened in Bethlehem? The Religious Power and Apocalyptic Pathos of the Religious Phenomenon. Paper presented at the Third Annual Conference on Elvis Presley, Memphis, August 15.
Glassman, Ronald
1975 Legitimacy and Manufactured Charisma. Social Research 42:615–636.
Gmelch, Sharon B.
1986 Groups That Don't Want In: Gypsies and Other Artisan, Trader and Entertainer Minorities. Annual Review of Anthropology 15:307–330.
Goldberg, Harvey E.
1983 The Mellahs of Southern Morocco: A Report of a Survey. The Maghreb Review 8(3):61–69.
1984 Greentown's Youth: Disadvantaged Youth in a Development Town in Israel. Assen, The Netherlands: Van Gorcum.
Gomez-Quiñones, Juan
1994 Roots of Chicano Politics, 1600–1940. Albuquerque: University of New Mexico Press.
Gonen, Rivka
1998 To the Tombs of the Saints: Pilgrimages and Hillulot in Israel. Jerusalem: The Israel Museum.

Gottdiener, Mark
1997 Dead Elvis as Other Jesus. *In* The Search for Elvis: Music, Race, Art, Religion. Vernon Chadwick, ed. Pp. 189–200, 272–274. Boulder, CO: Westview.
Graburn, Nelson H. H.
1989 Tourism: The Sacred Journey. *In* Hosts and Guests: The Anthropology of Tourism. Valene Smith, ed. Philadelphia: University of Pennsylvania Press.
Grant, Neil
1991 James Dean in His Own Words. New York: Crescent.
Guevara, Ernesto Che
1995 The Motorcycle Diaries: A Journey around South America. Ann Wright, trans. New York: Verso.
2001 Otra Vez: Diario Inédito del Segundo Viaje por Latinoamérica. Barcelona: Ediciones B.
Guillermoprieto, Alma
2001 Looking for History: Dispatches from Latin America. New York: Pantheon.
Halle, David
1993 Inside Culture: Art and Class in the American Home. Chicago: University of Chicago Press.
Harder, Michael
2002 The Story about the Image of Che Guevara. http://www.pix.dk/korda2.htm.
Hariot, M. Jean
2000 Feminist Spirituality, Theology and Anthropology. *In* Anthropology and Theology: Gods, Icons, and God-talk. Walter Randolph Adams and Frank A. Salamone, eds. Pp. 115–135. Lanham, MD: University Press of America.
Harrison, Ted
1992 Elvis People: The Cult of the King. London: Fount.
Hartley, John
1992 The Politics of Pictures: Creation of the Public in the Age of Popular Media. London: Routledge.
Hatch, Nathan O.
1989 The Democratization of American Christianity. New Haven, CT: Yale University Press.
Hattori Shôta (on behalf of the Hon no Mori/Jidôsha group)
1998 hide We miss you. Tokyo: Hon no Mori Shuppan Center.
Hayward, Paul Antony
1999 Demystifying the Role of Sanctity in Western Christendom. *In* The Cult of Saints in Late Antiquity and the Early Middle Ages. James Howard-Johnston and Paul Antony Hayward, eds. Pp. 115–142. New York: Oxford University Press.
Head, Thomas, ed.
2001 Medieval Hagiography: An Anthology. New York: Routledge.
Heelas, Paul
1996 The New Age Movement: The Celebration of the Self and the Sacralization of Modernity. Cambridge, MA: Blackwell.

Heinich, Nathalie

1996 The Glory of Van Gogh: An Anthropology of Admiration. Paul Leduc Browne, trans. Princeton, NJ: Princeton University Press.

Heliodoro y Fabiola [Heliodoro González Valdés and Fabiola López de la Fuente Villarreal]

1997 Una luz en el desierto. El campo de dolor. Vida del Niño Fidencio. Monterrey, México: Print Impresora.

Henneberger, Melinda

2002 The Saints Just Keep Marching. New York Times, Ideas and Trends, March 3:A6.

Herberg, Will

1955 Protestant, Catholic, Jew. New York: Garden City.

Hills, Matt

2002 Fan Cultures. New York: Routledge.

Hitchens, Christopher

1995 The Missionary Position: Mother Teresa in Theory and Practice. New York: Verso.

Hobsbawm, Eric J.

1983 Introduction: Inventing Traditions. *In* The Invention of Tradition. Eric J. Hobsbawm and Terence O. Ranger, eds. Pp. 1–14. Cambridge: Cambridge University Press.

Hobsbawm, Eric J., and Terence O. Ranger, eds.

1983 The Invention of Tradition. Cambridge: Cambridge University Press.

Holden, William C.

1978 Teresita. Owings Mills, MD: Stemmer House.

Holland, Dorothy, William Lachicotte, Debra Skinner, and Carol Cain

2002 [1998] Identity and Agency in Cultural Worlds. Cambridge, MA: Harvard University Press.

Hopgood, James F.

1979 Settlers of Bajavista: Social and Economic Adaptation in a Mexican Squatter Settlement. Latin American Series, 7. Athens, OH: Ohio University.

1998a Another *Japanese Version:* An American Actor in Japanese Hands. *In* The Social Construction of Race and Ethnicity in the United States. Joan Ferrante and Prince Brown, Jr., eds. Pp. 470–477. New York: Longman.

1998b Inside Passages to the Self: Deaners and Pilgrimage in Fairmount. *In* Wish I Were: Felt Pathways of the Self. Linda Rogers, ed. Pp. 101–114. Madison, WI: Atwood.

2000 "Back Home in Indiana": Semiotics of Pilgrimage to Honor an American Icon. *In* Anthropology and Theology: Gods, Icons, and God-talk. Walter Randolph Adams and Frank A. Salamone, eds. Pp. 337–361. Lanham, MD: University Press of America.

Horowitz, Sam, and Moshe Lissak

1989 Trouble in Utopia: The Overburden Polity of Israel. Albany: University of New York Press.

Hudson, Wilson M.

1951 The Healer of Los Olmos and Other Mexican Folklore. Austin: Texas Folklore Society.

Hufford, David J.

1988 Contemporary Folk Medicine. *In* Other Healers: Unorthodox Medicine in America. N. Gevitz, ed. Pp. 228–264. Baltimore: Johns Hopkins University Press.

Huntington, Richard, and David Metcalf

1979 Celebrations of Death: The Anthropology of Mortuary Ritual. Cambridge: Cambridge University Press.

Hutton, Patrick H.

1993 History as an Art of Memory. Hanover, NH: University Press of New England.

Illades Aguiar, Lilián

1993 La rebelión de Tomóchic 1891–1892. México, D.F.: Instituto Nacional de Antropología e Historia.

Inbar, Michael, and Chaim Adler

1977 Ethnic Integration in Israel. New Brunswick, NJ: Transaction.

Irwin-Zarecka, Iwona

1994 Frames of Remembrance: The Dynamics of Collective Memory. New Brunswick, NJ: Transaction.

James, William

1902 The Varieties of Religious Experience: A Study in Human Nature. 2nd edition. New York: Longmans, Green.

Jefferies, Randy

1994 Jackie Kennedy's Grave Heals the Sick. Weekly World News, September 13: 8–9.

Josei Jishin

1998 Hide okite! Mô ichi do "gambare!" tte itte! (Wake up, hide! Tell me to fight hard one more time!). Pp. 43–47. Tokyo: Kôbunsha.

Kantorowicz, Ernst H.

1957 The King's Two Bodies: A Study in Medieval Political Theology. Princeton, NJ: Princeton University Press.

Kapferer, Bruce

1988 Legends of People, Myths of State: Violence, Intolerance, and Political Culture in Sri Lanka and Australia. Washington, DC, and London: Smithsonian Institution Press.

Kehoe, Alice

2000 Shamanism and Religion: An Anthropological Exploration in Critical Thinking. Prospect Heights, IL: Waveland.

Keisatsucho anzenseikatsukyoku chiikka [The National Police Agency's Office for Livelihood Safety, Regional Section]

2003 Heiseinenju ni okeru jisatsu no gairyo shiryo [summary data for suicides for 2002]. Tokyo: National Police Agency.

Kelly, William W., ed.

2004 Fanning the Flames: Fans and Consumer Culture in Contemporary Japan. Albany: State University of New York Press.

Keyes, Charles F.

1977 Millennialism, Theravada Buddhism and Thai Society. Journal of Asian Studies 36(2):283–302.

Kieckhefer, Richard

1984 Unquiet Souls: Fourteenth-Century Saints and Their Religious Milieu. Chicago: University of Chicago Press.

Kimmerling, Baruch

2001 The Invention and Decline of Israeliness. Berkeley: University of California Press.

King, Christine

1992 His Truth Goes Marching On: Elvis Presley and the Pilgrimage to Graceland. *In* Pilgrimage in Popular Culture. Ian Reader and Tony Walter, eds. Pp. 92–104. New York: Macmillan.

Klapp, Orrin E.

1962 Heroes, Villains, and Fools: The Changing American Character. Englewood Cliffs, NJ: Prentice-Hall.

Kleinberg, Aviad M.

1992 Prophets in Their Own Country: Living Saints and the Making of Sainthood in the Later Middle Ages. Chicago: University of Chicago Press.

La Constitución

1896 El Asalto de la Aduana de Nogales. La Constitución (Hermosillo, México), September 18: 2.

La Ilustración Espirita

1892 Noticias acerca de la medium Teresa Urrea. La Ilustración Espirita (México, D.F.), January 1: 255–260.

La Voz del Estado

1896 Asalto a la Aduana Fronteriza de Nogales. La Voz del Estado (Magdalena, México), August 16: 2.

Lafaye, Jacques

1984 Mesías, cruzadas, utopías: el judeo-cristianismo en las sociedades ibéricas. México, D.F.: Fondo de Cultura Económica.

Landau, Misia

1991 Narratives of Human Evolution. New Haven, CT, and London: Yale University Press.

Lapham, Lewis

2001 Lights, Camera, Democracy: Selected Essays. New York: At Random.

Larralde, Carlos

1976 The Teresita Movement: 1888–1905. *In* Mexican American Movements and Leaders, by Carlos Larralde. Pp. 58–71. Los Alamitos, CA: Hwong.

Lasarow, Bill

2002 [1998] Alberto Korda. http://artscenecal.com/ArticlesFile/Archive/Articles1998/Articles1198/AkordaA.html.

Lasch, Christopher

1979 The Culture of Narcissism: American Life in an Age of Diminishing Expectations. New York: W. W. Norton.

Lewis, Lisa A., ed.

1992 The Adoring Audience: Fan Culture and Popular Media. New York: Routledge.

Lindholm, Charles

1990 Charisma. Cambridge, MA: Basil Blackwell.

Ling, Richard
1987 The Production of Synthetic Charisma. Journal of Political and Military Sociology 15:157–170.
Little, Graham
1999 The Public Emotions: From Mourning to Hope. Sydney: Australian Broadcasting Corporation.
Llorca, Carmen
1978 Las mujeres en los dictadores. Madrid: Hyspamérica.
López Jordán, Rafael
1985 ¿Cómo se "fabrica" un santo? Esquíú, Jan 27.
Los Angeles Record
1903 Santa Teresa Takes a Hand in the Strike. Los Angeles Record, April 28:front.
Los Angeles Times
2001 Alberto Korda Dies at Age 72; Photographer of Castro, Che, Sunday, May 27, p. CO8.
Luca de Tena, T., L. Calvo, and E. Peicovich
1981 Yo, Juan Domingo Perón, relato autobiográfico. 2nd edition. Barcelona: Planeta.
Luckmann, Thomas
1967 The Invisible Religion: The Problem of Religion in Modern Society. New York: Macmillian.
Luna, Félix
2000 Eva Duarte de Perón. Madrid: Planeta.
MacAloon, John J.
1982 Sociation and Sociability in Political Celebrations. *In* Celebration: Studies in Festivity and Ritual. Victor Turner, ed. Pp. 255–271. Washington, DC: Smithsonian Institution Press.
McAuslan, Fiona, and Matthew Norman
2000 The Rough Guide to Cuba. London: Penguin.
McBrien, Richard P.
1997 Lives of the Popes: The Pontiffs from St. Peter to John Paul II. San Francisco: HarperSanFrancisco.
2001 Lives of the Saints: From Mary and St. Francis to John XXIII and Mother Teresa. San Francisco: HarperSanFrancisco.
MacCannell, Dean
1976 The Tourist: A New Theory of the Leisure Class. New York: Schocken.
McDannell, Colleen
1986 The Christian Home in Victorian America, 1840–1900. Bloomington: Indiana University Press.
1995 Material Christianity: Religion and Popular Culture in America. New Haven, CT: Yale University Press.
McGeagh, Robert
1987 Relaciones entre el poder político y eclesiástico en la Argentina. Buenos Aires: Itinerarium.

Macklin, June

1967 El Niño Fidencio: un estudio de curanderismo en Nuevo León. Anuario Humanitas 8:529–563. Anuario de Centro de Estudios Humanisticos, Universidad de Nuevo León (Monterrey, México).

1974a Belief, Ritual, and Healing: New England Spiritualism and Mexican-American Spiritism Compared. *In* Religious Movements in Contemporary America. Irving I. Zaretsky and Mark P. Leone, eds. Pp. 383–417. Princeton, NJ: Princeton.

1974b Folk Saints, Healers and Spiritist Cults in Northern Mexico. Revista Interamericana Review III(4):351–367.

1988 Two Faces of Sainthood: The Pious and the Popular. Theme issue, "Saints, Near-Saints, and Society." Luise Margolies and June Macklin, eds. Journal of Latin American Lore 14(1):67–91.

1997 El chamanismo y el neo-chamanismo en la declinación del milenio: los usos de los estados alterados de conciencia. *In* Religión y Etnicidad en América Latina, vol. III. G. Ferro Medina, ed. Pp. 35–44. Bogotá: Instituto Colombiano de Antropología.

Macklin, B. June, and N. Ross Crumrine

1973 Three North Mexican Folk Saint Movements. Comparative Studies in Society and History 15(1):89–105.

MacLachlan, Colin M., and William H. Beezley

1999 El Gran Pueblo: A History of Greater Mexico. 2nd edition. Upper Saddle River, NJ: Prentice Hall.

McWilliams, Carey

1968 North from Mexico: The Spanish Speaking People of the United States. Westport, CT: Greenwood.

Main, Mary

1956 La mujer del látigo: Eva Perón. Buenos Aires: La Reja.

Maino, Guido

1975 The Healing Hand: Man and Wound in the Ancient World. Cambridge, MA: Harvard University Press.

Mallay, Jack D., and Warren Vaughn

1992 Elvis: The Messiah? Mount Horeb, WI: TCB Publishing.

Mansilla, César

1983 Los partidos provinciales. Buenos Aires: Centro Editor de América Latina.

Marcus, Greil

1991 Dead Elvis: A Chronicle of a Cultural Obsession. New York: Doubleday.

Marcus, M. A.

1985 The Saint Has Been Stolen: Sanctity and Social Change in a Tribe of Eastern Morocco. American Ethnologist 12:454–467.

Marin, Louis

1988 Portrait of the King. Minneapolis: University of Minnesota Press.

Marling, Karal Ann

1993 Elvis Presley's Graceland, or the Aesthetics of Rock 'n' Roll. American Art 7(4): 72–105.

1996 Graceland: Going Home with Elvis. Cambridge, MA: Harvard University Press.

Marshall, P. David
1997 Celebrity and Power: Fame in Contemporary Culture. Minneapolis: University of Minnesota Press.

Martínez Estrada, Ezequiel
1956 ¿Qué es esto? Buenos Aires: Catilinaria.

Massuh, Víctor
1995 Toda mitificación lleva a la idolatría. La Nación (Buenos Aires), March 3:7.

Meier, Matt S.
1997 Teresa Urrea (1873–1906). Mexican American Mystic, Curandera (Herbalist, Faith Healer). *In* Notable Latino Americans: A Biographical Dictionary, by Matt S. Meier with Conchita Franco Serri and Richard A. Garcia. Pp. 389–392. Westport, CT: Greenwood.

Meier, Matt S., and Feliciano Rivera
1981 Teresa Urrea. *In* Dictionary of Mexican American History, by Matt S. Meier and Feliciano Rivera. Pp. 359–360. Westport, CT: Greenwood.

Merck, Mandy, ed.
1998 After Diana: Irreverent Elegies. New York: Verso.

Meri, Josef W.
1999 The Etiquette of Devotion in the Islamic Cult of Saints. *In* The Cult of Saints in Late Antiquity and the Early Modern Ages. James Howard-Johnston and Paul Antony Hayward, eds. Pp. 263–286. Oxford, U.K.: Oxford University Press.

Meyrowitz, Joshua
1985 No Sense of Place: The Impact of Electronic Media on Social Behavior. New York: Oxford University Press.

Mills, C. Wright
1956 The Power Elite. New York: Oxford University Press.

Mirandé, Alfredo, and Evangelina Enríquez
1982 Chicanas in the History of the Southwest. *In* Introduction to Chicano Studies. 2nd edition. Livie Isauro Duran and H. Russell Bernard, eds. Pp. 156–179. New York: Macmillan.

Moell, C. J.
1967 Sacred Heart, devotion to. *In* New Catholic Encyclopedia, vol. 12, pp. 812–828. New York: McGraw Hill.

Monaghan, John
1995 The Covenants with Earth and Rain: Exchange, Sacrifice, and Revelation in Mixtec Sociality. Norman: University of Oklahoma Press.

Moody, Raymond, Jr.
1987 Elvis after Life: Unusual Psychic Experiences Surrounding the Death of a Superstar. Atlanta: Peachtree.

Mooney, Catherine M., ed.
1999 Gendered Voices: Medieval Saints and Their Interpreters. Philadelphia: University of Pennsylvania Press.

Moore, R. Laurence

1994 Selling God: American Religion in the Marketplace of Culture. New York: Oxford University Press.

Morgan, Ronald J.

2002 Spanish American Saints and the Rhetoric of Identity: 1600–1810. Tucson: University of Arizona Press.

Morgan, David, ed.

1998 Visual Piety: A History and Theory of Popular Religious Images. Berkeley: University of California Press.

Morin, Edgar

1960 The Stars. Richard Howard, trans. New York: Grove.

Muller, Herbert J.

1966 Freedom in the Modern World. New York: Harper and Row.

Munck, Victor de

2000 Introduction: Units for Describing and Analyzing Culture and Society. Ethnology 39(4):279–292.

2002 Contemporary Issues and Challenges for Comparativists: An Appraisal. Anthropological Theory 2(1):5–19.

Muñoz, Carlos, Jr.

1989 Youth, Identity, Power: The Chicano Movement. New York: Verso.

Murashima, Eiji

1988 The Origin of Modern Official State Ideology in Thailand. Journal of Southeast Asian Studies 19(1):80–96.

Murray, William Breen

1980 Prologo a la Cuarta Edición: Perspectivas Antropológicas sobre Fidencio y el Fidencismo. *In* El Niño Fidencio y el Fidencismo, by Fernando Garza Quirós. 4th edition. Pp. 10–36. Monterrey, México: Talleres de Impresora Monterrey.

2001 Atlatl Hunters of the Sierra Madre Oriental. *In* American Indian Rock Art, vol. 27. S. Freers and A. Woody, eds. Pp. 261–267. Tucson, AZ: American Rock Art Research Association.

Myers, Greg

2000 Entitlement and Sincerity in Broadcast Interviews about Princess Diana. Media, Culture & Society 22:167–185.

Newell, Gillian E.

1999 Teresa Urrea, Early Chicana? The Politics of Representation, Identity, and Memory. M.A. thesis, Anthropology Department, University of Arizona, Tucson.

Newey, Glen

1998 Diarrhoea. *In* After Diana: Irreverent Elegies. Mandy Merck, ed. Pp. 147–158. New York: Verso.

Nietzsche, Friedrich

1996 [1886] Human, All Too Human. R. J. Hollingdale, trans. Cambridge: Cambridge University Press.

Nithi Aeusrivongse

1993 Lathi phi thi sadet pho ro ha (The Cult of King Rama the Fifth). Sinlapa Watthanatham chabap phiset (Special Edition of Art and Culture), Matichon (Bangkok), August.

Nolan, Mary Lee, and Sidney Nolan

1989 Christian Pilgrimage in Modern Western Europe. Chapel Hill: University of North Carolina Press.

Nora, Pierre

1989 Between Memory and History. Representations 26:7–25.

Nugent, Daniel

1993 Spent Cartridges of Revolution: An Anthropological History of Namiquipa, Chihuahua. Chicago: University of Chicago Press.

Oasis

1896 Nipped in the Bud. Lauro Aguirre's Revolution Materializes, the Customs House at Nogales Captured. Oasis (Nogales, Arizona), August 15:1.

Obeyesekere, Gananath

1968 Theodicy, Sin and Salvation in a Sociology of Buddhism. *In* Dialectic in Practical Religion. Edmund R. Leach, ed. Cambridge Papers in Social Anthropology No. 5. Cambridge: Cambridge University Press.

O'Connor, Bonnie B.

1998 Healing Practices. *In* Handbook of Immigrant Health. S. Loue, ed. Pp. 145–162. New York: Plenum.

Olalquiaga, Celeste

1992 Megalopolis: Contemporary Cultural Sensibilities. Minneapolis: University of Minnesota Press.

Orsi, Robert

1991 The Center Out There, In Here, and Everywhere Else: The Nature of Pilgrimage to the Shrine of Saint Jude, 1929–1965. Journal of Social History 25(2):213–232.

Osorio, Rubén

1995 Tomóchic en llamas. Mexico, D.F.: Consejo Nacional para la Cultura y las Artes.

Page, Joseph A.

1983 Perón: A Biography. New York: Random House.

Pavón Pereyra, Enrique

1973 Coloquios con Perón. Madrid: Edítores Internacionales Técnicos Reunidos.

Peers, E. Allison

1960 The Life of Teresa of Jesus: The Autobiography of St. Teresa of Avila. New York: Doubleday Image.

Perón, Eva

1951 La razón de mi vida. Buenos Aires: Ediciones Peuser.

Pierce, Patricia Jobe

1994 The Ultimate Elvis: Elvis Presley Day by Day. New York: Simon and Schuster.

Pinguet, Maurice

1993 Voluntary Death in Japan. R. Morris, trans. Cambridge, MA: Polity.

Plotkin, Mariano Ben

2003 [1993] Mañana es San Perón: A Cultural History of Perón's Argentina. Keith Zahniser, trans. Wilmington, DE: Scholarly Resources.

Poole, Stafford
1995 Our Lady of Guadalupe: The Origins and Sources of a Mexican National Symbol, 1531–1797. Tucson: University of Arizona Press.
Popular Memory Group
1982 Popular Memory: Theory, Politics, Method. *In* Making Histories: Studies in History Writing and Politics. Richard Johnson, Gregor McLennan, Bill Schwarz, and David Sutton, eds. Pp. 205–252. London: Hutchinson.
Porterfield, Amanda
2001 The Transformation of American Religion: The Story of a Late-Twentieth-Century Awakening. New York: Oxford University Press.
Potash, Robert A.
1980 The Army and Politics in Argentina, 1945–1962, Perón to Frondizi. Stanford, CA: Stanford University Press.
Pountain, Dick, and David Robins
2000 Cool Rules: Anatomy of an Attitude. London: Reaktion.
Powdermaker, Hortense
1950 Hollywood, the Dream Factory: An Anthropologist Looks at the Movie-Makers. Boston: Little, Brown.
Pringle, Heather
2001 The Mummy Congress: Science, Obsession, and the Everlasting Dead. New York: Hyperion.
Propp, Vladimir
1968 [1928] Morphology of the Folktale. Laurence Scott, trans. Austin: University of Texas Press.
Putnam, Frank B.
1963 Teresa Urrea, "The Saint of Cabora." Southern California Quarterly 45(3):245–264.
Rabinow, Paul
1975 Symbolic Domination: Cultural Forms and Historical Change in Morocco. Chicago: University of Chicago Press.
Raglan, Lord
1934 The Hero of Tradition. Folklore 45:212–231.
Richardson, Miles
2001 The Gift of Presence: The Act of Leaving Artifacts at Shrines, Memorials, and Other Tragedies. *In* Textures of Place: Exploring Humanist Geographies. Paul C. Adams, Steven Hoelscher, and Karen E. Till, eds. Pp. 257–272. Minneapolis: University of Minnesota Press.
Riese, Randall
1991 The Unabridged James Dean: His Life and Legacy from A to Z. Chicago: Contemporary.
Rock, David
1993 La Argentina autoritaria: los nacionalistas, su historia y su influencia en la vita política. Buenos Aires: Ariel.
Rodrígues Brandào, Carlos
1988 El banquete de los brujos: relaciones sociales y simbólicas en la prática del curan-

derismo en Brasil. *In* Mito y ritual en América. Manuel Gutiérrez Estévez, ed. Madrid: Alahambra.

Rodriguez, Jeanette
1994 Our Lady of Guadalupe: Faith and Empowerment among Mexican-American Women. Austin: University of Texas Press.

Rodriguez, Richard, and Gloria L. Rodriguez
1972 Teresa Urrea: Her Life, as It Affected the Mexican-U.S. Frontier. El Grito 5(4): 48–68.

Rojek, Chris
2001 Celebrity. London: Reaktion.

Romano, Octavio
1965 Charismatic Medicine, Folk Healing and Folk Sainthood. American Anthropologist 67:51–73.

Roof, Wade Clark
1993 A Generation of Seekers: The Spiritual Journeys of the Baby Boom Generation. New York: Harper.

Rosaldo, Renato, Robert A. Calvert, and Gustav L. Seligmann, eds.
1973 Chicano: The Evolution of a People. Minneapolis: Winston.

Rosenbaum, Ron
1995 Among the Believers. New York Times Magazine, September 24:50–57, 62, 64.

Roth, Beulah, and Sanford Roth
1983 James Dean. Corte Madera, CA: Pomegranate.

Roth, Sanford, and Seita Ohnishi
1987 James Dean: The Memory of the Last 85 Days. Tokyo: Shinnippon Calendar.

Russo, Richard
1999 How 'I' Moved Heaven and Earth: We've Lived with the Me-Centered Universe Long Enough Now to Wonder if This Is a Good Thing. New York Times Magazine, Oct. 17:85–89.

San Francisco Call
1896 Santa Teresa to Be a Freak. San Francisco Call, August 27:np.

San Francisco Examiner
1896 Fierce Yaquis Eager for War. San Francisco Examiner, August 18:1.

Sánchez, Camio
1995 San Gardel. Viva (Buenos Aires), June 18:64–65.

Sánchez Zinny, E. F.
1958 El culto de la infamia, Historia documentada de la segunda trianía argentina. 2nd edition. Buenos Aires.

Sauras, E.
1972 Culto. *In* Gran Enciclopedia Rialp, vol. VII. Madrid: Rialp.

Schatt, Roy
1982 James Dean: A Portrait. New York: Delilah.

Schickel, Richard
2000 [1985] Intimate Strangers: The Culture of Celebrity in America. Chicago: Ivan R. Dee.

Schulenburg, Jane T.
1998 Forgetful of Their Sex: Female Sanctity and Society, ca. 500–1100. Chicago: University of Chicago Press.
Schutte, Anne J.
2001 Aspiring Saints: Pretense of Holiness, Inquisition, and Gender in the Republic of Venice, 1618–1750. Baltimore: Johns Hopkins University Press.
Semyonov, Moshe
1981 Effects of Community on Status Attainment. Sociological Quarterly 22:359–372.
Seremetakis, C. Nadia
1994 The Senses Still: Perception and Memory as Material Culture in Modernity. Chicago: University of Chicago Press.
Shamayyim, Maia C. M.
1995 Elvis and His Angelic Connection. Angel Times 1(4):20–25.
Shils, Edward
1975 Center and Periphery: Essays in Macrosociology. Chicago: University of Chicago Press.
Shirai, Ken'ichi, ed.
1998 hide e no tegami—eien no ai w komete . . . (Letters to hide: With love forever . . .). Tokyo: Okurashuppan.
Shukan Josei
1998a hide wa gisei ni natta no ka? 'korosareta' X Japan saigo no ketsudan (Was Hide Sacrificed? The Last Decision of the 'Dead' X Japan). Pp. 31–36. Tokyo: Shufu to seikatsusha, May 26.
1998b X JAPAN Forever hide. Tokyo: Shufu to seikatsusha, June 20.
Smith, Waldemar R.
1977 The Fiesta System and Economic Change. New York: Columbia University Press.
Spiro, Milford E.
1982 Buddhism and Society: A Great Tradition and Its Burmese Vicissitudes. Berkeley: University of California Press.
Stanley, David
1997 Cuba: A Lonely Planet Travel Survival Kit. Hong Kong: Colorcroft.
Stark, Rodney, and William Sims Bainbridge
1985 The Future of Religion: Secularization, Revival and Cult Formation. Berkeley: University of California Press.
Steffen, Vibeke
1997 Life Stories and Shared Experience. Social Science and Medicine 45(1):99–111.
Steif, William
1956 What Makes Elvis Presley Tick—No. 3, The Pelvis Explains That "Vulgar" Style. San Francisco News, October 17.
Steinberg, Leo
1996 The Sexuality of Christ in Renaissance Art and in Modern Oblivion. 2nd edition. Chicago: University of Chicago Press.
Stengs, Irene
2000 The Commodification of King Chulalongkorn: His Portraits, Their Cultural Biog-

raphies and the Enduring Aura of a Great King of Siam. Working Paper No. 10, WOTRO-Research Programme Globalization and the Construction of Communal Identities, The Hague.

2003 Worshipping the Great Moderniser: The Cult of King Chulalongkorn, Patron Saint of the Thai Middle Class. Ph.D. thesis, University of Amsterdam.

Stevens, Carolyn

2002 Saved by the Love Song: Japanese Rock Fans, Memory and the Pursuit of Pleasure. *In* Japan at Play: The Ludic and the Logic of Power. Massimo Ravieri and Joy Hendry, eds. Pp. 99–114. New York: Routledge.

Stevens, Carolyn, and Shuhei Hosokawa

2001 So Close and Yet So Far: Humanizing Celebrity in Japanese Music Television, 1960s–1990s. *In* Asian Media Productions. Brian Moeran, ed. Pp. 233–246. Surrey: Curzon.

Stewart, Kathleen

1988 Nostalgia—A Polemic. Current Anthropology 3:227–241.

Stillman, Norman A.

1982 Saddiq and Marabut in Morocco. *In* The Sephardi and Oriental Jewish Heritage. I. Ben-Ami, ed. Pp. 489–500. Jerusalem: Magnes.

1995 Sephardi Religious Responses to Modernity. Luxemburg: Harwood Academic.

Stock, Dennis

1978 James Dean Revisited. New York: Viking.

1987 James Dean Revisited. San Francisco: Chronicle.

Stromberg, Peter

1990 Elvis Alive? The Ideology of American Consumerism. Journal of Popular Culture 24(3):11–19.

Subsecretaría de Informaciones

1952 Eva Perón en la bronce. Homenaje de la Honorable Cámara de Diputados. Buenos Aires: Subsecretaría de Informaciones, Presidencia de la Nación.

Swidler, Ann

2002 Saving the Self: Endowment versus Depletion in American Institutions. *In* Meaning and Modernity: Religion, Polity, and Self. Richard Madsen, William M. Sullivan, Ann Swidler, and Steven M. Tipton, eds. Pp. 41–55. Berkeley: University of California Press.

Taibo, Paco Ignacio, II

1997 Guevara, Also Known as Che. Martin Michael Roberts, trans. New York: St. Martin's.

Takahashi, Yôji, ed.

1993 Nihon no ROCK [Japanese Rock] 1950s–1990s. Tokyo: Heibonsha.

Take Hideki

1999 Yomu J-Pop 1945–1999 shitekizenshi [Reading J-pop: 1945–1999, a Personal History]. Tokyo: Tokuma Shoten.

Take Hideki, and Yôji Maeda

1995 J-pops CD de kiku: meiban meikyoku 716 [Listening to J-pop on CD: 716 Famous Recordings and Music]. Tokyo: Nihonbungeisha.

Tambiah, Stanley J.
1984 The Buddhist Saints of the Forest and the Cult of the Amulets. Cambridge: Cambridge University Press.
1985 Culture, Thought and Social Action: An Anthropological Perspective. Cambridge, MA, and London: Harvard University Press.
1988 [1984] The Buddhist Saints of the Forest and the Cult of Amulets: A Study in Charisma, Hagiography, Sectarianism and Millennial Buddhism. Cambridge Studies in Social Anthropology, No. 49. Cambridge: Cambridge University Press.

Taylor, Charles
2002 Varieties of Religion Today: William James Revisited. Cambridge, MA: Harvard University Press.

Taylor, Eugene
1994 Desperately Seeking Spirituality. Psychology Today 27(6):54–62, 64, 66, 68.

Taylor, J. M.
1979 Eva Perón: The Myths of a Woman. Chicago: University of Chicago Press.

Telgen, Diane, and Jim Kamp, eds.
1993 Notable Hispanic American Women. Detroit: Gale Research.

Terán Lira, Manuel
1980 El Niño Fidencio. Torreon, Coahuila: Editorial Macondo.

Terwiel, Baas
1994 [1975] Monks and Magic: An Analysis of Religious Ceremonies in Central Thailand. 3rd, rev., edition. Bangkok: White Lotus.

Troncoso, Francisco P.
1905 Las guerras con las tribus Yaqui y Mayo del Estado de Sonora. México, D.F.: Tipografía del Departamento de Estado Mayor.

Trouillot, Michel-Rolph
1995 Silencing the Past: Power and the Production of History. Boston: Beacon.

Trow, George W. S.
1997 Within the Context of No Context. New York: Atlantic Monthly Press.

Turner, Bryan S.
1994 Orientalism, Postmodernism and Globalism. New York: Routledge.

Turner, Kay
1986 Home Altars and the Art of Devotion. *In* Chicano Expressions: A New View in American Art. Inverna Lockpez, ed. Pp. 40–48. New York: Intra Latin American Gallery.
1992 "Because of This Photography": The Making of a Mexican Folk Saint. *In* Niño Fidencio: A Heart Thrown Open, by Dore Gardner. Pp. 120–134. Santa Fe: Museum of New Mexico Press.

Turner, Victor W.
1967 The Forest of Symbols: Aspects of Ndembu Ritual. Ithaca, NY: Cornell University Press.
1969 The Ritual Process: Structure and Anti-Structure. Chicago: Aldine.
1974 Dramas, Fields, and Metaphors: Symbolic Action in Human Society. Ithaca, NY: Cornell University Press.

Turner, Victor W., and Edith Turner

1978 Image and Pilgrimage in Christian Culture: Anthropological Perspectives. New York: Columbia University Press.

Vallen, Mark

2004 [2001] Alberto Korda (Rest in Peace). Electronic document, http://www.art-for-a-change.com/Month/korda.htm, accessed June 25, 2004.

Vanderwood, Paul

1998 The Power of God against the Guns of Government: Religious Upheaval in Mexico at the Turn of the Nineteenth Century. Stanford, CA: Stanford University Press.

Vargas Somoza, Federico

2001 Los ciclos del sol, pinturas sobre roca en Arroyo Seco, Victoria (Guanajuato). México Desconocido XXV(292):54–61.

Vauchez, Andre

1997 Sainthood in the Later Middle Ages. Jean Birrell, trans. Cambridge: Cambridge University Press.

Vikan, Gary

1994 Graceland as *Locus Santos*. *In* Elvis + Marilyn 2 × Immortal. Geri DePaoli, ed. Pp. 150–166. New York: Rizzoli.

Wales, Quaritch H. G.

1992 [1931] Siamese State Ceremonies: Their History and Function (with Supplementary Notes). Richmond, Surrey: Curzon.

Warner, Marina

1982 Joan of Arc: The Image of Female Heroism. New York: Vintage.

Weber, Max

1946 From Max Weber: Essays in Sociology. H. H. Gerth and C. Wright Mills, trans. and eds. New York: Oxford University Press.

1963 [1922] The Sociology of Religion. Ephraim Fischoff, trans. Boston: Beacon.

1968 Economy and Society: An Outline of Interpretive Sociology, vol. 1. Guenther Roth and Claus Wittich, eds. New York: Bedminster.

Weiner, Tim

2001 A New Saint Revives Old Battles Over the Church. New York Times International, Dec. 27:A2.

Weingrod, Alex

1985 Studies in Israeli Ethnicity: After the Ingathering. New York: Gordon and Breach.

1990 The Saint of Beersheba. Albany, NY: State University of New York Press.

Weinstein, Donald, and Rudolph M. Bell

1982 Saints and Society: The Two Worlds of Western Christendom, 1000–1700. Chicago: University of Chicago Press.

Wertheimer, Alison

1991 A Special Scar: The Experiences of People Bereaved by Suicide. London: Routledge.

Westermarck, Edward A.

1926 Ritual and Belief in Morocco. London: Macmillan.

Williams, Mark
1997 The Effect of the Media. *In* Cry of Pain: Understanding Suicide and Self-Harm, by Mark Williams. Pp. 130–157. London: Penguin.

Williams, Raymond
1977 Marxism and Literature. Oxford: Oxford University Press.

Wills, Garry
2002 Why I Am a Catholic. New York: Houghton Mifflin.

Wilson, Bryan
1970 Religious Sects: A Sociological Study. New York: McGraw-Hill.

Wilson, Stephen
1983 Introduction. *In* Saints and Their Cults: Studies in Religious Sociology, Folklore, and History. Stephen Wilson, ed. Pp. 3–25. Cambridge: Cambridge University Press.

Windsor, John
1992 Faith and the State of Graceland Enterprises. Independent (London), August 15.

Wolf, Eric R.
1959 The Virgin of Guadalupe: A Mexican National Symbol. Journal of American Folklore 71:34–59.

Wollenberg, Charles
1973 Working on El Traque: The Pacific Electric Strike of 1903. Pacific Historical Review, 42 (3)(Aug.):358–369.

Womack, John, Jr.
1986 The Mexican Economy during the Revolution, 1910–20. *In* Twentieth-Century Mexico. W. Dirk Raat and William H. Beezley, eds. Pp. 73–83. Lincoln: University of Nebraska Press.

Woodward, Kenneth L.
1990 Making Saints: How the Catholic Church Determines Who Becomes a Saint, Who Doesn't and Why. New York: Simon and Schuster.

Wuthnow, Robert
1994 Sharing the Journey: Support Groups and America's New Quest for Community. New York: The Free Press.

Young, Adrienne
1994 Taking Care of Business: Elvis Fans and Moral Community. M.A. thesis, George Washington University, Washington, DC.

Zarfati, Leora
2000 The Cult of the Saints in Israel at the End of the Millennium: Religiosity, Mysticism, and Modernity (in Hebrew). M.A. thesis, Tel-Aviv University.

Zavaleta, Antonio N.
1998 El Niño Fidencio and the Fidencistas. *In* Sects, Cults, and Spiritual Communities: A Sociological Analysis. William W. Zellner and Marc Petrowsky, eds. Pp. 95–115. Westport, CT: Greenwood.

Contributors

Walter Randolph Adams (Ph.D., Michigan State University; Postdoctorate in Community Health, Brown University) is affiliated with the Facultad de Ciencias de la Salud at the Universidad Rafael Landivar in Guatemala City, where he instructs Master's candidates in all phases of their thesis work. For the past 10 years he has served as co-director of the Brigham Young University anthropological field school in three indigenous communities in highland Guatemala. An applied anthropologist, he has conducted research in the United States, Mexico, Guatemala, El Salvador, and Paraguay. He has taught at Kansas State University, Brown University, and the University of the South. He is author of *Anthropology and Theology: Gods, Icons, and God-talk* (contributor and co-editor, 2000); "Social Structure in Pilgrimage and Prayer: Tzeltales as Lords and Servants" (in *Pilgrimage in Latin America*, 1991); and "Political and Economic Correlates of Pilgrimage Behavior" (*Anales de Antropología*, 1983), among other publications.

Yoram Bilu (Ph.D., Hebrew University) is Professor of Anthropology and Psychology at Hebrew University of Jerusalem. His research interests include culture and mental health, folk religion, Moroccan Jews, and the sanctification of space in Israel. His awards include the Bryce Boyer Prize (1986), the Stirling Prize (1997), and the Bahat Prize (2003). He was the Gilon Visiting Professor for Israel Studies at the Jewish Theological Seminary (2002). He is author of *Without Bounds: The Life and Death of Rabbi Ya'aqov Wazana* (2000); *Grasping Land: Space and Place in Contemporary Israeli Discourse and Experience* (co-editor, 1997); and numerous articles in professional journals.

Roberto Bosca (Ph.D., Universidad de Buenos Aires) is Professor of Law at the Universidad Austral in Buenos Aires, Argentina. He is the former Dean of the School of Law and is currently Director of the Department of International and Institutional Affairs at Austral. Professor Bosca is currently working with the Carnegie Council (USA) on issues related to international ethics. His research interests include the interrelations of religion and politics, the cultural impact of religion, and religious liberty and fundamentalism. He is the author of *La Iglesia nacional peronista, Factor religioso y poder político* (1997); *New Age: La utopía religiosa del fin de siglo* (1993); and many other publications in English and Spanish.

Erika Doss (Ph.D., University of Minnesota) is Professor of Art History at the University of Colorado, Boulder, and specializes in 20th-century and contemporary American art. She is the author of *Twentieth-Century American Art* (2002); *Looking at Life Magazine* (editor, 2001); *Elvis Culture: Fans, Faith, and Image* (1999); *Spirit Poles and Flying Pigs: Public Art and Cultural Democracy in American Communities* (1995); and *Benton, Pollock, and the Politics of Modernism: From Regionalism to Abstract Expressionism* (1991).

James F. Hopgood (Ph.D., The University of Kansas) is Professor Emeritus of Anthropology and former department chair at Northern Kentucky University. In addition to his research on the "Deaners," his areas of research interest include belief systems, worldview, religious movements, and urbanization, with fieldwork in northeast Mexico, Japan, and the United States. Publications include "Monterrey, Mexico" (in *Encyclopedia of Urban Cultures,* 2002); "Identity, Gender, and Myth: Expressions of Mesoamerican Change and Continuity" (*Latin American Research Review,* 2000); *Settlers of Bajavista: Social and Economic Adaptation in a Mexican Squatter Settlement* (1979); and several recent chapters on the Deaners. He is a recent recipient of a Sasakawa Fellowship, Japan Studies Institute, San Diego. A former president of the Central States Anthropological Society, he is currently editor of the society's *CSAS Bulletin.*

June Macklin (Ph.D., University of Pennsylvania) is Rosemary Park Professor Emerita of Anthropology, Connecticut College, and a former chair of the department. Her areas of research interest include popular and folk religion, new religions, and medical anthropology, and she has conducted field research in Mexico, South America, and the United States. Among her publications are "New Religious Movements and Ritual Transformations of the Modern Self" (*Scripta Etnológica,* 2000); "El chamanismo y el neo-chamanismo en la declinación del mileno: los usos de los estados alterados de conciencia" (in *Religión y Etnicidad,* 1997); "Saints, Near-Saints, and Society" (contributor and co-editor, *Journal of Latin American Lore,* 1988); *The Chicano Experience* (contributor and co-editor, 1979); *Cultural Change and Structural Stability in a Mexican American Community* (1976); "Folk Saints, Healers, and Spiritist Cults in Northern Mexico" (in *Revista/Review Interamericana,* 1974); and *The Human Nature Industry* (co-author, 1973).

William Breen Murray (Ph.D., McGill University) is Professor of Anthropology and a former department chair at the Universidad de Monterrey, Monterrey, Mexico. His research interests, in addition to folk saints and religion, include medical anthropology, archaeoastronomy, and prehistoric rock art. Murray is a recipient of the Capt. Alonso de León Medal awarded by the Sociedad Nuevoleonesa de Historia, Geografía y Estadística and the Kenneth B. Castleton Prize from the American Rock Art Research Association. Murray is the author of "Atlatl Hunters of the Sierra Madre Oriental" (co-author, in *American Indian Rock Art*, 2000); "The Contributions of the Ethnosciences to Archaeoastronomical Research" (in *Archaeoastronomy*, 2000); and "Recent Rock Art Research in Mexico and Central America" (in *Rock Art Studies: News of the World*, 1996).

Gillian E. Newell (M.A., University of Arizona) is a Ph.D. candidate in anthropology at the University of Arizona and is currently conducting field research in Mexico on the role of archaeology in Mexican identity. She has conducted research in ethnohistory and archaeology, as well as cultural anthropology. She is author of "Teresa Urrea: ¿Una precursora chicana? Retos de memoria social, historia e identidad de los chicanos de los Estados Unidos" (in *Revista Frontera Norte*, 2003) and *Surveying the Archaeology of Northwest Mexico* (co-editor, in press), among other publications.

Phyllis Passariello (Ph.D., University of California at Berkeley) is Professor of Anthropology and a former program chair at Centre College. She is a member of Phi Beta Kappa and a former Woodrow Wilson Fellow. Passariello has extensive field experience with the Maya and other peoples of Mexico, as well as with the peoples of Ecuador, Peru, Bolivia, Guatemala, Belize, and Cuba. She has strong research interests in the anthropology of tourism, semiotics, religious pilgrimage, and "faith" communities, and has published on those topics. Among her publications are "Sustainable Omnivores" (in *Sustainable Cuisine*, 1999); "Mother of All Tricksters: The Virgin of Guadalupe" (*American Journal of Semiotics*, 1998); "'Never, Without Her Gladiator': Christina Rossetti, Mary Magdalen, and the Disguises of Desire" (in *Wish I Were: Felt Pathways of the Self*, 1998); and *Eating Culture: The Italian Yankee Cookbook, An Ethnographic Reminiscence* (co-author, 1997).

Irene Stengs (Ph.D., University of Amsterdam), a cultural anthropologist, is researcher at the Institute for Research and Documentation of Language and Culture of the Netherlands (Meertens Institute, Amsterdam), where she is investigating contemporary rites, rituals, and festive culture in the Netherlands. She has conducted research on modern cults, material culture, and social imagery in urban Thai society and on changing peasant culture in northeast Thailand. Since 1988 she has served as co-editor of *Etnofoor*, an anthropological journal published in the Netherlands. Her publications include *The Commodification of King Chulalongkorn: His Portraits, Their Cultural Biographies and the Enduring Aura of a Great King of Siam* (WOTRO, The Netherlands, 2000); "Imitating the State: Chulalongkorn Day at a Northern Thai Spirit Medium's

Residence" (*Tai Culture*, 1999); and "A Kingly Cult: Thailand's Guiding Lights in a Dark Era" (*Etnofoor*, 1999).

Carolyn S. Stevens (Ph.D., Columbia University), a cultural anthropologist, is senior lecturer in Japanese Studies at the Melbourne Institute of Asian Languages and Societies, University of Melbourne, Australia. She is a former Fellow of the Institute of International Studies, Meiji Gakuin University, Tokyo. Her current research includes investigations of fan culture and organization of Japanese popular music. Stevens is the author of "So Close and Yet So Far: Humanizing Celebrity in Japanese Music Television, 1960s–1990s" (*Asia Media Productions*, 2001); "Rocking the Bomb: A Case Study in the Politicalization of Popular Culture" (*Japanese Studies*, 1999); On the Margins of Japanese Society: Volunteers and the Welfare of the Urban Underclass (1997); "Whose *etto* Is It Anyway? New Year's Activities in a Yokohama *yoseba*" (*American Asian Review*, 1995); and other publications in English and Japanese.

Index